International and Development Education

The *International and Development Education Series* focuses on the complementary areas of comparative, international, and development education. Books emphasize a number of topics ranging from key international education issues, trends, and reforms to examinations of national education systems, social theories, and development education initiatives. Local, national, regional, and global volumes (single authored and edited collections) constitute the breadth of the series and offer potential contributors a great deal of latitude based on interests and cutting-edge research. The series is supported by a strong network of international scholars and development professionals who serve on the International and Development Education Advisory Board and participate in the selection and review process for manuscript development.

Titles:

Higher Education in Asia/Pacific: Quality and the Public Good
Edited by Terance W. Bigalke and Deane E. Neubauer

Affirmative Action in China and the U.S.: A Dialogue on Inequality and Minority Education
Edited by Minglang Zhou and Ann Maxwell Hill

Critical Approaches to Comparative Education: Vertical Case Studies from Africa, Europe, the Middle East, and the Americas
Edited by Frances Vavrus and Lesley Bartlett

Curriculum Studies in South Africa: Intellectual Histories & Present Circumstances
Edited by William F. Pinar

Higher Education, Policy, and the Global Competition Phenomenon
Edited by Laura M. Portnoi, Val D. Rust, and Sylvia S. Bagley

The Search for New Governance of Higher Education in Asia
Edited by Ka-Ho Mok

International Students and Global Mobility in Higher Education: National Trends and New Directions
Edited by Rajika Bhandari and Peggy Blumenthal

Curriculum Studies in Brazil: Intellectual Histories, Present Circumstances
Edited by William F. Pinar

Access, Equity, and Capacity in Asia Pacific Higher Education
Edited by Deane Neubauer and Yoshiro Tanaka

Policy Debates in Comparative, International, and Development Education
Edited by John N. Hawkins and W. James Jacob

Increasing Effectiveness of the Community College Financial Model: A Global Perspective for the Global Economy
Edited by Stewart E. Sutin, Daniel Derrico, Rosalind Latiner Raby, and Edward J. Valeau

Forthcoming titles:

Curriculum Studies in Mexico: Intellectual Histories, Present Circumstances
Edited by William F. Pinar

Taiwan Education at the Crossroad: When Globalization Meets Localization
Chuing Prudence Chou and Gregory Ching

Increasing Effectiveness of the Community College Financial Model

A Global Perspective for the Global Economy

Edited by
Stewart E. Sutin, Daniel Derrico, Rosalind Latiner Raby, and Edward J. Valeau

INCREASING EFFECTIVENESS OF THE COMMUNITY COLLEGE FINANCIAL MODEL

First published in 2011 by
PALGRAVE MACMILLAN®

10 0663058 1

in the United States—a division of St. Martin's Press LLC,
175 Fifth Avenue, New York, NY 10010.

Where this book is distributed in the UK, Europe and the rest of the world,
this is by Palgrave Macmillan, a division of Macmillan Publishers Limited,
registered in England, company number 785998, of Houndmills,
Basingstoke, Hampshire RG21 6XS.

Palgrave Macmillan is the global academic imprint of the above companies
and has companies and representatives throughout the world.

Palgrave® and Macmillan® are registered trademarks in the United States,
the United Kingdom, Europe and other countries.

ISBN: 978–0–230–10536–2

Library of Congress Cataloging-in-Publication Data

Increasing effectiveness of the community college financial model :
a global perspective for the global economy / edited by Stewart E. Sutin...
[et al.].
    p. cm.—(International & development education)
    ISBN 978–0–230–10536–2 (hardback)
        1. Community colleges—Finance. I. Sutin, Stewart E.

LB2328.I625 2011
378.1'18—dc22   2011005482

A catalogue record of the book is available from the British Library.

Design by Newgen Imaging Systems (P) Ltd., Chennai, India.

First edition: September 2011

10 9 8 7 6 5 4 3 2 1

Printed and bound in Great Britain by
CPI Antony Rowe, Chippenham and Eastbourne

This book is dedicated to our families for their continued strength and conviction to believe in a project of this magnitude. In particular, we want to thank our spouses, Rowna Sutin, Debra Derrico, Vera Valeau, and Ronald Raby for their patience and support during this long process. They have given so much and we love them dearly. We also dedicate this book to all present and future community college leaders whose decisions will impact learning across nations and generations.

Contents

Tables and Figures

Tables

Figures

Foreword

Community colleges and similar institutions, sometimes called technical colleges, technical universities, higher colleges of technology, polytechnics, further education (FE) colleges, or technical and further education (TAFE) colleges have proved to be the most flexible institutions for higher or further education and training, throughout the world. They readily shape their curricula to meet the needs of local economies, and they can move quickly to meet emerging needs for training or retraining. They maintain close ties to their community leaders and to local businesses. The institutions are sometimes referred to as "economic engines" because of their impact on local economies and preparing people with the skills needed for employment. However, the colleges are now under increasing pressure to deliver education and training to a surge of students in an environment of fiscal constraint and calls for greater accountability. The colleges have become the center of attention because policy makers are setting goals for increased levels of education and for higher levels of program and degree completion to improve the economic standing and standard of living in countries throughout the world. Students in these institutions must be prepared to succeed in an increasingly global society and economy.

The authors of *Increasing Effectiveness of the Community College Financial Model: A Global Perspective for the Global Economy* provide a wide-ranging look at what leaders of these colleges are doing and can do to meet calls for increased access, affordability, quality, and responsiveness to global economic needs—and to be more accountable for outcomes—in an environment of reduced resources. The authors first make the case for an improved financial model, calling for a new thematic and pragmatic application of financing the colleges to facilitate educational reform, to assist internationalization efforts, and to create systemic support systems to maintain the mission. Chapters deal with globalization, financial reform, governance, strategic planning, accountability, budget development, performance metrics, facilities management, cost containment strategies, and nontraditional revenue streams. Practical case studies describe how college leaders in several different institutions were able to meet challenges through such actions as changing institutional culture, developing new revenue streams through training and workforce development programs, securing new revenue from the public through a bond campaign, developing college foundations in rural areas, cost reduction and containment, international education as a revenue stream, using a return-on-investment model to focus on improving student success, and using student government to internationalize a campus.

Strategic planning is a central theme of the book, guiding leaders to set priorities that are in alignment with the institution's mission and values. The plan should effectively link to budget development and should be multiyear. Accountability for program effectiveness and for student success is emerging as a critically important leadership requirement. Colleges will need to be more effective and more efficient. College administrators all too often are not willing to make the difficult decisions needed to maintain the health of an institution during difficult financial times, making across-the-board cuts or cutting items like international programs, staff development, and travel budgets. Often institutional research is underfunded at a time when developing a culture of evidence and accountability is becoming more important to improve student success and to advocate effectively for needed support. The authors of *Increasing Effectiveness of the Community College Model* provide the information that leaders need to make the difficult but correct decisions that will move their colleges forward even in challenging times.

GEORGE R. BOGGS

Preface

It is the best of times and the worst of times for community colleges, for colleges of further education, and for all of their global counterparts. The good news for community colleges is that leaders around the globe are recognizing the roles that community colleges can and must play in economic development and economic revitalization. Peter Drucker once referred to community colleges as being the "twenty-first century graduate school." In the United States, our national leaders have proposed to invest billions of dollars to support community college initiatives with workforce development as well as economic and community revitalization. The recognition and respect that community colleges are receiving around the globe is unparalleled in the history of these institutions.

On the other hand, these institutions are facing crisis levels never before imagined. The good news is that student and community demands for quality services from these institutions have never been higher. Students are lined up to access community college programs that will lead them to enhanced personal and financial opportunities in the future. Enrollment figures have been increasing dramatically in these institutions since the turn of the twenty-first century.

The bad news for community colleges is that state and local funding for all of higher education has continued to decline over the past 25 years. I am fully aware that many politicians would say that actual dollar appropriations for community colleges have increased during this time period, but not as a percentage of the colleges' operating budgets. In many states, community college appropriations are at an all-time low. And in those states where local tax support is possible, many of the taxing possibilities available for community college districts are maxed-out—i.e., community colleges could not increase local tax levies without a vote from the citizens of the district.

In 2005, Barbara Jones and I edited *The Entrepreneurial Community College*. We compiled our volume to provide actual benchmarks and examples of best financial practices with which community colleges could expand and broaden their revenue sources. In this book, Stewart Sutin and his colleagues provide guidelines and pathways for institutions seeking to curtail costs while simultaneously expanding learning and service opportunities to the various constituencies that comprise the community college district.

Older readers will remember well those times in community college history when the need for additional revenues would have been laughable. I remember many times in my own career when colleagues referred to me as an "educational entrepreneur," implying that I was associated closely with used-car salesmen and snake oil peddlers. Today, every college and university around the globe is fully aware that continued public support for higher education (and our community colleges) is much in danger. I have heard many legislators refer to higher education as a "discretionary item" in state budget plans for the future. In fact, several governors have proposed more autonomy for the state universities in their states if those institutions would forego the expectation of state funding on a regular basis. I envision a time when a number of our major universities will become independent, autonomous, and almost totally self-reliant.

This will not be an easy course for community colleges to follow. Our institutions are in, of, and for the communities that support them. And it is more than likely that these communities will look to, and totally depend upon, community colleges to help them identify and solve, through education, the difficult challenges that lie ahead in an increasingly global society.

So much in the transformational leadership literature has focused on the need for leaders to have vision, suggesting that those who have clarity around visionary goals and expectations will be able to apply new directions and strategies for their attainment. What I have learned in my 40 years as director of the Community College Leadership Program, at the University of Texas at Austin, is that many, if not most, of our leaders have very clear ideas about the goals they have for their institutions. It is critical, of course, that leaders have a clear vision of what their colleges can and should become. Leaders must be able to see beyond the reality of the present to the potential of the future. No one would minimize the importance of vision clarity in transforming organizations.

What is overlooked, many times, is the critical importance of execution and implementation qualities in those leaders. It is not unusual to have a college president articulate very clear goals and focus for the future, but not be at all clear about the strategies and/or execution efforts needed to achieve them.

Execution is the true genius in effective leadership and this book, *Increasing Effectiveness of the Community College Financial Model: A Global Perspective for the Global Economy* provides the reader with the information, case studies, and effective benchmarks to transform planning into full-scale action plans. This book is focused properly on strategies for financial change. It is timely, well written, and of use to community college leaders, trustees, legislators, and others who have limitless expectations for these open-access institutions.

JOHN E. ROUECHE
Sid W. Richardson Regents Chair
Director, Community College Leadership Program
The University of Texas at Austin

Reference

Roueche, John E., and Barbara R. Jones. 2005. *The Entrepreneurial Community College.* Washington, DC: The Community College Press.

Acknowledgments

The editors would like to thank several people for their contributions to the production of this book. First, we are thankful to our community college and global counterpart colleagues, without whose voices, this book would not have been possible. In particular, we would like to recognize John Roueche for inspiring us to write a book focused upon the financial model of the community college. Second, we would like to thank all of the contributing authors who have been wonderful in embracing the project and sharing their stories for successful reform. Third, compilation of this book would not have been possible without the extensive research and assistance conducted by Yan Li, an extremely conscientious graduate student, in the Master's in Higher Education Management program at the University of Pittsburgh and Jacey Simon, a graduate of University of California at Davis, who assisted with the Index. Fourth, we would like to thank the series editors, W. James Jacob and John N. Hawkins for their guidance and insight. Fifth, the authors wish to thank the American Association of Community Colleges and their former president, George Boggs, for their encouragement as we proceeded with our project. Finally, we would like to thank the staff at Palgrave Macmillan for their support to which the editorship offers its deep appreciation.

Acronyms and Abbreviations

AACC	American Association of Community Colleges
AACU	Association of American Colleges and Universities
ABC	Activity-Based Costing
ACCD	Alamo Community College District
ACCs	American Community Colleges
ACCC	Association of Canadian Community Colleges
ACCT	Association of Community College Trustees
ACE	American Council on Education
ADEA	Association for the Development of Education in Africa
AfDB	African Development Bank
AFT	American Federation of Teachers
AtD	Achieving the Dream
BMCC	Borough of Manhattan Community College
BOG	Board of Governors
BTVET	Business Technical Vocational Education and Training
CCAC	Community College of Allegheny County
CCIE	California Colleges for International Education
CCLC	Community College League of California
CDF	Capital Development Funding
CEO	Chief Executive Officer
CFO	Chief Financial Officer
CHEA	Council for Higher Education Association
CIEFR	China Institute for Educational Finance Research
CIP	Capital Improvement Program
CMB	Contribution Margin Budget
CMOE	China Ministry of Education
CMOF	China Ministry of Finance
CMR	Construction Manager at Risk
COMBASE	Cooperative for the Advancement of Community-Based Postsecondary Education Colleges
CPI	Consumer Price Index
CPO	Chief Personnel Officer

CPs	Community Polytechnics
CUNY	City University of New York
ESB	Energy-Sector Business
FE	Further Education
FE college	Further Education Colleges
FEMA	Federal Emergency Management Agency
FICA	Federal Insurance Contributions Act
FTEs	Full-Time Equivalent Credit Hours
GMP	Guaranteed Maximum Price
GO Bonds	General Obligation Bonds
GoU	Government of Uganda
GTZ	Deutsche Gesellschaft für Technische Zusammenarbeit
GWIT	Global Workforce in Transition
HCCD	Houston Community College District
HEIs	Higher Education Institutions
HVAC	Heating, Ventilating, and Air Conditioning
HVCs	Higher Vocational Colleges
IACCP	Iowa Association of Community College Presidents
IACCT	Iowa Association of Community College Trustees
ICASB	Iowa Council of Area School Boards
IDED	Iowa Department of Economic Development
IGAs	Income Generating Activities
IIE	Institute of International Education
ILB	Individual-Learner Business
IT	Information Technology
KPIs	Key Performance Indicators
LEED	Leadership in Energy and Environmental Design
MBO	Management by Objectives
MOES	Ministry of Education and Sports (Uganda)
NAFSA	National Association of Foreign Student Advisers
NASULGC	National Association of State Universities and Land Grant Colleges
NCES	National Center for Educational Statistics
NEA	National Education Association
NGO	Nongovernmental Organization
NJTP	Iowa New Jobs Training Program Act
OECD	Organisation for Economic Co-operation and Development
PBB	Performance-Based Budgeting
PEST	Political, Economic, Social, and Technology
RC 2020	Renewal and Change 2020

REAP	Rural Education Action Project
RFP	Request for Proposals
ROI	Return on Investment
SAIT	Southern Alberta Institute of Technology (also referred to as SAIT Polytechnic)
SEIU	Service Employee International Union
SES	Socioeconomic Status
SGA	Student Government Association
SMWBE	Small, Minority, Women Owned Business Enterprise
SOLIS	SAIT Open Learning Instructional System
STEEP	Social, Technical, Economic, Educational, and Political
STOCS	Study/Travel Opportunities for CUNY Students
SUNY	State University of New York System
SWOT	Strengths, Weakness, Opportunity, Threats
TAFE	Technical and Further Education
TOPS	Taxonomy of Programs and Services
UBOS	Uganda Bureau of Statistics
UK	United Kingdom
UNESCO-UNEVOC	UNESCO International Centre for Technical and Vocational Education Training
UPE	Universal Primary Education
US	United States
USGBC	US Green Building Council
VET	Vocational and Education Training
WASC	Western Association of Schools and Colleges
WIB	Workforce Investment Boards

Series Editors' Introduction

Years of prolonged financial crises in national and global environments provide a precarious backdrop for higher education institutions at the beginning of the second decade of the twenty-first century. Financial constraints, reduced government funding, and requirements for tighter fiscal controls are areas of increasing importance for senior higher education administrators in the United States and abroad. *Increasing Effectiveness of the Community College Financial Model: A Global Perspective for the Global Economy* helps address these timely financial issues in higher education. The book was conceived as a CIES Higher Education Special Interest Group research project by an editorial team of four scholars and practitioners with a wealth of administrative experience at community colleges and universities.

The initial two chapters position the volume within the broader comparative and international higher education literature, emphasizing the dearth of published works and firsthand case studies of actual higher education financial programs and processes. This is especially the case at the community college level. Divided into two primary sections, the volume provides ten chapters on various higher education finance topics such as leadership, strategic planning, budget management, and facilities management. The second half of the book includes ten country and institutional case studies of higher education models with firsthand accounts from the editors and other contributing authors. This case study chapter approach offers readers a unique and catchy way of learning about a variety of practical topics including culture, training a global workforce, financing, the role of foundations in the fund-raising process, and a "value-added" international education department. The concluding chapter serves in many ways as an epilogue to the entire volume with suggestions from the editors on the way forward.

Many of the chapters in this volume draw from empirical research, with clear descriptions of data collected along with their methods of analysis. Multiple national case studies offer readers a comparative look at the volume's focus on the role a global perspective plays in increasing effectiveness of the higher education institutional financial model. The editors have structured this book to address current policy and practice issues that relate to higher education institutions generally and community colleges in particular. With country examples from China, Uganda, the United Kingdom, and the United States, the case-study approach provides examples of how senior higher education administrators deal with some of the leading finance issues of our day.

The book opens with a foreword and preface by George R. Boggs and John Rouche respectively, both highly reputed community college leaders. As the newest addition to our Palgrave Macmillan *International and Development Education Book Series*, this volume puts forward a financial higher education institutional model of relevance to senior higher education administrators everywhere.

JOHN N. HAWKINS
University of California, Los Angeles

W. JAMES JACOB
University of Pittsburgh

Chapter 1

A Changing World and Changing Community College

Stewart E. Sutin, Daniel Derrico, Edward J. Valeau, and Rosalind Latiner Raby

Introduction

Although community colleges are called by various names around the world, they all tend to serve as an alternative pathway that offers options for university overflow, adult learners, displaced workers, bright students from low-income families, and therefore, a "second chance" for nontraditional students to gain a basic education that accommodates the educational needs of the communities they serve (Raby and Valeau 2009). These institutions are increasingly called upon as "first responders" to retool displaced workers and meet regional medium-term labor requirements in high-demand occupations (Levin 2001). Increasingly, courses offered at these colleges represent the only avenue for postsecondary education for many students, especially from underprivileged backgrounds. Student enrollment underscores the crucial role of community colleges worldwide as 900,000 full-time and 1.5 million part-time students attend over 900 Canadian community colleges, and 44 percent of all US students attend over 1,177 community colleges (see Raby and Valeau 2009; Elsner, Boggs, and Irwin 2008 for cross-country comparisons). While its core multipurpose mission (Cohen 2009) has not changed appreciably in almost 50 years, economic and sociopolitical globalization has forced community colleges worldwide to reprioritize their central focus and expand their mission.

The prevailing financial model of the community college was not designed for an environment in which demands and expectations for their services continue to rise while funding appropriations from traditional governmental resources decline dramatically. The economic realities of debt-heavy local, state/provincial, and federal governments weigh against the likelihood of material changes in the near future. *Increasing Effectiveness of the Community College Financial Model: A Global Perspective for the Global Economy* examines the causal factors behind an eroding financial model, comments on existing challenges at hand, proposes remedies, and offers case studies of community colleges and their global counterparts who have adopted creative and responsive solutions for change.

Although the roots of the community college lie in meeting local resident needs, increasing global connectivity underscores how greatly the world influences the curriculum, student services, and management of financial resources. Understanding global flows supports the development of contemporary information literacy skills that all leaders must possess. The 2008–2009 destabilization of the banking system in the United States negatively impacted world capital and labor markets, and reduced commerce. The consequences are visible on multiple levels. The eroding value of college saving accounts caused by the devaluation of global equity markets, high rates of un- and underemployment, and high levels of consumer debt accentuate the need for an affordable college education. Leaders are reconciling expectations in an environment of constrained funding, often, without a material change to the college's base line financial model. These challenges occur throughout the world and are not confined to any single country.

Cyclical underfunding from budget-constrained traditional government sponsors, coupled by a tendency of some policymakers to undervalue the critical role played by community colleges, accentuates the problem (O'Banion 2005). On the other hand, there is an unprecedented emphasis on the value of community colleges by policy makers and nongovernmental organizations (NGOs). Neither commission reports, speeches from elected officials, nor ceremonial visits have altered the reality that the allocation of real dollars has not kept pace with need. Demand for community college education often results in enrollment growth in excess of resource availability and support services' capacity to meet increasing demand. The convergence of economic turmoil, decline of public funding, and enrollment growth sets a pattern that "wherever short-cycle colleges are found, financing is the primary dilemma" (Ishumi 1988, 163). This disconnect is evident in community colleges throughout the world, and the problem escalates when colleges are cost-ineffective, have weak planning, rely upon legacy curricula and pedagogy, and graduate students in low-demand occupational and professional fields (Raby 2009).

Systemic reform is necessary if community colleges and their global counterparts are to continue to provide an affordable and accessible education, while improving the quality of their educational offerings and student services. Our generation has witnessed unparalleled and enduring global connectivity. Capital and labor markets, commerce, technology, communications, demographic flows, energy, environment, health, and education are drivers of change, which create exciting opportunities and at the time act as harbingers of risk. Uncertainty about future financial support for community colleges is real. It is the new role of community college leadership to resolve increasing student demand, inflated operating costs, and revenue shortages while educating a workforce that is technologically literate, competitive, productive, and capable of functioning in a globally dependent society (AACC and ACCT 2006). A viable performance-based financial construct is a fundamental attribute of success.

This book examines existing challenges in the context of economic and sociocultural change, changing roles of community college leadership, and identifies choices for financial reform options that are available to community college leaders. The contributors represent a united cadre of academic and practitioner voices. While the chapters define theories and processes, the case studies exemplify leadership strategies undertaken and their consequences. A common agreement among such disparate thinkers is that effectiveness in meeting the rapidity and complexity of change requires institutional agility and highly effective internal processes that provide a foundation for new holistic change.

Existing Challenges

There are very few comprehensive books on community college financial management. Of those books (Lombardi 1973; Wattenbarger and Starnes 1976; Augenblick 1978; Garms 1977, 1980; Breneman and Nelson 1981; Richardson and Leslie 1980; Honeyman, Williamson, and Wattenbarger 1991), most were authored prior to the era of global connectivity to which we have referred. Some of these publications emphasize the definitions of chief business officers and chief financial officers in financial concepts examined in higher education publications (Augenblick 1978; Harvey, et al., 1998; Burke and Modarresi 1999; Hauptman 2001; Burke and Minassians 2003), but so many of these are written without a holistic understanding of the community college.

This book advocates a merger of the skill set of management-oriented training of the 1980s that emulated private sector business models with the emphasis on transformational leadership theory in the 1990s and with the focus on teamwork, accountability, transparency, and institutional solvency in support of student access and success in the 2000s. In today's world, financial literacy, business competencies, and a global outlook toward transforming scholarship and professional leadership become the new vision. Unless community college leaders embrace this vision and adapt supportive behaviors, the pool of at-risk students will grow. Some will be priced out of the market, others may be denied access, and many will never understand how the world functions in a global socioeconomic setting.

Basic skills-based training, once a hallmark of the community college, is inadequate to grow economic and social capital so that students can effectively work and live in our interconnected world (Valeau and Raby 2007). The skills learned by students must include demographic change in view of the emergence of multicultural and multilingual workforces, outsourcing of labor, both within the United States and abroad, and the irrevocable move toward technologically driven manufacturing and services environments. We need to understand the global market, while evaluating program sustainability in this context (Levin 2005; Stark 2007; AACU 2009). It demands that all academic, technical, occupational, and vocational courses present learning-outcomes-based assessable education, along with updated curriculum, syllabi, and instructional pedagogy. As President Barack Obama observed, "Simple exchanges can break down walls between us, for when people come together and speak to one another and share a common experience, then their common humanity is revealed" (Obama 2009). Community colleges unable to adjust to our new paradigm risk becoming irrelevant (Dellow 2007) and guilty of inadequately preparing students with skills and behaviors required for sustainable employment (DeSiqueira 2004). Community colleges are the primary educational delivery system for the increasingly interdependent global workforce.

Basis for Improving a Financial Model

The authors in this book discuss three guiding principles for improved financial models: (a) the need for broad financial literacy and application of sound financial management practices; (b) the need for adherence to the community college philosophy and mission; and (c) the need for transformational leadership to guide systemic change of an improved financial model. The chapters illustrate how actions may either positively or adversely influence the quality of educational programming through intended or unintended consequences, while also commenting upon the critical nature of core management functions such as sustaining a balanced budget (Derrico's chapter 7), strategic planning (Trettle and Yeager's chapter 6), oversight (Kinsella, Valeau and Raby's chapter 9), and operations maintenance (Moran's chapter 8). New applications of financial management are profiled, including increasing use of consultants and outsourcing (Moran's chapter 8), multiyear planning (Derrico-Sutin's chapter 5), and creating a culture of self-reliance (Sutin's chapter 10). Since times are changing, new financial models must support the international relevance for workforce training and societal investment (Raby-Valeau's chapter 2) and design changes at the board level (Valeau-Peterson's chapter 3), chief executive officer (CEO) level (Frost-Raspiller-Sygielski's chapter 4), and among internal and external stakeholders.

An improved financial model will be applicable in most countries and will require creativity in an environment of transparency and accountability that connects actions to the college's mission, strategy, and priorities. Potential adverse consequences of failure are worrisome. Tuition increases could limit access for students from low-income families. Community colleges may have to cap enrollment as the norm rather than the exception. The quality of educational and student services may erode. Globalization of curriculum may prove elusive. Unbalanced budgets and financial losses from operations, over time, will reduce financial liquidity, restrict institutional access to credit markets, limit capacity to meet payment obligations, and eventually bring about insolvency.

Financial Literacy and Application of Sound Financial Management

Financial management literacy begins with leadership that shares and provides accurate, complete, and timely data about the financial condition of the community college, the causal factors, and the range of solutions. Arguably, the sharing of news regarding financial challenges will define the case for change. Until recently, the 1976 Wattenbarger and Starnes classifications of US state support were standard in the field that included (a) negotiated budget funding, (b) unit-rate formulas, (c) minimum foundation funding; and (d) cost-based program funding. The Mullin and Honeyman (2007) reclassification begins with three categories: (a) no formula funding; (b) responsive funding with cost of education, equalized, and option funding subcategories; and (c) functional component funding with the subcategories of generalized and tiered funding. While both constructs define our times, neither of them adequately comments upon the adverse consequences of a failing delivery system. This book advocates that a new era is emerging whereby we must learn from those around us, including global counterparts of the community college institution.

Funding Formulas

Traditional funding comes from federal, state/provincial, and local governments' appropriations along with student tuition/fees, as seen in the United States (Breneman and Nelson 1981; Murphy 2004; Mullin-Frost (case study 1), in England (Harbour and Oza 2007), in Uganda (Mugimu and Cullinane case study 2) and in China (Song and Postiglione case study 9). Before 1950, US funding formulas were a combination of tuition and simple allocation of state aid based on budget requests from individual institutions. From 1950 to 1995, complicated formulas were used to allocate money from state or provincial sources (Richardson and Leslie 1980; Mullin and Honeyman 2007; Watson, Melancon, and Kinchen 2008). Most of these appropriations were based on General Fund or General Revenue Fund from sales taxes (Alexander 2000; Behn 2001; Ewell 2002; Burke and Minassians 2002; Commons 2003; Harbour 2003; Harbour 2006; Kitagawa 2003). Worldwide, similar funding formulas cause uncertainty in institutional planning that affect mission, purpose, and effectiveness. Recent funding streams have expanded to include fair-market revenue generation of grants, private gifts, sales of services, auxiliary enterprises, and endowment income (Waller 2003; Kenton et al. 2005; DoBell and Ingle 2009). This book shows that the historical problem stemming from the old model reinforces socioeconomic inequities associated with a liberal market economy and overpowers attempts to redress this imbalance (Grubb and Lazerson 2004). In the wake of change and challenge, traditional remedies often prove insufficient since their impact has been moderate (Dougherty and Hong 2006).

A combination of internal and external factors, nationally and internationally, has caused tuition and fees to increase. Internal costs have risen. They include health care insurance premiums, energy costs, construction and facility maintenance, campus security, specific curriculum, labs, remediation, counseling, support services, and faculty. External costs of government-mandated compliance and reporting requirements and public demands to open additional local campuses and educational centers come with a price tag. Administrative overhead has expanded to meet service needs and expectations of students and communities. This is true in the United States (Romano 2005a), Canada (Levin 2001), and Scotland (Lowe and Vernon 2007). Sadly, the absence of year-to-year predictability and adequacy of funding streams is a common denominator of community colleges worldwide. Such factors are often beyond the control of college leadership. Nevertheless, student access and expectations for improvement of skills and a better life are increasingly problematic.

Incremental Generation of Revenue

Generation of revenue from traditional and nontraditional sources is worthy of attention as one key to improving institutional effectiveness. It is most visible in the adoption of global entrepreneurial ventures and sophisticated ways of marketing services (Dowd and Grant 2007; Newman, Couturier, and Scurry 2004). Profiles of community college entrepreneurial programs exist in England (Harbour and Oza 2007), Ireland (DoBell and Ingle 2009) and in many of the book's case studies (Anglin; Friedel and Covel; Giammarella; Styrbos; Nixon, and Sutin). Both must and can be done without sacrificing the quality of education and the traditional mission of the community college. Opponents of change are reminded that the end game objective is to sustain an affordable and accessible community college education.

Cost Containment

Increases of student tuition and fees are worrisome. The National Association of State Universities and Land Grant Colleges (2007) shows an average annual rate of increase of 3.93 percent (1996–2006) for US community colleges tuition/fees, while during the same period Consumer Price Index (CPI) only rose 2.44 percent (McPherson and Shulenburger 2008, 20). The College Board (2007), using constant or inflation-adjusted 2007 dollars, showed that US community college tuition/fees for a full-time student rose from $306 in 1977–1978 to $1,040 in 2007–2008. Moreover, there remains a disparity of tuition/fees between states as the 2007–2008 average tuition and fees per FTE (the conventional standard for Full Time Equivalent student is 24 credit hours per annum) in Minnesota was $4,443 compared to $633 in California (College Board 2007, 15). Finally, the cost of instruction per FTE fell from 52.8 percent of operating budget in 1995 to 50.2 percent in 2006 by using more part-time faculty and increasing student enrollment per section. Simultaneously, student services cost rose from 11.3 percent per FTE to 12.1 percent and administration and support rose from 35.7 percent to 37.7 percent (Wellman, Desrochers, and Lenihan 2009, 22). Similarly, from 1987 to 2007, part-timers filled 72.6 percent of increased faculty positions, while increases in management and back office staff were largely supported by full-time employees (Bennett 2009, 6–7). Shortfalls in public funding are countered with increased student tuition. This is not an issue confined to the United States as illustrated in case studies by Mugimu and Cullinane, Nixon, and Song and Postiglione. There is an increasing concern about the affordability of a community college education (Romano 2005b).

Containing tuition and fee increases should be a central focus of community college leadership. Future leaders need to assure the public that efforts are under way across the college to support maximum productivity and efficiency of back office staff, and that effective internal cost control policies and procedures are in place. They need to ensure that health care insurance, energy, and other procurement consortiums are managed to contain costs and that simplification of student services takes place but without deterioration of service quality. Finally, they need to show that nonfaculty functions are not overstaffed relative to existing needs.

Adherence to Community College Philosophy and Community College Mission

Notwithstanding the lack of predictability and occasional inadequacy of state appropriations, the mandate to sustain affordability and access to maintain educational quality and relevance is constant (Cohen and Brawer 2003; Mullin and Honeyman 2008; Katsinas and Tollefson 2009). Community colleges that manifest institutional behaviors reflected in improved curriculum, pedagogy, and educational performance measures can also adopt improved financial models. An emphasis on student success and accountability for performance has been added to college mission (Askin 2007). As an example, it has been observed in the Delta Cost Project that "while the public recognizes the importance of higher education and worries about declining affordability . . . widespread perception [holds] that college spending is not well managed" (Wellman and Desrochers 2008, 10). These perceptions are reflective of increasing public concern about institutional performance. Jephcote case study has found unintended consequences from the ways that further education colleges are funded in Wales. Consequences for failure to improve an institution's financial model may induce a drop in enrollments, loss of credibility support from public officials, and impair the effectiveness of advocacy efforts to restore funding. Community colleges and their global counterparts must adopt institutional and staff behaviors that assure optimum effectiveness (Commission on Future 2006). The need to connect the community college values-based mission, "open access," affordability, educational quality, and an improved financial model represents core competencies. Several suggestions for change are woven into the chapters and case studies in this book.

Transformational Leadership Expectations

Community colleges serve diverse constituencies and must satisfy broad and occasionally conflicting demands. A constant theme in this book is that systemic change by transformational leaders is integral to meeting performance expectations on a sustainable basis. Leaders need to understand and apply basic financial management practices. Resources must be aligned with college priorities. Operational efficiencies are of paramount importance. Workforce productivity is essential along with a commitment to innovation, experimentation, and quality. Communication binds the ability to inspire teamwork and set forth plans for change. Finally, the passion for learning, prioritization of institutional goals, and the ability to assume ownership of actions must characterize this millennium's leadership.

Due to the unique local demeanor of community college, no ideal funding formula exists. As Milliron (2007, 37) claims, "We are trapped in old models designed for a very different time." Therefore, we need leaders who adhere to the community college mission, and at the same time find ways to increase revenues and contain costs. Leaders should anticipate that cost-cutting measures and adopting entrepreneurial approaches to revenue generation may encounter resistance, and be prepared to deal with opposing points of views and behaviors. Sustainability of change mandates transformational leadership and the creation of new and more innovative institutional cultures.

Consequences of Change

Wellman (2008) suggests that strategic cost management has to be engaged to free up resources, fund new initiatives, and improve public credibility. Recent initiatives have driven systemic reforms toward attainment of improved learning outcomes and persistence for students. Fundamental reforms are essential if financial resources are to be sufficient to meet student and community needs. Caution is warranted. Decision-making criteria, due diligence, and analysis of relevant qualitative and quantitative data contained in business plans should be undertaken to assure the soundness of creative proposals.

One area of renown for community colleges is their ability to transform themselves quickly to meet the needs of local society. Watson, Melancon, and Kinchen (2008) suggest that manufactured and natural disasters quicken the process of forcing colleges to reenvision delivery of quality education with little state funding. Yet meaningful financial reforms in many cases are not occurring quickly enough in light of our current worldwide economic crisis. Perhaps too much attention has been afforded a rearguard action to restore public funding. This book endorses Wagner's (2008) change of action strategies.

The present times call for creativity, being globally relevant, and adopting the best attributes of improved financial models into community college operations. We must practice entrepreneurship, accountability, strategic marketing, plan execution, and frugality as the norm rather than the exception. Initiatives undertaken must be consistent with global sociocultural and economic patterns. Concurrently, the ability to remain agile remains critical. We must reconceptualize what equity means and how it relates to community college funding (Mullin and Honeyman 2007). One key is to apply sound budgeting procedures based on revenue projections and determine requirements based on analysis of function, workloads, and methodology. Steady, innovative, forceful, visionary leadership is required now and needs to be tested as colleges attempt to deal with the erosion of state and local tax revenue to support their programs.

Conclusion

We firmly believe that financial viability, affordable tuition, high-quality education, and a globally inclusive curricula are reconcilable objectives. Effective financial management should be defined by fidelity to mission, alignment of financial resources to college priorities, and comprehending the implications of global connectivity, willingness to ask hard questions and make the right decisions, adaptability, innovation, and transparent accountability (Mullin and Honeyman 2008). An inclusive approach to community college leadership merits respect and reinforcement. This is a tall order, but an achievable one. It requires passionate, visionary, and performance-driven leaders who can inspire, and empower staff and support teams using a collaborative approach.

As editors, we support continued systemic transformation of the financial model in ways that the *Learning College* has done for instruction and *Achieving the Dream* is doing for remedial education. This approach has global applicability since we live in a time "with the highest level of global interconnectedness in human history" (Boggs and Irwin 2007, 25). Thus, it is critical to examine prevailing policies, programs, and practices that govern financing and understand that similar institutions from around the world are also asking these hard questions. Worldwide there is concern about improving or expanding learning and if so, how, and for which students. As the knowledge- and productivity-based global economy continues to exist, community colleges are challenged to prepare students capable of problem-solving, innovation, technological competence, critical thinking, and a capacity to work within multicultural/multilingual teams. Such graduates will be ready to face emerging challenges, build our economies, lead our companies, and transform our communities.

The times are changing and so must the community college's financial model. We must redesign colleges to deliver globally relevant workforce development programs in high demand occupations, sustain high-quality transfer functions, and accommodate all who can profit from it. Community colleges and their global counterparts are facing complex and tenacious challenges linked to growing student enrollment, decreased revenues, increased demand for accountability, transparency, and an emerging cry for international education. The various chapters and case studies presented in *Increasing Effectiveness of the Community College Financial Model: A Global Perspective for the Global Economy* offer a foundation for such a reform.

References

American Association of Community Colleges (AACC). 2010. AACC Homepage. Washington, DC: AACC. Available online at: http://www.aacc.nche.edu.

AACC and Association of Community College Trustees (ACCT). 2006. *Building the Global Community: A Joint Statement on the Role of Community Colleges in International Education.* AACC Homepage. Washington, DC: AACC. Available online at: http://www.aacc.nche.edu.

Association of American Colleges and Universities (AACU). 2009. *Raising the Bar Employers' Views On College Learning in the Wake of The Economic Downturn.* Washington, DC: AACU.

Association of Canadian Community Colleges (ACCC). 2008. *Key Priorities 2006–2007.* Ottawa: ACCC. Available online at: http://www.accc.ca.

Alexander, Fieldon K. 2000. "The Changing Face of Accountability: Monitoring and Assessing Institutional Performance in Higher Education." *The Journal of Higher Education* 71 (4): 411–431.

Askin, Jacalyn A. 2007. "Community College Mission: Re(S)ources Make a Difference." *Community College Journal of Research and Practice* 31 (12): 977–997.

Augenblick, John. 1978. "Financing Community Colleges: An Examination of the State and Local Roles." *Education Finance*, No. 2: 56. Denver, CO: Education Commission of the States.

Behn, Robert D. 2001. *Rethinking Democratic Accountability.* Washington, DC: Brookings Institution.

Bennett, Daniel. 2009. *Trends in the Higher Education Labor Force.* Washington, DC: Center for College Affordability and Productivity.

Boggs, George R., and Judy T. Irwin. 2007. "What Every Community College Leader Needs to Know: Building Leadership for International Education." *New Directions for Community Colleges* 2007 (138): 25–30.

Breneman, David. W., and Susan C. Nelson. 1981. *Financing Community Colleges: An Economic Perspective.* Washington, DC: Brookings Institution.

Burke, Joseph C., and Shahpar Modarresi. 1999. *Performance Funding and Budgeting: Popularity and Volatility—The Third Annual Survey.* Albany, NY: Rockefeller Institute.

Burke, Joseph C., and Henrik P. Minassians. 2003. *Performance Reporting: "Real" Accountability or Accountability "Lite"—Seventh Annual Survey 2003.* Albany, NY: Rockefeller Institute.

Burke, Joseph C., and Henrik P. Minassians. 2002. "The New Accountability: From Regulation to Results." *New Directions for Institutional Research* 116: 5–19.

Cohen, Arthur M. 2009. "Community Colleges in the United States." In *Community College Models: Globalization and Higher Education Reform,* ed. Rosalind Latiner Raby and Edward J. Valeau. Dordrecht, The Netherlands: Springer.

Cohen, Arthur M., and Florence B. Brawer. 2003. *The American Community College.* 4th ed. San Francisco, CA: Jossey-Bass.

College Board. 2007. *Trends in College Pricing.* Washington, DC: The College Board.

Commission on the Future of Higher Education. 2006. *A Test of Leadership: Charting the Future of U.S. Higher Education.* Washington, DC: U.S. Department of Education. Available online at: http://www.ed.gov.

Commons, P. K. 2003. "The Contributions of Inspection, Self-Assessment, Investors in People and the Inclusive Learning Quality Initiative to Improving Quality in Further Education Sector Colleges: An Initial Exploration." *Journal of Further and Higher Education* 27 (1): 27–46.

Dellow, Donald A. 2007. "The Role of Globalization in Technical and Occupation Programs." *New Directions for Community Colleges* 2007 (138): 39–45.

DeSiqueira, A. 2004. *The Regulation of Education Through the WTO/ GATS: Path to the Enhancement of Human Freedom?* Paper presented at the Comparative International Education Society National Conference, Salt Lake City, March 2004.

DoBell, Daniel C., and Sarah A. Ingle. 2009. "Pathways to Participation: A Comparative Study of Community College Entrepreneurial Educational Programs in the United States and Ireland." In *Community College Models: Globalization and Higher Education Reform,* ed. Rosalind Latiner Raby and Edward J. Valeau. Dordrecht, The Netherlands: Springer.

Dougherty, Kevin J., and Esther Hong. 2006. Performance Accountability as Imperfect Panacea. In *Defending the Community College Equity Agenda,* ed. Thomas Bailey and Vanessa Smith Morest. Baltimore, MD: Johns Hopkins University Press.

Dowd, Alicia C., and John L. Grant. 2007. "Equity Effects of Entrepreneurial Community College Revenues." *Community College Journal of Research and Practice* 31 (3): 231–244.

Elsner, Paul A., George R. Boggs, and Judith T. Irwin. 2008. *Global Development of Community Colleges, Technical Colleges, and Further Education Programs.* Washington, DC: Community College Press, AACC.

Ewell, P. T. 2002. A Delicate Balance: The role of evaluation in management." *Quality in Higher Education* 8 (2); 159–171.

Garms, Walter I. 1977. *Financing Community Colleges.* New York: Teachers College Press.

Garms, Walter I. 1980. "On Measuring the Equity of Community College Finance." Unpublished manuscript. ERIC ED Document No. ED187378. Rochester, NY: University of Rochester.

Grubb, W., Northan, and Marvin Lazerson. 2004. *The Educational Gospel: The Economic Power of Schooling.* Cambridge, MA: Harvard University Press.

Harbour, Clifford P. 2003. "An Institutional Accountability Model for Community Colleges." *Community College Journal of Research and Practice* 27: 299–316.

Harbour, Clifford P. 2006. "The incremental Marketization and Centralization of State Control of Public Higher Education: A Hermeneutic Interpretation of Legislative and Administrative Texts." *International Journal of Qualitative Methods* 5 (3): 35–54.

Harbour, Clifford P., and Oza Jaquette. 2007. "Advancing an Equity Agenda at the Community College in an Age of Privatization, Performance Accountability, and Marketization." *Equity and Excellence in Education* 40 (3): 197–207.

Harvey, James, Roger M. Williams, Rita J. Kirshstein, Amy Smith O'Malley and Jane V. Wellman. 1998. Straight Talk about College Costs and Prices. Report of the National Commission on the Cost of Higher Educaiton. Washington, DC: National Commission on the Cost of Higher Education. Access at http://www.eric.ed.gov/PDFS/ED416762.pdf

Hauptman, Arthur. 2001. "Reforming the Ways in Which States Finance Higher Education." In *The States and Public Higher Education Policy: Affordability, Access, and Accountability*, ed. D. E. Heller. Baltimore: Johns Hopkins University Press.

Honeyman, David., Mary L. Williamson, and James L. Wattenbarger. 1991. *Community College Financing 1990: Challenges for a New Decade.* Washington, DC: American Association of Community and Junior Colleges.

Ishumi, Abel G. M. 1998. "Vocational Training as an Educational and Development Strategy: Conceptual and Practical Issues." *International Journal of Educational Development* 8 (3): 163–174.

Katsinas, Stephen G., and Terrence A. Tollefson. 2009. *Funding and Access Issues in Public Higher Education: A Community College Perspective.* Tuscaloosa, AL: Education Policy Center, University of Alabama.

Kenton, Carol Piper, Mary E. Huba, and John H. Schuh. 2005. " Financing Community Colleges: A Longitudinal Study of 11 States." *Community College Journal of Research and Practice* 29 (2): 109–122.

Kitagawa, Fumi. 2003. "New Mechanisms of Incentives and Accountability for Higher Education Institutions: Linking the Regional, National and Global Dimensions." *Higher Education Management and Policy* 15 (2): 99–116.

Levin, John S. 2001. *Globalizing the Community College: Strategies for Change in the Twenty-First Century.* New York: Palgrave.

Levin, John S. 2005. "The Business Culture of the Community College: Students as Consumers, Students as Commodities." *New Directions for Higher Education* 2005 (129): 11–26.

Lombardi, John V. 1973. *Managing Finances in Community Colleges.* San Francisco, CA: Jossey-Bass.

Lowe, Janet, and Vernon Gayle. 2007. "Exploring the Work/Life/Study Balance: The Experience of Higher Education Students in a Scottish further Education College." *Journal of Further and Higher Education* 31 (3): 225–239.

McPherson, Peter, and David Shulenburger. 2008. *University Tuition, Consumer Choice and College Affordability.* Washington, DC: National Association of State Universities and Land Grant Colleges.

Milliron, Mark David. 2007. "Transcendence and Globalization. Our Education and Workforce Development Challenge." *New Directions for Community Colleges* 2007 (138): 31–38.

Mullin, Christopher M., and David S. Honeyman. 2007. "The Funding of Community Colleges: A Typology of State Funding Formulas." *Community College Review* 35 (2): 113–127.

Mullin, Christopher M., and David S. Honeyman. 2008. "Statutory Responsibility for Fixing Tuition and Fees: Community Colleges and Undergraduate Institutions." *Community College Journal of Research and Practice* 32 (4–6): 284–304.

Murphy, Patrick J. 2004. *Financing California's Community Colleges.* San Francisco, CA: Public Policy Institute of California.

National Association of State Universities and Land Grant Colleges (NASULGC). 2007. *University Tuition, Consumer Choice, and College Affordability: Strategies for Addressing a Higher Education Affordability Challenge.* Washington, DC: NASULGC.

Newman, Frank, Lara Couturier, and Jamie Scurry. 2004. *The Future of Higher Education: Rhetoric, Reality, and the Risks of the Market.* San Francisco, CA: Jossey-Bass.

Obama, Barack H. 2009. Remarks Made at a Press Conference to the Grand National Assembly of Turkey, Ankara, February 24, 2009. Available online at: http://www.whitehouse.gov.

O'Banion, Terry. 1997. *A Learning College for the 21st Century.* Phoenix: Oryx Press.

Raby, Rosalind Latiner. 2009. "Globalization and Community College Model Development." In *Community College Models: Globalization and Higher Education Reform*, ed. Rosalind Latiner Raby and Edward J. Valeau. Dordrecht, The Netherlands: Springer Publishers.

Raby, Rosalind Latiner, and Edward J. Valeau. 2009. *Community College Models: Globalization and Higher Education Reform.* Dordrecht, The Netherlands: Springer Publishers.

Richardson, Richard C. Jr., and Larry L. Leslie. 1980. *The Impossible Dream? Financing Community College's Evolving Mission*. Washington, DC and Los Angeles, CA: American Association of Community and Junior Colleges; Council of Universities and Colleges; ERIC Clearinghouse for Junior Colleges.

Romano, Richard M. 2005a. "Seeking the Proper Balance Between Tuition, State Support, and Local Revenues: An Economic Perspective." In *Sustaining Financial Support for Community Colleges. New Directions for Community Colleges (Vol. 132)*, ed. Stephen G. Katsinas and James C. Palmer. San Francisco, CA: Jossey-Bass.

Romano, Richard M. 2005b. "Privatizing the Community College." *Community College Journal* 75 (5): 22–26.

Stark, Paul S. 2007. "The New Rule Paradigm Shift: Transforming At-Risk Programs by Matching Business Archetypes Strategies in the Global Market." *Community College Journal of Research and Practice* 31 (6): 491–492.

Valeau, Edward J., and Rosalind Latiner Raby, eds. 2007. *Special Issue: International Reform Efforts and Challenges in Community Colleges. New Directions for Community Colleges* 2007 (138): 1–96.

Wagner, Tony. 2008. *The Global Achievement Gap*. New York: Basic Books.

Waller, Lee R. 2003. "Disparities in Community College Finance: In-District." *Community College Journal of Research and Practice* 27 (5): 409–419.

Watson, Lisa M., Girard Melancon, and Nancy Kinche. 2008. "Financing Higher Education: Three Case Studies in a Post-Disaster Recovery Environment." *Community College Journal of Research and Practice* 32 (3): 203–219.

Wattenbarger, James L., and Paul M. Starnes. 1976. *Financial Support Patterns for Community Colleges*. Gainesville, FL: Institute of Higher Education.

Wellman, Jane V. 2008. "Foreword." In *Cost Containment: A Survey of Current Practices at America's State Colleges and Universities*. Washington, DC: American Association of State Colleges and Universities Press.

Wellman, Jane V., and Donna M. Desrochers. 2008. *The Growing Imbalance: Recent Trends in Post Secondary Education*. Washington, DC: Delta Cost Project and American Institutes for Research.

Wellman, Jane V., Donna M. Desrochers, and Colleen M. Lenihan. 2009. *Trends in College Spending*. Washington, DC: Delta Cost Project and American Institutes for Research.

Chapter 2

Global and National Context

Rosalind Latiner Raby and Edward J. Valeau

Introduction

Globalization is not a local phenomenon, but a condition that impacts every aspect of our lives worldwide. As a dynamic force, globalization perpetuates a borderless world where practices and ideas are shared across space and time, aided by technology, wide mobility, communication, socioeconomic relationships, and environmental interdependence. Since globalization affects the economic, social, and political stability of communities that depend on a trained workforce and an educated citizenry for its identity and survival, it profoundly influences higher education, and in particular the community college. As an identified concept, globalization directly impacts community college institutional mission and curricula that internationalizes the campus and in so doing, supports intercampus, intercommunity, and intercountry relationships as a "requisite seed for internal change that reflects how the institution responses to [globalization] pressures" (Levin 2001, x).

The impact of globalization on our lives has been made even more acute in the post 9/11 era and most recently through cross-country interaction that delimits the financial foundation that governs each local community. Global economic flows are simply part of our lives and define the basis for the skills that were once essential for employment and which are not viable in today's world. This is even more important for community colleges than for other postsecondary institutions whose education is so closely linked to social change. However, while change is a hallmark feature of the community college, it is often too slow to happen and is often hindered by financial constraints. For example, most community colleges still use an industrial factory model based on an agrarian calendar to meet the needs of an information age. There remains concern for the relevancy of the educational programs offered. As Milliron (2007, 37) claims, "we are trapped in old models designed for a very different time." There is a need to adopt new models because, as the U.S. secretary of education Arne Duncan stated, community colleges are invaluable resources for adults seeking to acquire new skills needed by employers (Kellog and Tomsho 2009). These new models embody principles of globalization at their core.

The skills that community colleges need to embrace are those that have an international foundation. As President Obama noted in his speech (Obama 2009a) to Congress on February 24, 2009, "our children will compete for jobs in a global economy that too many of our schools do not prepare them for." In the *Chronicle of Higher Education*, (Fisher 2008, 1) notes that "Community-college leaders want to ensure that their institutions produce students who can collaborate with co-workers from other countries and cultures, who have an understanding of global economics, and who, perhaps, even speak a foreign language." This reinforces the American Association of Community Colleges (AACC) and Association of Community College Trustees (ACCT) 2006 Joint Statement that affirms that "we live in a time of continuous economic and social change driven by increasing globalization" (Boggs and Irwin 2007, 27). In response to this affirmation, community college leaders should take the steps necessary to secure a financial, educational, and social environment that encourages and prepares faculty, students, and the community to be globally engaged.

If this chapter had been written prior to 2010, the tone and message might have been different. Amid the economic crisis, the deep funding cuts to institutional budgets began. By late 2010, and throughout 2011, the severity of the funding crisis became more apparent. The cuts to community colleges were significant and made swiftly. Programs deemed optional, or at the periphery, suffered the most. Periphery status defines the field of international education[1]. In 2005, the American Council on Education (ACE) reported 61 percent of community colleges having a "low" level of internationalization (Green and Siaya 2005). In California, which has the largest community college system in the world, international education was among the first programs cut. This despite the long history of supporting international education that dates back to 1975, and that 17 of the top 20 colleges nationally in the field of education abroad and 18 of the top 50 colleges nationally in the field of international students are California community colleges. By early 2010, 47 percent of all California community colleges either eliminated or suspended support for their international programs. By 2011, many of these were restored and yet the initial actions contradict overall leadership acknowledgment of the link between the global economy and community college education (California Colleges for International Education [CCIE] 2011).

While all programs are perceived by their stakeholders to be important, we nonetheless advocate that the consequences of not supporting internationalization of the community college are severe enough to stand reconsideration. It is difficult to convince educational leaders that international education that has at best maintained a marginalized status is where a limited budget should go (Frost and Raby 2009). Yet, the chapter will precisely attempt to make this the case.

This chapter examines how community colleges are affected by and perpetuate conditions that advance globalization in terms of (a) changing definitions of community, (b) economic and sociocultural applications of globalization, and (c) reforming community college finance for the globalization era.

Changing Definitions of a Community College

The common definition of the community college is to provide education to all those who can learn. A unique mission supports this vision by reinforcing policies of open access, local commitments, and multicurricular emphasis backed by sound economic planning. While this mission has remained constant over the decades, the students who attend the colleges and the purpose of the education offered has changed significantly. Therefore, current and future financial decision-making needs to encompass the interconnectedness of (a) student population, (b) local/global dichotomy, and (c) educational purpose.

Student Population

Over the past 25 years, a common feature of the community college student worldwide is their nontraditional characteristics. Beginning with the shift from "junior" to "community" college, the student increasingly remains one who has been denied any privileged educational opportunities (Cohen 2009). The nontraditional characteristic is defined by gender in Japan, working class in Scotland, and second-tier elite in Mexico, Thailand, and Senegal. In the United States, all of these characteristics are present among community college students. These are students, who for some reason cannot or choose not to attend the traditional university (Raby and Valeau 2009). The nontraditional characteristics are frequently intertwined with the local-global dichotomy because nonlocal students may enroll in a community college and increasingly, such enrollment is linked to their only opportunity for postsecondary study. This is a primary reason for the explosion in the enrollment of international students on community college campuses. It is also connected to educational purposes since course offerings are often dictated by student need, ranging from remedial instruction and vocational education to education abroad. Effective community colleges support the unique needs of their students without denying opportunity for anyone.

Local-Global Dichotomy

The local-global dichotomy concept has existed since the formation of district boundaries, which defined the college mission to serve the needs of its geographic community in terms of transfer to local four-year institutions or for employment at local businesses. This variable has been adopted by most community colleges throughout the world (Raby and Valeau 2009) as mission statements connect the college to "serve the needs of the general community" (College of North Atlantic, Qatar), provide "opportunities for social mobility" (Nong Bualumpu Community College, Thailand) and "make colleges accessible to local students" (Scottish Further Education). While the mission is clearly connected with the local, the application is global. Valeau and Raby (2007) suggest that when defined globally, *community* expands networks that demand colleges to abandon thinking in linear relationships across borders and favor of educating students as *global citizens*. Thus, in the proposed holistic interconnection, these changes redefine student populations and educational purpose as demonstrated by examples of student mobility and on-line instruction and have created a situation where the local service nature of the college is no longer its sole intent. Those colleges that support these changes will necessarily be in a stronger position to serve their local populations in the years ahead.

Educational Purpose

The educational purpose is at the heart of the community colleges' need for existence and, as the student population becomes increasingly "bifurcated" (Levinson 2005, 18–20), the split between traditional transfer-bound students and degree/certificate students becomes more pronounced (Cohen 2009, 39). Institutions have a need to serve a wide range of students for an even larger range of purposes, and at affordable levels. Yet, this concept will remain a focus of discussion for it is directly connected with financial decisions and vision. On the student personal level, regardless of intent, i.e., be it transfer, lifelong learning, or trade/service careers, all community college students are to benefit from the higher education they receive. Therefore, financial decisions, which are programmatic designs, must aim to support the multiopportunities that help provide personal student growth. On the societal level, an educated citizenry promotes a common humanity and culture (Cohen and Brawer 2003). Therefore, financial decisions must support actions that integrate academic/skill-set knowledge with international literacy skills to support personal, societal, and skills training needs for our current generation.[2] In a comparative context, Raby (2009) advances the idea that community colleges lead to widespread higher educational reform when they tend to educate nontraditional postsecondary students and demonstrate in a practical way the means by which new generations can receive skills and training that ensure employment and social mobility that can transform communities. Here, financial decisions connect to ensuring an education that supports societal transformation. When an educational purpose has such ramifications, it clearly remains something that should be centered in all financial planning and operations that support mission, vision, goals, and values of the institutions.

Economic and Sociocultural Applications of Globalization

Globalization influences financial structure and planning of community colleges through two trajectories. The first trajectory views colleges as a supplier of human capital and defines economic flows as the primary objective. The second trajectory is sociocultural wherein community colleges play a key link in overcoming inequalities that stem from differential access to higher education.

Economic Globalization

Economic globalization links the college to the principles of neoliberalism, which depict the global market as redefining technical and career sectors, new workplace skills, and credentialization. The business world understands that the world is a global marketplace where four out of every five jobs have an international connection. Therefore, success depends on acquiring a far different set of knowledge, skills, and perspectives than previous generations. In this context, students worldwide "must be prepared to trade with, work alongside and communicate with persons from radically different backgrounds than their own" (Fiske 2006, 2). While the need to secure international literacy skills is generally understood by most stakeholders, these are skills that are still rarely taught in our colleges. College budget woes influence negative financial flows that perpetuate a lack of courses and training. In this context, the repercussions could lead to the miseducation of many students. Such results should leave no doubt as to the recognition and need to move economic globalization to the center of all community college financial planning and decision-making. There are three elements related to providing or preparing human capital via an economic strategy.

College Support to Promote Financial Gain

College support to promote financial gain is not a construct that is readily adopted by many community colleges. Yet, without the support, their future financial growth will be limited. A good example is that international student programs are now the fourth largest service sector export in the US economy (Open Doors 2009a). In California, it is most telling that in 2009, international students alone contributed more than $137,145,000 to the tuition of the various community colleges and *an additional* $613,581,000 to California's economy (Open Doors 2009b). While nationwide, international student programs have experienced a 126 percent growth since 2005, it is important to note that not all community colleges fully support the fact that students from other countries bring diverse ideas into classrooms, and introduce domestic students to worldviews, and provide an avenue for improving international relations among future leaders of today and tomorrow. International student programs remain underfunded and at perpetual risk of cuts. The continued lack of funding to support these programs remains critical.

Training and Credentialization

Training and credentialization are at the core of market-oriented policies that correlate the building of a relevant skills base, supported by lifelong learning with the explicit purpose of reducing unemployment (Schugurensky and Higgins 1996; Levin 2005; Carnoy and Luschei 2008). A disconnect exists today since too many community colleges do not understand the current ramifications of this correlation. Specifically, education related to lower-level skills, which used to be the hallmark of community colleges, is not needed in a globalized economy (Wolf 2009).[3] Globalization reinforces the need for specific credentials that demonstrate minimum competencies for the local workforce (Lim 2008). This is the area where community colleges can be most effective in the future. The community college experience therefore can no longer just link the relevance of education to a useful role in the local community but instead must make connections to those that have a global context (Ng et al. 2009). Community colleges can make this transformation since one of its basic characteristic is its ability to easily and quickly modify work-based and trade credentials to respond to the changing economic demands by providing low-cost, relevant, training for large numbers of people (Elsner, Boggs, and Irwin 2008). The key, however, is for community college leaders to recognize the role of globalization in this process.

Vocational Fallacy

Vocational fallacy defines the relevance of educational programs as central in today's global economy. Institutions that offer irrelevant and inflexible curriculum may not be an optimal means for solving labor needs (Selvarathnam 1998; Ishumi 1998). Community colleges are easily victim to this fallacy (George 2006). This is not a statement on graduation or transfer rates, but on the college providing an illusion of openness that veils a lack of opportunities. Worldwide, while a community college does provide an array of educational opportunities, they do not necessarily increase access for disenfranchised and may merely perpetuate an already unequal higher educational system (McMurtrie 2004; Raby 2009). In part, this is connected to the chronic underfunding and low prestige despite their share of the higher education student population (Lowe and Gayle 2007). The economic divide is furthered as community college education lacks the same market value, social prestige, or general reception in the society as other degrees or diplomas.

Sociocultural Globalization

Sociocultural globalization defines the second trajectory and is related to access, social stability, global workforce development, and academic integrity, which are discussed below. While not consistent in all countries, low tuition, nonexistent entrance exams, and local location do provide access for nontraditional students, many of whom have suffered social and political disorder and need to be reintegrated back into society (Lowe and

Gayle 2007; Smith 2007). It is central for community college leadership to develop the means to preserve open access as it is directly correlated with social stability, global workforce development, and academic integrity.

Social Stability

Social stability is linked to education throughout the world by politicians, economists, and academics. There is a belief that an outgrowth of education is the deliverable of opportunities that leads to employment, which supports economic development and improves social conditions (Strydom and Lategan 1998; Kintzer 1998; Jones 2002, Nisah-Gyabaah and Obour 2008, Labi 2009). By serving their communities, "the most crucial function of the community colleges then has been to provide students with training and retraining programmes which help them to achieve social mobility and contribute to the economic well-being of a country" (ITAP International 2009; Smith 2007; Ural 1998, 119). Globalization of education maintains cohesive relationships, by giving students the skills to work with different types of people, and form a valuable foundation by which they can contribute to their thriving community.[4]

Global Workforce Development

Global workforce development mirrors the needs of a globalized economy in which cultural knowledge and modern language skills are in increasing demand by employers, most of whom increasingly compete in a global arena one way or another. A multicultural and multilingual, and increasingly, international workforce is common (ITAP International 2009) and those with adaptable workers build a supportive economic environment that adds value to the free flow of capital, information, and technology that characterizes the global economy (Porter 2002, 1). Those students who have global competency skills, i.e., those who have a diverse and knowledgeable worldview (NASULGC 2004), are those who will excel. The others will simply be left behind (Block 2008).

Academic Integrity

Academic integrity prescribes that academic standards are transparent and facilitates portability worldwide, which are increasingly important in our era of institutional ranking. Simply speaking, courses and programs that do not reference international themes are incomplete. For example, studying nursing without acknowledging health issues that arise from pandemics or studying engineering without including international environmental impacts is remiss and shortsighted. Students know the value of international literacy and increasingly in competitive economic times will choose to attend those community colleges that provide appropriate curriculum and programs. Campuses with supportive education abroad and international student programs are favored over those who do not offer these options. It is now commonly accepted that community colleges need to "expand exchange programs, and increase scholarships, like the one that brought my father to America... invest in online learning for teachers and children around the world; and create a new online network, so a young person in Kansas can communicate instantly with a young person in Cairo" (Obama 2009b).

Reforming Community College Finance for a Globalization Era

A multicultural workforce defines the economy in which a college resides whether or not the local companies are global companies (ITAP International 2009). As community, colleges "weave together people and projects that reach beyond traditional educational boundaries" (Gordon 1999, 1), those community colleges that do not recognize global flows are at an extreme disadvantage. This suggests the need for leaders to pay close attention to coherently connecting the mission, curriculum, and programs so that local students can serve the local economy that exists within a global context. There are five areas in which realistic reforms in our economically strapped era can occur: (1) global workforce development, (2) innovation, (3) nontraditional educational pathways, (4) adaptability, and (5) support of campus internationalization.

Global Workforce Development

Institutional leaders and policy makers need to make a concrete connection between the academic, vocational, occupational, and technical programs of the college with globalization as the foundation upon which future success exists. The skills needed for our current global workforce place international skills in high demand. Yet, in a study of skills that employers want from community college graduates, Hart (2008, 4) notes that employers are less convinced of recent graduates' preparedness in terms of global knowledge. When asked about preparation of global knowledge, 46 percent say recent grads are not very well prepared. The most recent survey (Association of American Colleges and Universities [AACU] 2009) confirms that employers want colleges to place more emphasis on global issues (67 percent), intercultural competence (71 percent), and intercultural knowledge of global issues (67 percent). Although community college students stand to benefit from an international perspective, they often lack an explicit focus on international learning within their curriculum. Therefore, it is necessary to build the skills of the demand-driven workforce development mode (Porter 2002) that understands global flows and their connections to local demand and supply-sides of the labor market.

Innovation

There is a pressing demand for refocusing the delivery of curriculum to express innovation and to define skills that students really need and want. A critical question is whether or not community colleges are even beginning to address those skills in a systematic, coordinated manner evenly throughout all community colleges globally and in the United States. Such an undertaking begins with the critical examination of college policies, programs, and practices. It asks the hard questions about whether or not the college is improving or expanding international literacy skills that will impact future job attainment. Community colleges thus are challenged to focus on preparing intelligent, creative, and courageous learners able, ready, and willing to face challenges and transform communities (Ng et al., 2009). Currently, the primary issue remains with the ability of visionary community college leadership to understand and make changes at the colleges so that their students have the competitive edge to "integrate and apply their academic, technical and practical knowledge and skills to solve real-world problems, to continue learning in formal and informal ways throughout their lifetimes on-the-job, in schools and in their communities, and to work effectively with other people as customers, coworkers and supervisors" (Porter 2002, 4).

Nontraditional Educational Pathways

Colleges are encouraged to expand their awareness of the need to recognize alternative means for achieving lifelong education. Such possibilities include adult literacy, community service, apprenticeships, and experiential learning. One way to achieve this is by institutionalizing international educational that ensures that learning comes in various means either through an internationalized curriculum, international activities on a college or university campus, international student exchange and outreach, and education abroad. All stakeholders must embrace the fact that few intensive learning experiences provide the type of transformative learning that international education can achieve.

Adaptability to Change

The ability of community colleges to respond to the local economy by adopting product-oriented curricula and flexible short-term programming for differentially skilled laborers and career education helps to maintain their viability. For some colleges, success lies in the use of local resources to create organic relationships between the teacher and the learners. Since the community college is connected to the local, it can easily recognize this change. The key remains to respond accordingly (Dellow and Romano 2006). Colleges need to improve the responsiveness of education and training to prepare youth and adults for the demands of the global market place and those who lack such adaptability are destined to fall further behind (Porter 2002, 2).

Conclusion

Internationalization of the campus and curriculum are responses that the field of higher education and the community colleges in particular is making in the twenty-first century as the landscape changes. All community college associations, including AACC, ACCC, further education, TAFE, vocational education and training (VET), and others, have policy documents that support internationalization. Ironically, as students and the disciplines they study become more internationalized, and the workforce to which the students will eventually enter becomes more globalized, the community college is increasingly going in the opposite direction. In these economically challenging times, those colleges that honor their mission to endorse internationalization will find a way to support their various international programs. This is the key to future success.

Part of this new redirection is financing a global perspective for the global economy. Past arguments about financing primarily focus on how to find funding. We argue that we need to fundamentally redesign our colleges to imprint internationally relevant and transcendent skills that is not only good for workforce development, but for societal investment as well. If community colleges fully support the conviction that they provide opportunities for the disenfranchised and assist with social and economic restructuring by empowering students with economic and social opportunities, then internationalization follow suit. However, this must be an honest and real conviction that filters throughout the campus to promote career/ personal advancement opportunities, influence local business and industry by reinforcing new curricular emphasis, and reduce culture conflict in multicultural societies resulting from the education of the underprivileged. Care must be taken as reverberations from the economic crisis can force community colleges to abandon their unique characteristic of open access or be unable to sustain the educational ideals envisioned and expected by diverse sections of the society. The ramification of not internationalizing the campus then is that many students are denied an education that is given in abundance to other students elsewhere.

As Cohen and Brawer (2003) stated, for many students the choice is not between community college and a four-year institutions, but instead, it is between the community college and nothing. Without international education in community colleges, many students do not have the chance to expand their understanding of the global world or change their perceptions and attitudes about global relationships. The philosophy of open access is placed at risk if four-year college students have access to international literacy but community college students do not.

Uldrick (2008) suggests that society is nowhere near the outer limits of the growth in terms of all technological, science, and information technology fields. However, this concept can also be applied to colleges as Thornton (2009, 3) opines "college leaders must be prepared and able to jump the curve." As such, community colleges have become the place to expand opportunities and challenge the notion of higher education as an elitist venture intended for only the few and thus represent an important and significant branch of American postsecondary education. In this context, we believe our work is important for new and aspiring college presidents and policy-making boards who must lead in a challenging and changing environment.

Notes

1. For discussion on periphery status see Valeau and Raby (2007) and Frost and Raby (2008).
2. The 1947 Report from the Commission on Higher Education, also known as the Truman Commission Report, encouraged all higher educational institutions, including community colleges to produce an international citizenry (Frost and Raby 2009). In defining and refining the connection between international literacy and global citizenry, the global citizen is one who is trained to observe, reflect, interpret, and particularly, contribute to improving global society and who embodies the traits and learning outcomes associated with intercultural, multicultural, and international education, particularly including *the desire to*

learn more about other peoples and possess the skills to live, work and transact with those from radically different backgrounds within and across borders.

3. Jobs requiring an "associate degree" represent 49 percent of future United States jobs (U.S. Department of Labor Monthly Labor Review); 80 percent of future Canadian jobs (AACC 2008); and 50 percent of new British jobs (United Kingdom *White Paper* as quoted in Wolf 2009).

4. Mission statements reinforce this philosophy: United Arab Emeritus Higher Colleges of Technology "builds leadership potential to make the fullest possible contribution to the development of the community for the good of all its people"; Riverdale Community College (Ireland) "gives each pupil opportunity to develop his/her aptitudes and talents fully;" Nova Scotia Community College (Canada) "builds economy and quality of life through education and innovation;" Thai community colleges "provides locals with a chance for post-secondary education that they otherwise would be denied;" and Ghana colleges "provides support to industry and commerce in areas of human resource" to communities in which they are located (Nisah-Gyabaah and Obour 2008). Indeed, emphasis on open access is found in mission statements worldwide.

References

Association of American Colleges and Universities (AACU). 2009. *Raising the Bar Employers' Views on College Learning in the Wake of the Economic Downturn.* Washington, DC: AACU.

Fiske, Edward B. 2006. "Educating Leaders for a Global Society." Goldman Sachs and Asia Society Homepage. Available online at: http://www2.goldmansachs. com.

Block, Gene. 2008. "Presentation." Presented at the Education and Business Symposium by NAFSA: Association of International Educators (International Education & Global Workforce Development: A Dialogue with Business and Higher Education Stakeholders), Los Angeles, October 23, 2008. Available online at: http://www.international.ucla.edu.

Boggs, George R., and Judy T. Irwin. 2007. "What Every Community College Leader Needs to Know: Building Leadership for International Education." *New Directions for Community Colleges* 2007 (138): 25–30.

California Colleges for International Education (CCIE). 2011. *Annual Survey.* Los Angeles: CCIE. Available online at: http://www.ccieworld.org.

Carnoy, Martin, and Thomas F. Luschei. 2008. "Skill Acquisition in 'High Tech' Export Agriculture: A Case Study of Lifelong Learning in Peru's Asparagus Industry." *Journal of Education and Work* 21(1): 1–25.

Cohen, Arthur M. 2009. "Community Colleges in the United States." *Community College Models: Globalization and Higher Education Reform,* ed. Rosalind Latiner Raby and Edward J. Valeau. Dordrecht, The Netherlands: Springer.

Cohen, Arthur M., and Florence B. Brawer. 2003. *The American Community College.* 4th ed. San Francisco, CA: Jossey-Bass.

Dellow, Donald A., and Raymond M. Romano. 2006. "Globalization, Offshoring, and the Community College." *Community College Journal* (August/September): 18–22.

Elsner, Paul A., George R. Boggs, and Judith T. Irwin. 2008. *Global Development of Community Colleges, Technical Colleges, and Further Education Programs.* Washington, DC: Community College Press.

Fischer, Karin. 2008. "Community College Educators Focus on Globalization." *Chronicle of Higher Education 54, 26 March 7.* Available online at: http://chronicle.com/article/Community-College-Educators/18749/

Frost, Robert, and Rosalind Latiner Raby. 2009. "Creating Global Citizens: The Democratization of Community College Open Access" In *The Handbook of Practice and Research in Study Abroad: Higher Education and the Quest for Global Citizenship,* ed. R. Lewin. New York: Routledge Taylor and Francis Group.

George, Elizabeth St. 2006. "Positioning Higher Education for the Knowledge Based Economy." *Higher Education* 52 (4): 589–610.

Gordon, Michelle. 1999. "International Programs at Middlesex Community College." *Pioneering Leadership Exemplary Programs Occasional Papers Series.* Available online at: http://ccid.kirkwood.cc.ia.us.

Green, Madeline F., and Laura M. Siaya. 2005. "Measuring Internationalization at Community Colleges." Washington, DC: American Council on Education.

Hart, Peter D. 2008. "How Should Colleges Assess and Improve Student Learning? Employers' Views on the Accountability Challenge. A Survey of Employers Conducted on Behalf of the Association of American Colleges and Universities." Washington, DC: AACU. Available online at: http://www.aacu.org.

Ishumi, Abel G. M. 1998. "Vocational Training as an Educational and Development Strategy: Conceptual and Practical Issues." *International Journal of Educational Development* 8 (3): 163–174.

ITAP International. 2009. "Mission." ITAP Homepage. Newtown, PA: ITAP International. Available online at: http://www.itapintl.com.

Jones, Philip. 2002. "Globalization and Internationalism: Democratic Prospects for World Education." In *Globalization and Education: Integration and Contestation Across Cultures,* ed. Nelly P. Stromquist and Karen Monkman. Lanham, MD: Rowman and Littlefield.

Kintzer, Federick. 1998. Community Colleges Go International: Short-Cycle education around the world. *Leadership Abstracts World Wide Web Edition* 11 (6): 1–4.

Kellog, Alex P., and Robert Tomsho. 2009. "Obama Plans Community College Initiative." *Wall Street Journal Online,* July 14. Available online at: http://online.wsj.com.

Labi, Aisha. 2009. "Jill Biden Shines a Global Spotlight on American Community Colleges." *Chronicle of Higher Education.* July 5. Available online at: http://chronicle.com.

Levin, John S. 2001. *Globalizing the Community College: Strategies for Change in the Twenty-First Century.* New York: Palgrave.

Levin, John S. 2005. "The Business Culture of the Community College: Students as Consumers: Students as Commodities." *New Directions for Higher Education* 2005 (129): 11–26.

Levinson, David L. 2005. *Community Colleges: A Reference Handbook.* Santa Barbara, CA: ABC-CLIO.

Lim, David L. 2008. "Enhancing the Quality of VET in Hong Kong: Recent Reforms and New Initiatives in Widening Participation in Tertiary Qualifications." *Journal of Education and Work* 21 (1): 25–41.

Lowe, Janet, and Vernon Gayle. 2007. "Exploring the Work/Life/Study Balance: The Experience of Higher Education Students in a Scottish Further Education College." *Journal of Further and Higher Education* 31 (3): 225–239.

McMurtrie, Beth. 2001. "Community Colleges Become a Force in Developing Nations Worldwide." *Chronicle of Higher Education*, May 25: A44–45.

Milliron, Mark D. 2007. "Transcendence and Globalization. Our Education and Workforce Development Challenge." *New Directions for Community Colleges* 2007 (138): 31–38.

National Association of State Universities and Land Grant Colleges (NASULGC). 2004. "A Call to Leadership: The Presidential Role in Internationalizing the University." Washington, DC: NASULGC. Available online at: http://www. nafsa.org.

Ng, Kog-Yee, Linn Van Dyne, and Soon Ang. 2009. "Developing Global Leaders: The Role of International Experience and Cultural Intelligence." *Advances in Global Leadership* 7 (2): 225–251.

Nisah-Gyabaah, Kwasi, and Samuel Ankama Obour. 2008. "Developing Industry and College Partnerships: The Dilemma of Ghanaian Polytechnics." Paper presented at The World Federation of Colleges and Polytechnics, New York, February 18–20, 2008. Available online at: http://www.worldcongress2008. com.

Open Doors. 2009a. *Report on International Educational Exchange Study Abroad: U.S. Student Profile.* New York: Institute of International Education (IIE) Network. Available online at: http://opendoors.iienetwork.org.

Open Doors. 2009b. *Economic Impact.* New York: IIE Network. Available online at: http://opendoors.iienetwork.org.

Porter, Michael E. 2002. "GWIT." Paper presented at the Inter-American Development Bank, Washington, DC, November 18, 2002.

Obama, Barack H. 2009a. Remarks Made at a Press Conference to the Grand National Assembly of Turkey, Ankara, February 24, 2009. Available online at http://www.whitehouse.gov.

Obama, Barack H. 2009b. Remarks Made at a Press Conference at Cairo University, Cairo, Egypt on June 4, 2009. Available online at http://www. whitehouse.gov.

Raby, Rosalind Latiner. 2009. "Globalization and Community College Model Development." In *Community College Models: Globalization and Higher Education Reform*, ed. Raby, Rosalind Latiner and Edward J. Valeau. Dordrecht, The Netherlands: Springer.

Raby, Rosalind Latiner, and Edward J. Valeau, eds. 2009. *Community College Models: Globalization and Higher Education Reform*. Dordrecht, The Netherlands: Springer.

Schugurensky, Daniel, and Kathy Higgins. 1996. "From Aid to Trade: New Trends in International Education in Canada." In *Dimensions of the Community College: International and Intercultural, and Multicultural Perspectives*, ed. R. L. Raby and N. Tarrow. New York: Garland Publishing.

Selvaratnam, Viswanathan. 1998. "Limits to Vocationally-Oriented Education in the Third World." *International Journal of Educational Development* 8 (2): 129–143.

Smith, David J. 2007. "How Community Colleges Can Work for World Peace." *Chronicle of Higher Education, Community Colleges* 54 (9), October 23, B30. Available online at: http://chroncile.com.

Strydom, A. H., and L. O. K. Lategan, eds. 1998. *Introducing Community Colleges to South Africa*. Bloemfontein, South Africa: University of the Free State Publications.

Thornton, Sue J. 2009. "Embracing the Change." *Presidency* (Winter Supplement): 1–3. http://www.acenet.edu/Content/NavigationMenu/ProgramsServices /Publications/presidency/W09Sup_Toc.htm .

Uldrick, Jack. 2008. *Jump the Curve: 50 Essential Strategies to Help Your Company Stay Ahead of Emerging Technologies*. New York: Platinum Press.

Ural, Ipek. 1998. "International Community College Models: A South African Perspective." In *Introducing Community Colleges to South Africa*, ed. A. H. Strydom and L. O. K. Lategan. Bloemfontein, South Africa: University of the Free State Publications.

Valeau, Edward J., and Rosalind Latiner Raby, eds. 2007. *Special Issue: International Reform Efforts and Challenges in Community Colleges. New Directions for Community Colleges* 2007 (138): 1–96.

Wolf, Laurence. 2009. "Challenges and Opportunities for Post-Secondary Education and Training in Barbados, Bahamas, Guyana, Jamaica, and Trinidad and Tobago." In *Community College Models: Globalization and Higher Education Reform*, ed. Rosalind Latiner Raby and Edward J. Valeau. Dordrecht, The Netherlands: Springer Publishers.

Chapter 3

Systemic Change, Approval Processes and Governance: The Role of the Board of Trustees

Edward J. Valeau and John C. Petersen

Community College Boards of Trustees, whether, elected or appointed, have similar charges. Boards serve as stewards for the college and are mandated to govern the colleges by a set of adopted policies and procedures designed to guide the interaction between various constituencies who serve within the college. The origin and purpose of boards, their racial and ethnic profiles, role definition, and individual behaviors define the changing nature and growing complexities related to community college management. The high cost of education in an era of economic crisis demands that we understand some of the challenges boards face today and their overall preparation for their job.

This chapter reviews the historic and contemporary role and function of community college boards of trustees. The duties of the board are viewed in the context of external and internal challenges that relate to governing in an era of global dependency, declining resources, shifting demographics, and increased demand for transparency and accountability. Three areas are highlighted to depict the crucial functions of the board and their need for competence and commitment: (a) early beginnings, (b) environmental shifts and board profiles, and (c) board challenges. The boards of trustees work to provide governance over the operation of multimillion dollar enterprises that affect the lives of millions of students in their pursuit of a rewarding and prosperous life in a globally dependent society; they play a critical role in the new financial model.

Early Beginnings

Boards are not a recent historical phenomenon as it relates to governance in universities or community colleges. Early European universities were under auspices of the church or managed by various combinations of community authorities, students, and faculty. When colleges were formed in the English Colonies, lay boards whose members represented the church governed them. The inclusion of prominent community members not affiliated with the church is a Scottish import that altered many US public institutions. The independent colleges gradually reduced the proportion of clergy in favor of citizens with deep pockets. Increasingly, public colleges had boards appointed by civic authorities (mayors for city colleges, and governors or legislators for state colleges) or elected officials. The point is that governing boards, not internal faculty or student groups, have been the pattern since the beginning (Cohen 2010).

Community colleges grew with two distinct traditions. Where they were formed by school districts, the school board governed them just as it did K-12, with a locally elected board. Following the post-1960s expansion of community colleges, board members were both elected and appointed. Most elected terms are four years without restrictions on the number of times a person can contest an election. Board or county officials under special circumstances (often connected to a death or a change in personal status) can also appoint locally elected board members. Those who are elected subject themselves to the will of the voters and the need to campaign for their message and position. Appointed boards are generally at the systems level made by a governor, or because of a local or state mandate. Governor-appointed examples (Tollefson et al. 1999) include the 17-member board of governors of the California Community Colleges; 11 members Illinois Community College Board (also confirmed by the Senate for six-year terms); 17-member Kentucky Community and Technical College System, of whom eight are appointed by the governor; and Pennsylvania whose 15 members have a six-year renewable term. Often, appointed boards are highly political in nature and members can represent the interest of the elected official at the expense and sometimes detriment to the college. Indeed, college district employee unions have backed measures to eliminate at-large elections for trustees, allowing union resources to be concentrated on trustee election races, increasing the unions' influence on the composition of the board. Issues of importance, not unlike today related to influence, control, power, and dominated this paradigm at varying levels of the hierarchal structure (Richardson et al. 1972).

Historically, the charge of the board is based upon two models. The "president model" emerged with the chartering of Harvard University in

1636, and gave a lay governing board and the president the responsibility for charting the direction, mission, role, scope, and destiny of the university (Vaughan and Weisman 2003). The "approval model" has its roots in local public schools in which boards viewed themselves as "watchdogs." Their support of the public interest allowed involvement in hiring, expenditures, and mundane issues related to their own interests (Potter and Phelan 2008). Under both models, expectations of board's behavior as keepers of the public's money and its wise use persisted. The early behavior of boards was based in micromanagement and included discussion of everything including equipment purchase, travel mileage, and conference attendance. Such practices are today a continued source of contention between boards and their leadership. However, Schuetz (1999) claims that the community college governance today is uniquely different from high school and public four-year colleges and are more specific to state vs. local; elected vs. appointed; state appointed vs. locally appointed; taxing authority vs. no taxing authority; or voluntary shared governance vs. mandated shared governance.

Historically, board members have a fiduciary responsibility to uphold the mission and values of the college, set policy, monitor their effectiveness, hire the chief executive officer (CEO), review, and approve the recommended budget by the CEO. Additionally, they answer, through various reporting relationships, to some local, state, or federal governmental agency depending on their organizations' economic dependency. General principles of trusteeship are promulgated as policy by organizations such as The Association of Governing Boards, American Association of Community College Trustees, and state associations like the California Community College League. Trustees hold an institution "in trust" on behalf of the public- or private-sponsoring entity and as such provide a counterpoint to the professional staff of the institution, balancing the faculty's professional interests with a broader public policy perspective.

Environmental Shifts and Board Profiles

In this millennium, four primary environmental shifts reshaped board profiles: (a) compensation for service, (b) local power shift to state level, (c) diversity of members, and (d) charge of duty.

Compensation for Service

Many trustees serve as uncompensated citizens who monthly volunteer their time as well time spent with other duties associated with the college.

A little-noticed provision in some laws allows districts to compensate trustees with a payment schedule based on enrollment size and meeting frequency. In some cases, this resulted in an increase in meetings, as trustees understandably sought to increase this source of individual income. Over time, a combination of factors diminished the distinction between boards and employees, which allowed compensation increases, and alignment of board members as "professionals" with employee union concerns. Earned income of members today can earn upwards of $100,000 annually (Association of Community College Trustees 2009).

Local Power Shift to the State Level

Watershed changes in law and custom changed the nature of boards. In Arizona, California, Florida, Illinois, Kentucky, and Texas, establishment of the board of governors or state systems created state-level boards with uncertain authority, while weakening the authority of local boards. For example, in California, passage of Proposition 13 in 1978 removed the authority of local boards to levy property taxes for support of the college. All entities of local government found that the center of gravity suddenly shifted to the state capital.

Diversity of Members

Boards have evolved little from their past when they were predominately male, white, wealthy, and influential. While demographically, boards should resemble the community they represent, Vaughan and Weiseman (1997) confirm that the average board still consists of white males. The ACCT 2009 study (Brown 2010) of 750 local boards from 39 states and 34 state boards, for a total population of 1,600 trustees, found that 82 percent are white, 9 percent are African American, 4 percent are Latinos, and 2 percent are Asian Pacific Islanders or American Indian, and less than 1 percent are of mixed-race decent. Nearly 32 percent were from the business sector, 29 percent came from the ranks of education, and the remainder from professional services such as health care and manufacturing. Half of those surveyed did not have an education above the BA level. Boards still have a long way to go to take advantage of what diversity can do for a college, the students, and the community.

Charge of Duty

Linking community colleges to the nation's economic growth is clear in President Obama's economic stimulus policy and in Jill Biden's 2009

UNESCO address that confirms the international role that community colleges play at the societal level. Now part of a world stage that identifies them as a major player in the development of an educated citizenry and a competitive workforce, the duty of boards has shifted. It now moves from a "watchdog" mentality that emphasizes micromanaging to the moral compass for change for a generation affected by the Enron fiasco, Bernie Madoff's exploitation of ordinary citizens, and exorbitant salaries of bank officials during the nation's worst economic downturn since the depression. The Sarbanes-Oxley Act and in some cases appointment of external oversight committees who monitor and report on the use of public funds (especially related to bond revenue) are ushering in a renewed call for "trustee ethics," intended to make public and corporate boards become more engaged and sensitive to their governing role.

Board Challenges

The role of the board of trustees is well defined. The challenge is management to achieve a desired state of excellent stewardship. Challenges include (a) ramifications of shared governance, (b) public opinion and maintaining open access, (c) transparency, and (d) entrepreneurship.

Shared Governance

Community colleges governance is both a process for distributing authority (Cloud and Kater 2008), and a social system of self-government wherein decision-making responsibilities are shared among stakeholders (Lau 1996) that give voice to governing boards, district administrators, faculty, staff, and students. In some states like California, shared governance is a required element in the hiring processes. The roots for shared governance come from faculty who want an increasingly larger voice in the day-to-day operations of the college and from unions who continue to exert their power. Undeniably, the faculty best handles curriculum, tenure, and budget management at the unit level, along with control of student services. Yet, current involvement has become so political that it is hard to distinguish faculty academic responsibilities from their bargaining efforts. In fact, unions more often associate their academic freedom with a form of working conditions and therefore expect them to be addressed accordingly. Garfield (2008) posits that in this context, faculty members see themselves as the true management of their colleges. This leads to problems for administration and for boards who increasingly find themselves being threatened come the next election and find it quite difficult to confront faculty who are removed from accountability with little or no consequences for the outcomes associated with their actions.

Granted, everyone benefits from a well-informed staff and an environment, where discussion of ideas and the issues are encouraged and supported. However, that is not the same as decision-making and many boards and their presidents have lost their understanding of the difference. Boards must win back their authority along with presidents to lead. Regrettably, in the name of shared government, a leadership vacuum allows power to drift into the hands of people with no consequences for their actions and CEO and boards cave in because they are afraid to lead. While discussion and consultation is for the many, decision-making within the purview of the board and the president is theirs and theirs alone and supported in law.

Public Opinion and Maintaining Open Access

Students in the United States lag often behind other nations related to preparation in areas like math and science and in higher-education graduation rates. Too many American students seem to be unable to perform beyond remedial levels. At the same time, there is public expectation that community college education will lead to workforce preparation (Raby and Valeau 2009), and allow graduates to compete in the global economy. Meeting public expectations coincides with a call for more focused accountability and challenges status quo behaviors related to assessing outcomes, standards, and quality in colleges today. All of this leads to a demand to attend community colleges that exceeds capacity and thus threatens access. Thus, while the public understands the link between higher education and higher standards of living, it also believes that college is financially out of reach and they are suspicious of escalating costs (Immerwahr and Johnson 2009).

Transparency

Boards now operate in massive public media defined by Google, the Internet, and blogs that provide rapid dissemination of information and laser-like focus on leadership, decision-making, and effectiveness. The emphasis on transparency is the public backlash to irresponsible behaviors of private and public officials entrusted with the people's trust. In this context, the community is demanding closer monitoring and accountability of their CEOs and activities within the organization hammer boards, especially when they work outside of the norm of defined duties and responsibilities and behave as what O'Banion (2009) refers to as rogue trustees. For example, there is public concern about the use of new and existing bond dollars and even expenditure patterns of board members who use public funds for personal, private, or political gain. Such exposure is posing a major challenge for trustees as some reveal that they do not feel prepared. The call for transparency correlates to increasing stories of how board members and CEOs behave badly in the execution of their responsibilities. Focusing on trustees, O'Banion (2009) cites examples where some board members break protocol by leaking information to the press, funnel closed session information to faculty during district negotiations, threaten the job of CEOs by calling for resignations publicly, threaten faculty by making unplanned visits to the classroom, and demand excessive reports when little is needed for sound decision-making.

"Watchdog" behavior in modern times is crippling and counterproductive to finding meaningful solutions to complex problems. It seems that unless and until boards arrest such behaviors, institutions will not attract good leadership and when they do, the candidate could anticipate a short tenure. Concurrently, boards that appear out of control automatically lessen the goodwill of the community, truncate funding opportunities, and keep their respective institutions teetering in time of needed stability. Such behaviors unchecked can also affect institutional morale.

Entrepreneurship

Proprietary institutions have "come of age" and thus adds pressure on community colleges to rethink the way they do business. In this endeavor, trustees will be challenged to continue to convince their communities that their colleges are an important investment and necessary to community, development, economic health, an educated citizenry, and a well-trained and competitive global workforce. Conclusively, trustees will need to bolster their ability to deliver.

Staying the Course: Meeting the Challenges

Higher education historian Frederick Rudolph (1990) rightly explained that in the early 1800s changes related to business, image, and expanded knowledge of the citizenry, coupled with growing and powerful administrators, shifted the role of boards. The shift made possible the influx of new and different voices and most particularly those of the larger community, faculty, and students. Their incorporation into the mix brought complexity in governance, sharing of power, and conflict with entities like unions and competing political, social, and economic interest groups. Their focus evolved around offering and sometime demanding in the name of democracy where their views and voices could be heard.

Issues today carry a heightened awareness related to funding, student markets, international education, government, and global workforce development making the fiduciary responsibilities of the board harder to navigate. To their credit, boards across the nation have not been entirely oblivious to what confronts them, nor have their associations been dormant. However, board members are sufficiently engaged in systemic training on issues of accountability to enhance their effectiveness as stewards of the college. Noted strategies will help create and influence systemic change to make a difference in the way community colleges serve the public.

New Rules for Board of Trustees

Brown and Burke (2007) understanding Friedman (2005) connection to globalization outline new rules that focus on (a) accountability, (b) advocacy, (c) training, and (d) meeting specific roles.

Accountability requires explaining to the legislature what community colleges do and how they account for their existence beyond the traditional model of degrees earned, graduation, and transfer rates.

Advocacy deals with the issue of college affordability and countering the public's waning support. Board members need to show policy makers that it is counterproductive to cut community college funding at the exact same time colleges are proving more important to the country's need for a competitive trained workforce and an educated citizenry.

Training defines the professionalism of the field. Board members need to advance their knowledge in areas of community college budgeting, community relations, and leadership training. Some colleges and organizations that have adopted the Carver Plan (1997)—which focuses on ends and means training—include ACCT, American Association of Community Colleges (AACC), and Council for Higher Education Accreditation (CHEA). These organizations are already focusing on specific and measurable strategies aimed at teamwork to enable greater board success. Despite existing measures, a study conducted on four-year trustees by Selingo (2007) can be extrapolated to many community colleges; findings indicated that many trustees feel ill-prepared for their job. Fain (2010) suggests this is a continuing concern among trustees. Therefore, there is still a need at the local, state, and national levels to advocate strongly for training on a sustained basis that creates a culture of awareness driven by data on governing successfully in today's environment. The Center for Higher Education Policy Analysis (2010) suggests that it is not enough to engage boards in training after selection, but that stature, expertise, and representation become the new criteria for selecting trustees. In particular, trustees should have demonstrated commitment to diversity, have unique skills or competencies that are of particular value to the institution, and have complementary skills and perspective to ensure that some concerns are represented.

Meeting specific roles provides insight as to how well boards are measuring up to challenges that they encounter. Among the key board roles is selecting the CEO, which, in essence, shows how the board will shape and influence programs and services for the next generation of leaders. Pocock (1988) opined that the essence of the relationship is highly specific to the nature of the institution and its ascribed practices, structure of the board, and the personal chemistry that connects and drives the two parties. McKay (2004) conclude that trustees and CEOs must be educated in and agree upon those principles that drive the purpose, culture, direction, governance, and overall effectiveness of the community college. We believe these areas significantly affect the mission, vision, and values of the institution and which ultimately influence student learning. Undeniably this role is pressing and is exacerbated by retirement predictions (Weisman and Vaughan 2002; Shults 2001) that are on target and as the AACC estimates 75 percent of CEOs will retire between now and the year 2011, just one year from the time this chapter was written. In fact, since so many senior administrators are in the same age cohort, the need to find new leaders will be increasingly difficult and one that demands board members who can take the leadership reins (Smith 2010).

Strategies to Affect Change

There are four specific areas where change should occur. This includes: (a) team building, (b) financial literacy, (c) diversity, and (d) international literacy.

Team Building

Individuals who serve on community college boards are members of a team bonded together with clear responsibilities, special influence, and power for change. The team approach helps board members assert their power for the overall good of the institution. The ultimate team is the board and the CEO closely joined as the glue that holds the institution together while making it transparent. To accomplish an atmosphere of team unity, Martin (1997) suggests activities that support the concept of a team, such as reviewing the college's bylaws, mission, and other official documents regularly; studying board meeting minutes to ensure completeness and accuracy; and adopting parliamentary procedures and conflict resolution process before there is a problem or conflict. Potter and Phelan (2008) identify five key elements needed to foster and enhance institutional and board success: (a) existence of a sense of trust between the president and board, (b) open and appropriate communication, (c) respect for each other's right to make decisions, (d) mutual protection, and (e) recognition by the board and president that they are members of a team. While not new or revolutionary, these suggestions are timeless in their contribution to supporting the concept of teamwork for board success. The team model reflects the tone of the organization, ensures adherence to policy, and overall creates an atmosphere of civility. Such behavior sends a clear message to the college community and the public that the institution's mission, vision, and values are consistent and that the leadership is coordinated. When this occurs, the institution wins and the board gains in stature incur respect for carrying out its role.

Financial Literacy

The public is very concerned with ballooning budgets and seemingly inadequate systemic cost containment measures. Since boards are financially responsible, they must go beyond superficial "training" that occurs in board orientations and periodic retreats. Financial education must be ongoing, monitored, and focused on colleges operating budgets, capital budgets, externally audited financial statements, revenues from ancillary enterprises, and quantitative results of cost-containment efforts where they exist. Reports by the internal auditor and spending in compliance with board-approved policies, multiyear financial plans aligned with strategic plans, and periodic management/financial variance reports strengthen the board's financial literacy. Informed leadership is responsible for the boards' development in this area. Providing timely information on financial matters, assigning staff to help board members clarify their understanding, identifying study session issues related to financing, and modeling transparency contribute to the board's ability to carry out their duties. Working with the board in this manner ensures on one level their success and that of the college. It also sends a signal that team success is valued and supported.

Diversity

Boards would do well based on their revealed profile to begin in earnest to embrace diversity in ideas and its membership. There is work associated with achieving more representation of racial and ethnic composition for the nation's community college boards. With the exception of large urban centers, the racial and ethnic composition of boards remains the same mainly white males, increasingly white females, and a sprinkle of minorities whose seats are normally evidenced by their residence in large urban districts. Such changes will influence and help establish the framework for new thinking and organizational structures that take advantage of diverse talent and experiences that are both local and global in nature and could add to the success of boards.

International Literacy

Boards need to shift their thinking and attitude regarding the support of international education. The evidence (Raby and Valeau 2009; Valeau and Raby 2007) is wide and clear that community colleges run the risk of being isolates if they do not increase their attention to the value of internationalizing their programs and services. They should take their lead from some of the nation's universities that present a comprehensive program of services related to serving the needs of the international market, and to addressing curricular reforms that support a global workforce. Issues of governance and policy development regarding how boards respond to international education remains an important issue for future success.

It is interesting to observe that in all that has been said the more things change the more they seem to stay the same. The following are guideposts that still hold promise for strengthening the nations' boards of trustees to ensure institutional excellence and accountability.

1. Establishing at the local level a board continuing education and training function that plans and monitors board activities aimed at development.
2. At the national level through ACCT, revive the conversation regarding getting more districts to adopt the Carver Model as a gold seal for governance.
3. Conduct regular research to show the impact of institutional effectiveness as practiced by colleges that use it.
4. Proactively organize institutional building strategies related to planning, accreditation, and learning around integrated teams of faculty,

board members, administrators, and students. Regularly asses their progress and make changes where needed.

5. Design policies that ensure monitoring, support, and firm decision-making for the removal of board members found guilty of violating board policies.

Conclusion

We began this chapter with Art Cohen's explanation that structurally, community colleges have had both boards appointed by civic authorities and elected officials. Boards were never internal faculty or student groups and this has been the pattern since the beginning. Clearly, boards have the fiduciary responsibility to ensure that community colleges respond to the needs of the students and the communities they reside in. Such boards bear responsibility for multi-million-dollar enterprises and face many challenges in carrying out their duties. Issues of competing groups relate to power, control, and influence, and operate at every level.

Governance in the early development of the community college rested in the hands of a few and too often those who had control of the money ruled budget development, resource allocation, and program support. While issues of course development, faculty evaluation, and curriculum design were eagerly handed over to the faculty, the monetary support and decision-making rested with the administration, and its influence over the board. New and advancing circumstances fueled by collective bargaining, lawsuits, the pressure to share power, and the call for transparency have converged to spawn a form of participation rooted in the name of shared governance. It has given rise to tension as the fight for power blurs the importance of academic accountability and student success that requires a united approach to organizational planning and decision-making among major constituent groups. Effective governance is complex, contentious, and at the heart of every accreditation report where colleges are often cited for a failed process. In this era, much of the public view of academic governance and board leadership is weighted with suspicion and distrust. Likely, it will continue to be a challenge.

Today boards cannot afford to simply serve as watchdogs but instead must become stewards of the enterprise and move away from behavior that is counterproductive to a sworn oath, and that is detrimental to the needs of the institutions. Most boards do a reasonable job at fulfilling their duties, but during the age of intense media scrutiny, the demand for accountability is greater and the need more urgent. Boards that have not responded well generally are out of control and sometimes inhabited by rogue trustees who operate to promote personal agendas. Boards today ought to be ready for what is asked.

The community college system has been and continues to be the only system of higher education where access to education and the training needed to enhance lives, develop communities, and prepare a global workforce is available to the masses. Who leads them and governs is a matter of national interest, and in that context, boards of trustees and the challenges they face are critically important to the community. State and local government entities that appoint or elect trustees should thoughtfully identify representative talent needed to serve on boards.

References

American Association of Community College (AACC) Trustees. 2009. "Who Are Community College Trustees." *Inside Higher Education*, April 6. Available online at: http://www.insidehighereducation.com.

Biden, Jill. 2009. "American Community Colleges: A Global Model for Higher Education." Remarks made to the Opening Ceremony of the 2009 World Conference on Higher Education, Paris, July 5, 2009. Available online at: http://www.unesco.org.

Brown, Noah J. 2010. "The Citizen Trustee: a Profile in Leadership." A Power Point presentation and an Original UN published Source Document. Washington, DC: United Nations.

Brown, Noah J., and Kenneth P. Burke. 2007. "New Rules for Business in a Flat World: A Call to Action." *Community College Journal of Research and Practice* 31 (4): 441–448.

Carver, John S. 1997. *Boards That Make a Difference*. 2nd ed. San Francisco, CA: Jossey-Bass.

Center for Higher Education Policy Analysis. 2010. Los Angeles: CHEPA. Available online at: www.usc.edu/dept/chepa.

Cloud, Robert C., and Susan T. Kater, eds. 2008. *Special Issue: Governance in the Community College. New Directions for Community Colleges* 2008 (141): 1–98.

Cohen, Arthur M. 2010. Personal email communication on May 27, 2010 to Edward Valeau in Hayward California from Arthur Cohen in Los Angeles California.

Fain, Paul. 2010. "Trustees, and Professors Don't Understand one Another Role." *The Chronicle of Higher Education*, January 24, 1–3.

Friedman, Thomas L. 2005. *The World Is Flat: A Brief History of the Twenty- First Century*. New York: Farrar, Straus, and Giroux.

Garfield, Timothy K. 2008. "Governance in a Union Environment" in Cloud, Robert C., and Susan T. Kater, eds. 2008. *Special Issue: Governance in the*

Community College. New Directions for Community Colleges 2008 (141): 39–52.

Immerwahr, John, and Jean Johnson, eds. 2009. *Squeeze Play 2009: The Public's Views on College Costs Today: Public Agenda and the National Center for Public Policy and Higher Education.* Washington, DC: National Center for Public Policy and Higher Education.

Lau, Ron. 1996. *"Shared Governance and Compton Community College District."* Assembly Bill 1725 (California 1989). Compton Community College, Compton, CA.

McKay, Shaun. L. 2004. "Chief Executive Officers and Board of Trustee Perceptions and Preferences of Their Level of Involvement in Institutional Governance Activities." PhD diss., Morgan State University, Baltimore, MD.

Martin, Montez Jr. 1997. "Opportunities and Challenges for Boards in Times of Change." *New Directions for Community Colleges* 1997 (98): 55–62.

O'Banion, Terry. 2009. *Rouge Trustee: The Elephant in the Room.* Phoenix: League for Innovation in the Community College.

Pocock, John W. 1988. *Fund-Raising Leadership: A Guide for College and University Boards.* Washington, DC: Association of Governing Boards of Universities and Colleges.

Potter, George, and David J. Phelan. 2008. "Governance Over the Years: A Trustee's Perspective." *New Directions for Community Colleges* 2008 (141): 15–24.

Raby, Rosalind Latiner, and Edward J. Valeau, eds. 2009. *Community College Models: Globalization and Higher Education Reform.* Dordrecht, The Netherlands: Springer.

Richardson, Richard C., Louis W. Bender, and Clyde E. Blocker, eds. 1972. *Governance for the Two Year Colleges.* Englewood Cliffs, NJ: Prentice Hall.

Rudolph, Frederick. 1962. *The American College and University: A History.* New York: Knopf.

Schuetz, Pam. 1999. "Shared Governance on Community Colleges." Los Angeles: Eric Digest Eric Clearinghouse for Community Colleges. Available at http://www.eric.ed.gov.

Selingo, Jeffery. 2007. "Trustees: More Willing than Ready." *Chronicle of Higher Education*, May 11. Available online at: http://chronicle.com/article/Trustees-More-Willing-Than/15883/

Shults, Christopher. 2001. "The Critical Impact of Impending Retirements on Community College Leadership." *AACC/Research Brief. Leadership Series No.1.* Washington, DC: American Association of Community Colleges.

Smith, Josh. 2010. Personal communication through e-mail on May 31, 2010 to Edward Valeau in Hayward, California from Josh Smith in Brooklyn, New York.

Tollefson, Terrence A., Rick L. Garrett, and William E. Ingram, eds. 1999. *Fifty State Systems of Community Colleges: Mission, Governance, Funding and Accountability.* Johnson City, TN: The Overmountain Press.

Valeau, Edward, and Rosalind Latiner Raby, eds. 2007. *Special Issue: International Reform Efforts and Challenges in Community Colleges. New Directions for Community Colleges* 2007 (138): 1–96.

Vaughan, George. B., and Iris M. Weisman. 1997. *Community College Trustees: Leading on Behalf of Their Communities.* Washington, DC: Association of Community College Trustees.

Vaughan, George B., and Iris M. Weisman. 2003. "Leadership Development: The Role of the President Board Team" *New Directions for Community Colleges* 2003 (123): 51–61.

Weisman, Iris. M., and George. B. Vaughan. 2002, eds. "The Community College Presidency 2001." *Research Brief Leadership Series* No. 3 (AACC-RB-02-1). Washington, DC: AACC.

Chapter 4

The Role of Leadership: Leaders' Practice in Financing Transformation

Robert A. Frost, Edward "Ted" Raspiller, and John J. "Ski" Sygielski

Introduction

The role of community college presidents and executive leaders in college finances is both all-encompassing and ethereal. College leaders advance the college mission based on trustee priorities, promote good stewardship of college funds, and somehow manage to prioritize students, and learning first. Transformational leadership theory indicates there is a greater potential in staff: that a leader has larger objectives than handling the day-to-day issues, and therefore, seeks to transform the people, organization, or society (Burns 1978; Bass and Avolio 1993). At the same time, many organizational theorists have described much more ambiguous, even opaque, decision-making processes in higher education that give doubt to a leader's ability to connect finance with improvement (Cohen and March 1974, 1986). However, as players on a global stage, community college leaders today are better aware of the need to attract new, creative, and often distant resources into the college.

This chapter connects leadership theory and practice with the realities of community college finances in today's contemporary and global context. The authors have written and spoken on the topic of community college finance, fund raising, globalization, internationalization, and entrepreneurial leadership in numerous forums. As Frost (2009a) was researching the impact of globalization on the missions of rural community colleges,

Raspiller was preparing a report on the State of Virginia's ability to fund its community college system in the twenty-first century. In addition, Sygielski (2010) was writing and presenting on the need to find alternative funding to enhance the community college mission (Esters et al. 2008). But colleges are governed by boards, respond to diverse needs of their particular communities, and so do they both deal with the fickleness of trustees (Frost 2009b) even as they develop, for example, the global studies programs that help their students achieve global competencies (Frost 2007; Frost and Raby 2009). In many ways, this topic allows for the coming together of several years of community college research, and dialogues, between the authors and numerous colleagues.

As colleges increasingly compete and collaborate in global settings, college leaders wrestle with very fundamental and practical dichotomies: how will a specific act contribute to the better good even as it affects an increasingly finite bottom line? How will international events influence local elections? How can we attract a diverse group of students from around the world, price tuition competitively, and still provide adequate learning resources for all of our students? How can we educate our local communities about our needs so they can pass bond referendums, if needed by their local institutions of higher education? Community college leaders still live in a world where their communities expect them to be able to induce change, inspire staff, develop curricula, and "right wrongs" on pretty short notice. In the first decades of the twenty-first century, even with "good to great" (Collins 2001) being the most popular catch phrase associated with college vision statements, college executives may still be leading the same "organized anarchies," a term which Cohen and March (1974) used to describe modern higher education institutions. When presidents, vice presidents, and similar executives are charged with improving a college's financial prospects, or financing a new area of college operations or programs, how much advantage do they actually hold?

Much of the qualitative data for this chapter was obtained from phone interviews, conference meetings, and similar informal conversations with presidents, vice presidents, and similar college leaders because, as it turned out, most leaders did not wish to speak on the record about the limitations of their own authority in matters of college finance. The leaders' comments were both diverse and in a few cases, even inflammatory as they pondered whether funding in some cases worked to subsidize profitable industries:

1. Do community colleges lead or lag behind economic development?
2. Should colleges take on components of Grades 10–12 education as public school systems further deteriorate?

3. Are the colleges producing additional graduates that fuel the economy, or slowly deflating the aspirations of students who lack maturity to contribute to the workforce (the "holding tank" metaphor)?
4. Should career programs convert to a market-driven model to better compete with private technical colleges?
5. Are developmental, international, lifelong learning, and other specialized curricula value-added or excess cost endeavors?
6. Are training relationships with the business community healthy, or do they produce unfunded subsidies (at public expense) for one sector of the economy?
7. Are Allied Health Programs a public subsidy for highly profitable health care providers?
8. Do community colleges save funding for the universities by assuming the mission of developmental education, minor league athletics, and various other costly sectors of higher education?
9. Does the publicly elected board system contribute to educational equity across academic and workforce programs, or does it create bias toward local workforce or "pet project" interests?
10. Do all sides in the collective bargaining process have the ability to do so in the best interests of the institution, or will community colleges go the way of the US auto industry?

The conversations took place over 2009–2010 with leaders primarily in the West and Midwest, and large and small institutions, but some of the stories were shared several years ago and then reconfirmed for inclusion in this volume. But because community college leadership is not only a campus-based endeavor, but an extended network of colleagues facing similar challenges, the process of writing this chapter became an exercise in collaborative learning.

The Importance of Finance

A college on an unstable financial foundation cannot adequately support its mission. Such a college can make its payroll through not filling vacancies when staff leave (attrition), increasing the use of adjunct instructors, and even pay heating bills by cutting maintenance hours. However, can the institution respond to a community initiative, show improvements in student learning, or claim to offer a comfortable and healthy learning environment when impoverished conditions (such as increased class sizes and a reduction in diverse offerings) are present over time? Such are the day-to-day issues of financing college operations. Many of the conversations that added to this chapter were with presidents in this very position of "just holding the line," and their frustrations were evident. Here is a quote from a president in the western United States:

> I am just holding the line. I have a Human Resource Director conspiring with the staff union, a faculty union on the warpath because we cannot replace retiring faculty, and a board that wants me to be entrepreneurial from the foundation to the faculty. Now how do you think the faculty will react when I encourage them to compete for grants as an alternative to state funding cuts?

In some cases, colleges today have little to market to attract funding; in other cases, college leaders know where funding is and how to get it, but either a dysfunctional internal culture, or staff are uncomfortable with the risks of entrepreneurship. As one president of a large community college said, "a new breed of employee is needed if we are to compete with the entrepreneurship of the privately-capitalized colleges and universities (e.g., Capella University, DeVry University, Walden University, etc.)." Indeed, some presidents indicated they would not develop a large grants office, recruit international students, or seek private money for buildings because of the potential for scandal through an optional activity they had promoted. Even though such activities are legitimate, they can attract critics who view the community college mission through a narrow lens. Of course, the president who ignores finances does so at her peril. The complexity of finance in today's college, from forecasting future funding to closing out the fiscal year, is one reason the vice president of administration position is now standard in community colleges. Jensen and Giles, who wrote the classic *Insiders Guide to Community College Administration*, made fiscal responsibility truth #2 in their "Ten Truths of Community College Leadership": "No Chief Executive Officer (CEO) ever got fired for having a lousy curriculum, but many have been fired for not balancing the books" (Jensen and Giles 2006, 87). Another recently retired president declared:

> There is no doubt in my mind that money is the number one challenge. Finding it, asking for it, raising it, using it efficiently, keeping it safe, investing it wisely, defending allocations, charging and justifying tuition, challenging established notions about it—all of those money-related topics perpetually vex and confound a president. (Trachtenberg 2008)

While there are numerous similar comments in the literature, the above quote makes clear that while presidents' deal with many headaches, and are responsible for them as well, only a few areas can really destroy a presidency. The above statement helps produce a working definition for finances as applied to this chapter: putting money to work. In the case of the community college, this means maximizing resources for student learning. However, as several participants in our interview indicated, there is nothing as financially costly to the institution as an extended period of decline when a presidency fails. As a result, funding, and the success of a presidency intimately are intertwined.

As a result, the topic of financing education, for leaders, is one that can span the dullness and tedium of poring over budgets day after day, to the heroism of saving a program, reallocating funding to needy developmental programs, or even investing in public-private endeavors that might attract excess revenue (that will finance other initiatives!). Recently St. Louis Community College in Missouri purchased a former Circuit City store in lieu of building additional buildings on campus (Moltz 2010). Even though the building is a short distance from the campus, this one act saved capital, invested in the community, and expanded learning space. It is also likely that this act will win votes in the next board election. This purchase demonstrated that college leaders understood not only how to get funding, but also how funding spent can either motivate or dampen staff enthusiasm, connect to learning goals, and transform their relationship in the community. It is the leader's vision that connects financial resources to human capital and can connect the transformational victory displayed in a press conference with the practical achievement of improving the physical plant, learning spaces, or program performance.

Of course, not all community college leadership is successful or transformational. Compare the St. Louis Community College example with the following notion that leaders actually have been complacent for decades.

> Despite this prosperity, some community college leaders seemingly have been lulled into complacency. In 1993, the Wingspread Group report predicted troubles for community colleges if the trend towards complacency were not reversed. The report warned of the lagging sociopolitical forces, the rapid rise of technology, and the growing need for entrepreneurialism in higher education. Several subsequent reports also echoed this sentiment (e.g., Spellings Commission Report on Higher Education 2006; The Coming Tsunami 2006). Such an ominous forecast ought to have inspired college personnel to rally and refocus. Sadly, this did not happen. Some merely hit the "snooze" button on the national wake-up call and now are less prepared for turbulent times and the subsequent changes that must be made. (Roueche and Jones 2006, x)

As a result, even as a transformational style of leadership was the expectation, Roueche, Jones, and others apparently saw the complacency in leaders as the very drag on the community college system. Several college presidents for this chapter shared stories of how they and their peers had "kicked the can down the road" for many years instead of addressing the state and local funding issues that could have mediated the cuts colleges are currently facing and will face for years to come. In fact, the following story exemplifies this concept very well:

> So there we were, nearly all the presidents of the state (some 30+ colleges) gathered in the same meeting room in the state capital. It was early 2008, the primary industry in the state was hemorrhaging jobs, unemployment was rising, and the governor's office indicated we were entering a recession. The governor was willing to "instruct" the presidents to initiate an efficiency campaign that would induce campus reviews of services, cut unnecessary costs, and, overall produce a statewide initiative that would release campus leaders from the direct criticism of cutting positions or programs. The governor would "take the hit" for the reductions. Some presidents advocated for a statewide event that would depoliticize local level cuts. Several of the old guard, one who was only a year from retirement, counseled a "wait until next year" approach, to which most of the presidents agreed. Unfortunately, by the next year, the governor was significantly weakened by other losses; the national stimulus monies diverted attention from an efficiency drive, and the potential to make cuts *as the economy sank* was lost. In early 2010, the governor advised colleges cuts would be between 3 and 20 percent, and they should not expect to know until well after the fiscal year had begun. Of course, by now, those old guard presidents will retire and leave the crisis to us!

Many will read the above paragraph and exclaim, "That's MY state!" There can be little doubt that in many states, leaders saw this crisis coming, did little to prepare for it, and are weakened as leaders now to lead out ahead of the cuts. Several presidents discussed the distinction between what they would like to do to help their college in the long run, and the fact that those ideas would probably result in the loss of their job. Whether it was a divide between faculty and board views, a lack of an entrepreneurial culture on campus, or a community that defined the college mission narrowly, these scenarios were not conducive to creative or innovative solutions.

Regardless of the economic backdrop, community colleges are still closely knit social organizations, where a "we are family, how can you do that?" response is issued when a position, or program, is cut. The close connectivity between personal-professional-transformational emotions and actions represents the leader nexus as well. How can the college leader balance the right mix of attracting new revenue sources, limiting or cutting costs on campus, and still inspire staff to engage in both entrepreneurship and "twice the work with half the staff" as one president stated.

Another said, "I feel as if I am on a perpetual teeter-totter. I have to balance internal and external demands and most of those demands take money. So, it is more important than ever to ensure the college is supporting its strategic plan when financial decisions are made."

One president said, "We are going to have to invest more heavily in technology since we are probably not going to be able to hire the amount of professionals we need to address our burgeoning enrollments and reduction in local and state financial assistance. Once we were supported by the state, then we were assisted by the state, now we are located in the state!"

As a result, the leaders should be identified as both the cause and the solution; the heroes and the crooks; the first called for direction and vision, but also held responsible for numerous uncontrolled variables in this equation. Personalities on campus, long-simmering poor relationships that may have nothing to do with the president (but fester between faculty, chief financial officer (CFO) and chairs, board and the mayor, or a host of other possibilities), or an outdated and/or crumbling commercial sector that can only mean reduction in tax revenues: all of these point to the limited "control" a president has to effect financial change. There are several areas referenced by the leaders where they felt they had, or could have the most impact:

1. Promote passage of bond measure
2. Start passive fundraising one year before announcing campaign; build momentum early and lead to victory
3. Secure state funding for capital projects
4. Don't waste a perfectly good crisis: promote quick change and use crisis as a way to avoid finger-pointing and blame internally.
5. Support incremental tuition increases
6. Student fee increases tied directly to services
7. Increase development work (but this can be a chimera where tail wags dog)
8. Reduce staffing; flatten the organization's administration and support staff
9. Leave positions vacant, even if for remainder of academic year
10. Alternative academic schedules, such as a four-day work week, or reduce summer offerings
11. Physical plant changes; upgrade to cost-efficient systems; green technologies
12. HR changes: self insure vs. outside coverage; 10-month administrative contracts.

13. Negotiated contract changes; link specific economic events to contract changes in advance.

It is for this reason we prioritize the transformational role of the president. The relational qualities of a president, based on passion for learning, values that prioritize care for others, and credit given away to all the players involved with improvement, may be the one component that, beyond the approaches in the figure, connects the college, and community members, onto the same positive path.

A Word about Leadership Theories

Transformational leadership does not stand apart from servant, path-goal, and leader-member exchange theories as they relate to leadership in community colleges. Most presidents today will apply components of each to fit their own style and value system. A skilled transformational leader will certainly possess the necessary traits and attributes, such as charisma, trustworthiness, sophisticated communication skills, and ethical decision-making, to help guide their institution through this current national financial crisis. But often there are very practical skill sets that integrate with personal attributes that make up the complete, and successful, leader. For example, a leader can be a compassionate coward with great accounting skills, but the cowardice may annul the other qualities. As a result, a successful leader with transformational qualities almost certainly combines the right mix of multiple attributes. Northouse (2010, 205) states that, as a result, authentic leadership has been intriguing to researchers: It was defined earlier in transformational research but never fully articulated. Northouse, George (2003), and George and Sims (2007) identified several characteristics of authentic leaders including passion, behavior, connectedness, consistency, and compassion (Esters et al. 2008). Clearly, given the nature of financing transformation, an effective leader must balance these characteristics with those necessary to identify and navigate financial decision-making through data driven processes. To make financial decisions with no regard for the people involved will set back the morale and, ultimately, the institution, in potentially more severe ways than making no decisions at all.

In 2005, the American Association of Community Colleges (AACC) published its W. K. Kellogg Foundation–funded work on Competencies for Community College Leaders (AACC 2005). This pioneering work outlines six competencies, as identified by a wide array of experts, which are critical to function as a successful community college president in this new century.

These include: organizational strategy, resource management, communication, collaboration, community college advocacy, and professionalism. Today, *resource management* may be the most critical competency. Resource management states that an effective community college leader equitably and ethically sustains people, processes, and information as well as physical and financial assets to fulfill the mission, vision, and goals of the community colleges (AACC 2007, 4). Given today's monetary climate, effective resource management skills are paramount for those in and those seeking leadership roles.

Finally, the financial challenges of the new century have given rise to the need for community colleges leaders to completely rethink what are appropriate financing, and educational products, for the institutions they lead. Roueche and Jones (2005, 142) explain the importance of understanding entrepreneurialism:

> The rise of the community college entrepreneur represents a new wave in the community college system. And the entrepreneurial college—truly an American invention—represents a new journey, an unchartered path that will lead to new discoveries, helping reshape colleges into self-sustaining, ever-evolving enterprises.

To be effective long-term, community college presidents will have to not just understand, but actually possess the traits associated with entrepreneurialism, as it is likely the combination of a creative (inherent) gift and formal training. As an example, some of the most elaborate organizational and systems theories are rarely discussed "on the job," but pertain to the fact that resources are not created from within: they arrive from outside the college or, as Roueche puts it above, pulling these resources in is what produces the "self-sustaining enterprise." Concisely, humans cannot avoid starvation by eating their arms. Resources come from resource acquisition. Just like any living organism, colleges must continuously attract new outside resources to nourish and sustain them. When this process of attracting outside resources stops, the college atrophies. In the conversations associated with this chapter, it was all too obvious which presidents were in entrepreneurial colleges (and some not of their making) and which were resource-starved. The most entrepreneurial colleges had a healthy mix of public and private grant funds, strong foundations, and alumni connections, and effective community partnerships with both private and public agencies. A few examples of entrepreneurship in action include the following:

1. The college that encourages faculty creativity and innovation through grants, contracts, and consultancies BUT requires a standard indirect cost and buy-out provision in exchange for college support.

2. The president who defines three or more areas of innovation he or she will support; defines how it will be supported; cheers the faculty and staff who take up this challenge; and avoids exacting "consequences" when the staff person tries, but fails in their efforts.
3. The college identifies creativity coaches who work with any college or community member to help connect innovative ideas with college and community capabilities, especially toward attracting new revenue streams.
4. Synergistic partnerships on campus, such as bringing artists, scientists, and business incubator staff together to work on widely known community needs.

Historically, the community college has evolved, and often added to its mission, but always with an eye toward relevance and resources. For today's leaders, staving off atrophy requires an entrepreneurial spirit shared by many, and the requisite leadership skills and techniques to guide people and colleges, toward a model of continuous resource acquisition. By now, adding concepts like entrepreneurial and authentic leadership into the mix, it should be clear that the leadership component in financing community colleges is multifaceted, driven by both style and skill, and far, far, from easy. Add to the above the fact that higher education today operates in a global resource development context, and all of our work becomes still more complicated.

Global Perspectives from Within a Sheltered Community

As anyone who has lived overseas for an extended period knows, when a global economic player (United States, China, Japan, Germany, or any G8 nation) catches a cold, the nearby economies catch pneumonia. For centuries, the United States has been insulated by two oceans. Because of underdeveloped global communications and transportation networks, the United States enjoyed distinct advantages in attracting talent to its shores. But as the United States has gone from benefactor to debtor nation, other nations are investing heavily in their higher education subsectors. Over the past decade, universities in Australia, the United Kingdom, China, Canada, South Africa, Dubai, and elsewhere are rerouting students traditionally bound for the United States. In this most recent deep recession, the United States and other G-8 countries perhaps have the least advantage in technology and communications than ever before; the playing field is at its most even. Some evidence would be very helpful. As a result, drops in financial support to community colleges, in student flows to the United States (although currently they show small annual increases), and a gradual devolution of funding toward in public higher education are likely trends in the current decade. Colleges willing to evolve, however, and apply more diverse financing strategies will better position themselves for the global education sector that will rise out of this recession.

Already in some states, community colleges are global enterprises. While California has been in the vanguard of this movement for some decades, the State of Washington is a remarkable example of this trend as well. Edmonds, Green River, Seattle Central, and Highline Community Colleges have simply produced amazing results in the form of attracting international students to their campuses (in two cases, approximately 1,000 students a year); developing learning partnerships with sister-colleges in Asia, Africa, and Latin America; and in leveraging grant resources to build relationships with local industry and international partners (Highline in particular). This is but one leading state, as Texas, Florida, Arizona, and many other states in the East as well could provide similar examples. In these cases, there is a distinction between dozens of students or hundreds impacted; one to two small grants a year or $1 million-plus resource development achievements within five years (Daytona State College, Kirkwood Community College, Eastern Iowa Community College District, among others).

In each of the above cases, community colleges are globalizing; they are doing so through a model that melds the benefits of international tuition rates and internationalization of learning into the campus culture. Furthermore, each college above is a case study in leadership connected between the presidential, instructional, and international resource development positions. In each of these cases, a president was willing to take on significant risk to his or her presidency early on; adopt a prointernational student mantra, and combine that outreach with investment in a team of international development staff. Most colleges, over a decade or more, came to specialize, and develop reputations, in specific areas of training (hospitality, small business development, banking, or social welfare training, aquaculture, and even allied health) or activities, like study abroad, and build long-term relationships in their region-of-focus.

At the same time, recruitment of traditional international students in that same region and elsewhere produced a self-fulfilling marketing plan as family members recommended the college to others in their family, neighbors, and so on. This no-cost "word-of-mouth" marketing has been common in the Midwest for decades (St. Louis, College of DuPage in Chicago, numerous Iowa colleges, and several of the upstate New York and Eastern Pennsylvania colleges) as well as in the East but even more so through immigrants inviting family to join them. In some cases, the relationships are so strong today that those college leaders are invited to presidential inaugurations (Daytona State), embassy education events, national education planning meetings abroad, and even UNESCO and World Bank forums. Most importantly, a vibrant international student presence is now so firmly rooted on these campuses that it would be almost impossible to turn back, as was done at many colleges during the last two major recent recessions. This is because these students are no longer international: after two decades of student, immigrant, and refugee arrivals, the college service areas were transformed into diverse, multilingual small business districts. Examples of this trend abound, but a few good examples are St. Louis Community College at Forest Park, as well as South Seattle Community College. In each of these areas, a dying manufacturing district gave way to a new entrepreneurial and immigrant class, and the college student population both influenced and was influenced by the shift.

As English as a second language (ESL) and study abroad directors, and international advising staff in the field know, the tone set by the college president ripples throughout the college, helping both staff and the community appreciate the value added through globalizing the campus. The complex, rich infusion of cultures, colors (in clothing alone!), languages, and ideas that happens through the infusion of diverse cultures requires an eloquent and passionate voice over many years. This is the work of a committed, transformational leader. The presidents who have promoted international education know that long-term, the financial benefits are great; but they also know that is less the reward than the result of focusing on the right investment in human capital and development at their colleges. One president put it this way:

> Because we started internationalizing over 20 years ago, by now our campus is transformed in ways we could not have imagined. We have over 1000 international students, which meant adding housing units on campus, which made this campus a village, where multiple languages and cultural connections collide throughout our learning experiences. Today our students leave as global citizens, with global competencies.

There are many areas of excellence that presidents can "incubate" toward the process of resource development, capacity-building, and transforming learning experiences at the college. For any college to become self-sustaining over time, the vision of college leaders (often multiple presidents) may be required over decades. Interestingly, international education may also be one of the best examples of how resource development efforts *can fail* when they are done with a short-term, one-dimensional (recruitment only) "money-making" agenda. As rapidly globalizing institutions, community colleges are at a point where leaders can decide how they want to respond to global education influences, which are their most valuable assets to compete in the global arena, and, most importantly, how to connect the global competencies their students need with this (integrated) entrepreneurial resource agenda.

Connecting the Internal and External Worlds

As shown in this chapter, there are numerous microdebates within the topic of leadership and finance, particularly given the rapid globalization of higher education. Any of these areas require clear positions by leaders in order for staff and community to appreciate, and follow through on, a funding initiative. Many of the items in both charts suggest there is potential for community colleges to become much more entrepreneurial, and selective, in their resource management activities. But even as community colleges add new components to their local missions, whether be it a "globalized" curriculum, on-campus housing, partnering locally in green technology implementation, or international development, some question the rationale behind expanding the community college mission (Gump 2006; Vaughn 2006).

Questions like the above show that often there is little to distinguish the veneer from what goes on beneath the surface in some college districts. As a result, what is funded, promoted, and then "invested in" over time can result from the influence of both internal and external stakeholders, to all of whom the president is beholden. Just as another chapter in this volume details the erosion of the historic one-third rule, the transformational president may prefer any alternative to raising tuition, but $2 increments have rarely been linked to a president's demise. Unfortunately, incremental increases have made the difference between students formerly funding one-third of their educational costs to now paying over 40 percent of the costs in some states. Contrast the incremental tuition approach above with a bold plan to shift from training small cohorts of health care students (health is but one example, not a preferred one) to starting an international health center that competes for international contracts; charges international-level tuition to all students; allows faculty to do international consulting; and works with regional medical providers to provide trained staff from multiple language backgrounds. The risks may be as great as the potential to transform the college.

Thus, while we would like to think our "core values" drive our decision-making at the executive level, shrewd presidents recognize that there is a close connection between the internal (setting tuition policy) and the external (supplying a trained workforce to the healthcare industry). Or, as Jensen and Giles (2006, 87) state as their #1 truth: "Every decision you make will have three elements: educational, fiscal, and political."

In the near future, as public funding further erodes, calls will be made for "market-driven" tuition rates for costly (health) programs. While it does not seem a popular position to take, it may be what transforms health programs to produce more graduates and cost-out each one. Other nations experienced this shift to market-driven models at the community-based tertiary levels, such as England in the 1990s and the South Africa Technikon movement. While both cases showed interesting applications of market principles, both were fraught with corruption as well, as numerous business models sprung up within colleges, often independently through an unbridled entrepreneurialism.

On another level that connects internal operations with (external) potential students, colleges already are redefining the "open access" philosophy in order to address both the limitations of current financing as well as achieve related improvements. Perhaps in homage to ideas expressed by Bailey and Smith (2006) and Vaughn (2003), colleges in various states have closed registration the Friday before classes start, resulting in a "no late registration" policy. In one state, two years ago, a singular president shocked peers in his state by announcing months ahead of the fall semester that, henceforth, registration would be closed one week before classes began. He predicted retention, and student success, would go way up. Combine this with a limited-window refund policy and there is less scramble to drop, swap, and rapidly advise and register students in that critical first week (and at considerable savings); far fewer students are unprepared at the end of the first week; persistence rates go up; and a significant and needy population is left to wait (and hopefully better prepare) for the next semester. The best-prepared students get into classes and are more ready to learn. Those "left out" hopefully learn a lesson, apply for financial aid in a timely manner, and arrive better prepared next semester. Perhaps most importantly in terms of this chapter, the college can better afford this slower-growth approach, and there are far fewer low-enrollment classes because those were cancelled or combined even several days before that last day of registration.

While such an idea would have been heretical in a 1990s open door context, in a data-driven, post-Spellings era, such a novel way to increase retention rates and even to promote student readiness for learning can be a transformational idea. The president referenced above was widely criticized at the time, but today that decision is considered a bellwether event of emerging student success practices. There was little disagreement among the group that, no matter how much we talk about money and attracting new resources, everything must be placed in the context of student success, local learning, and quality of instruction.

Conclusion

The ability to sample the ideas and recent experience of colleagues produced both rich and surprising data. While "globalizing" is the focal point for some colleges, others are more "place-bound" with no beaches, ports, or similar features that help them recruit international partners and students. Because of a combination of revised federal fiscal and trade policy and climate change fears in society, colleges may be at the beginning of a period when more efficient green technologies can help reestablish weakened manufacturing and related career programs. Still other colleges will invent whole new areas of resource acquisition. These nexus points of resource acquisition, where technological, social, and political factors align, serve as a corollary to Jensen and Giles' Rule #1 shown in the section above, and may provide direction to leaders in search of long-term financing opportunities.

The work of financing a community college takes place on many, many levels. Identifying, building, and marketing a college's strengths is a collective process that requires an authentic leader. Perhaps most importantly, in the globalization of higher education, leaders must continuously inspire, review, and focus resource development. Thus, a never-ending cycle of developing robust and creative educational initiatives produces ongoing reliable funding streams.

References

American Association of Community Colleges (AACC). 2005. *Competencies for Community College Leaders*. Washington, DC: AACC. Available online at: http://www.aacc.nche.edu.

Bailey, Thomas and Smith Morest, Vanessa, Eds. 2006. *Defending the Community College Equity Agenda*. Baltimore, MD: Johns Hopkins University Press.

Bass, Bernard M., and Bruce J. Avolio. 1993. "Transformational Leadership and Organizational Culture." *Public Administration Quarterly* 17 (Spring): 112–121.

Burns, James M. 1978. *Leadership*. New York: Harper and Row.

Cohen, Michael D., and James G. March. 1974. *Leadership and Ambiguity: The American College President*. New York: McGraw-Hill.

Cohen, Michael D., and James G. March. 1986. *Leadership and Ambiguity: The American College President*. 2nd ed. Boston, MA: Harvard Business School Press.

Collins, Jim. 2001. *Good to Great: Why Some Companies Make the Leap...And Others Don't*. New York: HarperCollins Publishers.

Esters, Lorenzo; Christine J. McPhail; Raj Singh, and John J. Sygielski. 2008. "Entrepreneurial Community College Presidents: An Exploratory Qualitative and Quantitative Study." *Tertiary Education and Management* 14 (4): 345–370.

Frost, Robert A. 2007. "Global Studies in the Community College Curriculum." *The Community College Enterprise* 13 (2): 67–74.

Frost, Robert A. 2009a. "Globalization Contextualized: An Organization-Environment Case Study." *Community College Journal of Research and Practice* 33 (12): 1009–1024.

Frost, Robert A. 2009b. "Critical Challenges in California Community Colleges." *Community College Journal of Research and Practice* 33 (10): 797–804.

Frost, Robert A. and Rosalind Latiner Raby. 2009. "Democratizing Study Abroad: Challenges of Open Access, Local Commitments, and Global Competence in Community Colleges." In *Study Abroad and the Making of Global Citizens*, ed. R. Lewin. New York: Routledge/ Taylor and Francis Group.

George, Bill. 2003. *Authentic Leadership: Rediscovering the Secrets to Lasting Value*. San Francisco, CA: Jossey-Bass.

George, Bill and Peter E. Sims. 2007. *True North: Discover Your Authentic Leadership*. San Francisco, CA: Jossey-Bass.

Gump, Steven E. 2006. "Research as Mission Creep? Reconsidering the Role of the Community College." In *Insider's Guide to Community College Administration*. 2nd ed., ed. R. Jensen and R. Giles. Washington, DC: AACC Press.

Jensen, Robert, and Gilles, Raymond. 2006. *Insider's Guide to Community College Administration*, 2nd ed. Washington, D.C.: American Association of Community Colleges.

Moltz, David. 2010. "Buyer's Market." *Inside Higher Ed*. Available online at: http://www.insidehighered.com.

Northouse, Peter G. 2010. *Leadership: Theory and Practice*. Thousand Oaks, CA: Sage Publishers.

Roueche, John E., and Barbara R. Jones, eds. 2005. *The Entrepreneurial Community College*. Washington, DC: Community College Press.

Sygielski, John J. 2010. "Driving Your Budget Message: The Art of Clear Communication in Good Times and Bad." *University Business*. Norwalk, CT: University Business Available online at: http://findarticles.com/p/articles/mi_m0LSH/is_2_13/ai_n57137087/?tag=mantle_skin;content

Trachtenberg, Stephen J. 2008. "What I Might Have Told My Successor." *The Chronicle of Higher Education*, June 13. Available online at: http://chronicle.com.

Vaughan, George B. 2003. Refining 'Open Access.' *Chronicle of Higher Education* (December 5: 1).

Vaughan, George B. 2006. *The Community College Story*. (3rd edition). Washington, DC: Community College Press.

Chapter 5

Leadership, Multiyear Planning, and Budget Management

Daniel Derrico and Stewart E. Sutin

Introduction

Community colleges function in an increasingly complex and challenging environment in which performance expectations are rising, while governmental appropriations to fund their operations are contracting and less predictable. In order to respond effectively to these conditions, community colleges need to perform at extraordinary levels of institutional effectiveness. While focusing on their academic mission and core values, community colleges rely upon exemplary leaders. Leadership skills of increasing importance include creativity, evidence-based problem-solving, comprehensive multiyear planning, and exacting application of results-driven administrative processes. This chapter examines the correlation between college mission, leadership behaviors, and their connection to multiyear planning, performance evaluation systems, and budget management. The highlighted best practices are universally applicable irrespective of the size, structure, or location of the institution.

The overarching thesis of our chapter is that improved financial models for community colleges must be collaboratively developed within a broad institutional context, and be under the direction of inspired leaders who reflect a will to make difficult choices, be consistent with multiyear strategic and financial plans, and be supportive of the academic mission. Medium-term strategic and financial plans should be aligned. This approach provides a sound basis upon which annual operating goals and budgets are defined and performance is evaluated so that the academic purposes and the financial model are compatible outcomes.

Mission and Vision

Mission and vision, as noted in Trettel and Yeager in chapter 6, help guide strategic and annual operating plans. The mission statement should be a brief answer to "what we are here to accomplish?" Vision clarifies the multiyear direction of the college and how it will appear upon arrival at its destination. Now community colleges are challenged to consider ways to adopt mission and vision statements supportive of an improved financial model. For example, the Alamo Community College District in Texas developed its first multiyear strategic plan (2005–2010), which began with a new mission statement: "The Alamo Community College District provides accessible, affordable educational and training opportunities for the citizens of Bexar and surrounding counties." This was ACCD's reason for existence. ACCD enhanced this mission statement in its strategic plan by defining its "vision" of seeking to produce responsible and contributing citizens ready for success in the workforce, prepared for future academic studies, lifelong learning, and civic responsibility.

Leadership

Institutional innovation and systemic and cultural change have long been characteristics of many leading community colleges. Roueche, Baker, and Rose (1989) benchmarked the best practices of community college leadership in their evidence-based study. Sound leadership practices were meticulously applied at the Community College of Denver under the leadership of Byron McClenney (Roueche, Eileen, and Roueche 2001) with a focus on retention and student achievement. Byron and Kay McClenney went on to head up *Achieving the Dream*, an evidenced-based, and planning approach devoted primarily to the persistence of minority students from low-income families. The League of Innovation, Renewal and Change 2020 (RC 2020), Cooperative for the Advancement of Community-Based Postsecondary Education (COMBASE), and the American Association of Community Colleges are among many community college associations devoted to improved educational performance and information sharing.

Community college application of data-based solutions to the educational, student services, and workforce development domains are not novel. The challenge is to apply a similar methodology to the development of a sustainable and improved financial model, which is supportive of the college mission, core values, and student-centric educational priorities.

The selection criteria used by the National Institute of Standards and Technology, US Department of Commerce—in naming winners of the prestigious Baldrige National Quality Program (2010)—offer insight into institutional benefits derived from effective leadership in which in today's environment if you are standing still, you are falling behind. Chief executive officers (CEOs) believe that making the right decisions at the right time is critical and deploying strategy is three times more difficult than developing strategy. Accordingly, institutions are urged to monitor progress and, implicitly, to hold administrators accountable. The selection criteria for this award represent a continuum of planning, actions, and accountability toward delivery of quality product and services, and define attributes supportive of change. The nine criteria include leadership, strategic planning, customer focus, measurement, analysis, knowledge management, workforce focus, process management, and results. Increasingly, higher education is aware of the merits of applying the Baldrige standards to their internal environments.

Core values must be supportive of meeting high and recognized standards of achievement. The emphasis on values reminds the community college faculty, staff, and administrators of why mission is so important, and that fundamental values should drive its goals. This is in alignment with Pohlman and Gardiner (2000) findings that the most successful private and public organizations are those that are value-driven (among examples cited were IBM under Thomas Watson and Wal-Mart under Sam Walton).

Linking Behaviors, Objectives, and Performance Evaluation

Plan development, goal setting, and articulation of values are ethereal in the absence of personal accountability. This requires adoption of performance evaluations based upon ownership of measurable and documentable objectives and behaviors. Community colleges that conduct job description–oriented performance reviews may wish to develop a transition plan, inclusive of training workshops, in order to help administrators understand new and more vigorous standards and especially ones that integrate key features of a new financial model into accountability.

Equitable performance evaluations should recognize achievements, while providing for appropriate personnel actions for those unable or unwilling to adapt to change.

Many community colleges already articulate their values and behavioral attributes. Integration of these values into the formal performance review process offers community college administrators an interactive process to assure that either outstanding or unacceptable behaviors are included in the performance evaluations. This system enables a college to promote ways of thinking and acting supportive of mission and goal realization. The process has validity to the extent that administrators note behaviors as they occur, provide timely feedback, and document what occurred. An extract of values stated in community college websites is revealing.

Inclusiveness

We value inclusiveness and respect for one another. We believe that teamwork is critical, that each team member is important and we depend on each other to accomplish our mission (Maricopa Community Colleges).

Integrity

Do what we say we do. Keep our word. Act responsibly, accountably, and ethically. Do the right thing no matter what. Take personal responsibility for your actions and the outcomes of your actions (Bunker Hill Community College).

Partnership with the Community

Provides accessible campus and outreach centers. Cooperates with other educational systems. Supports activities that enrich the community. Plans educational programs with business and industry to promote the economic development of the community. Increases the community's awareness of college programs and activities (Miami Dade College).

Learning Assured

Create optimal conditions for student learning. Partner with students to improve their contribution to achieving their potential. Close achievement gaps (Valencia Community College).

Communication

We engage in open and transparent communication, information sharing and collaboration (Alamo Community College District).

Stewardship

We are effective and ethical stewards of the resources placed in our trust. Seeking, using, and protecting financial, physical, technological, and human resources are a shared responsibility (Community College of Allegheny County).

Global Education

Prepare and empower students to excel in their academic and professional pursuits for lifelong success in an evolving global environment. Changing lives in the global community through excellence in education (Santa Monica Community College).

Teamwork

Teamwork is a behavior that warrants further comment. Realization of broad institutional goals often requires highly effective teamwork among two or more leaders from different areas of the institution and their support staffs. For example, in highly functioning community colleges, instructional deans and deans of student services are codependent for successful outcomes for students. Chief business or financial officers must be creative and aggressive advocates of cost containment, but the institutional efforts to achieve expense reduction targets and operating efficiencies are apt to fail if "ownership" of the community college financial condition is considered to be the exclusive purview of the CEO and the CFO. Leaders set the tone and the foundation of collaborative ownership and accountability, so sharing responsibility for annual operating goals must be the norm. Persons incapable of effective collaboration and teamwork will be sources of needless conflict, and a drain on the energies of those around them.

Leadership Roles and Responsibilities

This section comments upon several leadership positions, responsibilities, and behaviors supportive of an improved financial model for community colleges. We comment on the ways that certain leaders can contribute to furthering change rather than the full scope of responsibilities normally contained in job descriptions. Our commentary is not definitive, but is indicative of responsibilities and functions that make a difference.

Senior leadership must be role models of self-restraint in containing expenses. This is the right thing to do. Furthermore, systemic reforms may result in pushback from members of the college community who are resistant to change. Any perceived indiscretion in spending is subject to scrutiny and public criticism. Most of all, effective teamwork among all leaders and between the board of trustees, leaders, middle management, and faculty is an imperative condition for sustainable change. The ultimate litmus test of a broad and senior leadership in terms of institutional effectiveness is whether system-wide operations and student-centric activities produce superior educational results, while maintaining affordability and access for students.

Board of Trustees

Board members have a fiduciary responsibility to assure external and internal stakeholders of responsible stewardship of the fiscal, human, and physical resources of community colleges. Fidelity to mission is of paramount importance. Boards approve strategic and annual operating plans, operating and capital budgets, and annual goals as presented by the CEO and other members of the president's cabinet. They approve policies, operating procedures consistent with board-approved policies, and assign authority to the CEO for approval of expenses within budget and prescribed limits. The roles of the board chair, and of the chairs of the finance and human resource committees, where such board committees exist, are of particular importance in both the approval and oversight processes. In this context, it is perfectly reasonable for the board to mandate incremental revenue generation and cost containment in the event that leadership fails to build such initiatives into their plans and budgets. The board selects the president, normally approves senior-level appointments, and evaluates CEO performance annually. But it behooves board members to exercise restraint in travel and entertainment expenses on behalf of the college, and to never act in ways suggestive of conflict of interest in general or when it comes to procurement and personnel matters in particular. On the other hand, there is a need for their consistent support for administrative leadership to improve revenue streams from ancillary enterprises and to contain costs— the more so since certain actions may prove unpopular and may even result in votes of no confidence from faculty.

It is also essential that the board, while holding the CEO accountable for performance consistent with board actions, not endeavor to micromanage or engage in day-to-day decision-making. The board has no role in directing staff, other than their selection and evaluation of the CEO, and the internal auditor. All other college employees are responsible to the CEO, and to their respective line supervisors, not to board members. It is also important that board members exercise their legitimate authority only as a group, never as individuals, and only at open and scheduled board meetings. The CEO must insist on this relationship. Collectively and individually, board behavior must be above reproach, and actions must meet legal and ethical standards for transparency.

Chancellor or President

The CEO embodies the college value system and is the primary communicator of the college mission, vision, goals, and budget. The college relies upon the CEO to hold administrators and others accountable for achieving their respective objectives—inclusive of the revenue generation and/or cost containment targets set in the annual budget. The importance of the CEO as *change agent* cannot be underestimated. The CEO is accountable for delivery of plans, goals, and budgets for approval by the board of trustees. Board members must be kept fully informed of material change and news affecting the financial condition of the college. It is the CEO's obligation to assure that this occurs. CEOs must set a collaborative tone for problem-solving and creating an improved financial model. Perhaps most important of all, the CEO must be supported by administrators with like qualities, who are goal-oriented and work as unselfish members of a team. The CEO more likely to have a lasting impact on institutional change is a motivator, facilitator, inclusive, equitable, honest, a delegator, and supportive of open decision-making processes. Change is less likely to survive the tenure of the CEO in an institution that is hierarchical, controlling, and where decision-making authority resides only at the top of the organization. The CEO must demonstrate the qualities and skills of integrity, courage, judgment, energy, problem-solving, risk-taking, conflict resolution, and accountability. As one of Giuliani's (2002, 69) chapter headings states: "Everyone's accountable, all the time."

Chief Financial (Administrative or Business) Officer

CFOs play a critical role in the development of an improved financial model for the college. They oversee all financial matters and are accountable directly to the CEO. The CFO creates the forums for collaborative development of multiyear financial plans, the annual budget, and must be relentless in advocating for revenue generation and cost containment. After approval by the board, the CFO monitors and reports on budget revenues and expenses on an ongoing basis. More than any other position among senior administrators, the CFO "owns" college expense management and must encourage imaginative and realistic efforts to develop nontraditional revenue streams.

CFO talents include accounting and finance skills, along with having tough-minded questioning, critical thinking, problem-solving, comparative analysis of results, and collaborative leadership. CFOs should encourage broad participation in creating annual budgets, an improved financial model, and assuring their alignment with the college's strategic plan, annual operating plans, and institutional priorities. Moreover, the CFO must be an institutional change agent, and relentlessly pursue delivery of high-quality educational and student services at levels of tuition and fees that remain affordable. The CFO must assure that every cost-containment and revenue-generation option is fully and objectively studied. The CFO must also apply cost containment objectives to areas and personnel directly under his or her authority. To do otherwise will undermine the credibility of college-wide initiatives. The CFO position can be lonely. Those too congenial or unable to rise above the level of chief accountant may be unable to fulfill the institutional imperatives of this difficult assignment.

It is not unusual for procurement, facilities management, and risk management to report to the CFO. Open and competitive bidding processes help keep costs in line. No external provider of services or products should feel that they have a lock on community college business. The CFO should proactively explore outsourcing opportunities for wide ranges of services. In certain cases, data may support *in-sourcing*. Some community colleges now have their own internal legal counsel in order to save money relative to relying upon outside attorneys. A more subtle responsibility is to develop financial literacy among faculty, staff, and students so that they understand the college's financial condition and challenges. To conclude, CFO talents now must embrace ethical, strategic, and tactical behaviors along with the skills to communicate effectively, ask thoughtful questions, listen attentively, and act decisively. An effective CFO is the financial leader of the college.

Provost or Chief Academic Officer

This position defines the academic leader of the college and is accountable for the quality of educational services. Normally about one-half of the annual operating budget reflects the cost of instruction. Colleges count upon this leader to work with faculty and administrators to maintain academic quality, assume an important role in cost containment, and realize educational goals, and especially issues where cost containment initiatives may adversely impact student performance. This leader's view as to the correct mix of full time to adjunct faculty per department per location is of paramount importance. While the CFO may set optimum class size targets across the institution, this leader should determine which disciplines can support larger student enrollment, and which cannot. Low persistence and graduation rates are a hidden cost to the college if one includes such expenses as student orientation, marketing, advertising, and recruitment in the mix. As Anglin points out in case study 3, student persistence also offers beneficial financial results through revenue retention. Funding for learning labs, distance education, student support, and tutorial services may be deemed as essential to educational operations and realization of institutional goals. The role of the provost in hiring, promoting, and granting tenure to faculty is an essential component of institutional effectiveness. This leader must be an exceptional instructional leader, have outstanding people skills, command the respect of the board, the CEO, peers, faculty, and students, be a proficient data-based problem-solver, evidence an uncompromising commitment to student learning outcomes, demonstrate passion for results, and be fully accountable for educational achievement and budgetary performance.

Vice President of Student Services

A range of diverse responsibilities falls under the stewardship of the head of student services. Duties often include freshmen orientation, student activities (including clubs, student newspapers, student government, and intercollegiate sports), student recruitment and enrollment services, financial aid, counseling, student life, career placement, and student support services. Effective collaboration with the provost and CFO is of paramount importance as efforts are made to improve the student campus experience, graduation rates, and student persistence. As such, their role as advocate for the student interests and service provider in support of retention and developmental education must be appreciated. This is a job whose value to students and the community college environment is often well in excess of the budget assigned to this position. The head of student services can materially influence student retention and graduation rates. Accordingly, their role in promoting institutional effectiveness and an improved financial model must be appreciated.

Vice President for Workforce Development and Community Education

This leader should be the most entrepreneurial and market-driven leader in the community college. There are extraordinary opportunities to partner with business organizations in workforce training and other educational opportunities for their employees. This may lead to fees for services, and support from local businesses to include scholarships, contributions of equipment, technology, expertise, leadership skills, exposure to best business practices, and political influence and support. Community education, the noncredit extension of community college services, should be developed as a significant revenue-generating business. As mentioned elsewhere in our book, community colleges such as SAIT Polytechnic and Central Piedmont are proof-positive that significant ancillary revenues can come from such operations, and its leadership should be held accountable accordingly. In certain cases, it may be necessary to hire leaders and trainers from industry in order to realize the full financial benefits that this part of the college enterprise has to offer. Thoughtful and aggressive growth plans, and yearly performance targets should be integral to the college's multiyear plans and annual operating budgets. The leader of this activity must be outgoing, a good two-way communicator, creative, high energy, able to ask probing questions, command the respect of local business leaders, and focused on executing annual plans through hands-on management.

Chief Personnel Officer (CPO)

A highly functioning CPO can directly impact the financial condition of the college and their role on the leadership team should be understood. Efficient, ethical, fair, consistent, legal, and effective hiring, promoting, and disciplining practices can materially influence the cost of doing business. Familiarity with union and employee relations and grievance processes can foster change, while reducing the risk of successful litigation by dissidents. A respected CPO can directly contribute to morale among employees. Professional development and training programs are often needed to support community college priorities. In addition, the CPO should work with the CFO in evaluating employee health and benefit programs, which represents a significant part of the total operating budget. Experience, resilience, judgment, problem-solving abilities, negotiating and conflict resolution skills, communication abilities, and creativity support the transformation to an improved financial model. The CPO must also train and inspire the human resources department staff. The CPO must be the expert on the application of college personnel policy, and must be a role model for ethnical management behavior. In summation, an effective CPO will command respect among employees at all levels of the community college, and willingly accepts the role of change agent in creating and delivering an improved financial model.

Leadership: Forums for Initiating and Monitoring Change

The CEO leadership team must meet on a regular basis to discuss concerns, issues, and progress related to goals, assignments, pending projects, and issues of budget, productivity, and related matters. It is this group that must drive improvement of the college's financial model. Data should be reviewed at these meetings that relate previous assumptions and projections to current reality, and the need to make adjustments. At the large and comprehensive community colleges of Miami Dade College, and the Alamo Community College District, such meetings were scheduled on a weekly basis, on the same day, time, and location. Action minutes were taken and distributed to all meeting participants and to many others for purposes of communication, transparency, and trust. The focus of these meetings should always be on what needs to be done, by whom, and when. When tasks and projects are assigned, then let those assigned to do it determine how to do it, and how to measure how well it gets done, and report back to the group. Their decisions and analysis of the results are always subject to review by the leadership group, and by the CEO. This process will work very well if the CEO has created a very strong and capable leadership team. Collins (2001, 41) describes this as "getting the right people on the bus." It is also necessary to hold people accountable for failure, and on occasion, to "get the wrong people off the bus."

Budget Management

Budget creation and postapproval management are key tools in bringing about an improved financial model. Clear decision-making criteria provide invaluable guidelines for budget creation and approval. They are best agreed upon up front by community college leadership and the board of trustees. Postboard budget approval is often where the rubber meets the road in management of change processes.

Alignment with multiyear strategic and financial plans and annual operating goals are imperative. Other guidelines are self-generated by each college and may include: (1) the community college "cannot be all things to all people," (2) adverse impact on educational or student service quality is nonnegotiable, (3) sustaining a balanced budget is essential, and (4) fidelity to the access and affordability component of the community college mission remains essential. In our proposed construct, annual budgets must also include financial targets for generation of revenues from ancillary enterprises and cost containment initiatives.

The Alamo Community College District offers a case in point regarding transition from school year to multiyear planning cycles. For many years, the college did not strategically plan, focus upon multiyear budget assumptions, and undertake medium-term financial projections. Budget priorities and allocations were determined one year at a time. This weakness of traditional annual budget models creates major problems of underfunding new and growing programs, preparing for predictable enrollment growth, and not anticipating the impact of cost inflation over time. Another major problem is illustrated by the large-scale capital building program, which had new buildings coming on-line each year from 2007 to 2010. The financial problem, briefly stated, is that buildings that open one year have most of their enrollment revenue (student fees) come in the next year, and state enrollment funding support will not arrive until another year after that in the Texas biennium funding cycle, which always lags behind enrollment increases, as in other states. This required a multiyear budget plan creating a budget surplus the first year to cover deficits for the next one or perhaps two years, until the revenues caught up with the operational expenses of the operating and staffing the new buildings.

Budget preparation and management should foster disciplined approaches to cost containment and revenue generation from nontraditional functions by creating forums for analysis and discourse. Community colleges have many options worthy of consideration. Organizational structures can be modified to improve service quality while eliminating redundant activities. As observed by Fletcher Byrom of Kopper's Corporation, "of all the things I have observed...the most disturbing has been a tendency toward over-organization, producing a rigidity that is intolerable in an era of accelerating change" (Peters and Waterman 1982, 50). Which services and support activities can be reengineered to reduce labor content, improve efficiency, lower cost, and improve service quality for students? How can this be accomplished? Available data at a national level notes that an increasing percent of operating budgets in higher education has been consumed by administration and back shop staff. A framework for evaluation may hypothesize; if we were building this college today what minimal level of administrative and staff would be required to meet community college needs. Use of outside consultants may assure a more objective evaluative process.

The staffing consequences of change may vary. During periods of high enrollment growth, improving operating efficiencies need not include staff reductions, but instead training and redeployment of displaced workers to other functions in the college. A "win-win" scenario is to service more students with current staffing levels. Involvement of faculty and staff in such projects may generate ideas, while inspiring confidence in solutions emerging in a collaborative bottom-up environment. But during periods of nonenrollment growth, such actions may result in contraction in the number of nonfaculty positions at the college, which is counterintuitive for those devoted to sustaining lifelong employment practices. In such cases, one must consider whether sustaining full employment trumps the college mission of sustaining affordability and access.

In order to meet the stated goals of the strategic plan, annual operating goals and budget, leaders must attempt accurate projection of enrollment, and revenues from (1) tuition and fees, (2) public appropriations, (3) auxiliary business activities, (4) continuing education, and (5) contractual arrangements and partnerships with the private sector to deliver workforce training and consulting services. Entrepreneurial skills, creativity, and sales talent are essential to building revenues from nontraditional activities. This may require hiring outsiders from industry- or business-focused associations such as chambers of commerce. Multiyear business plans must be developed for these activities, inclusive of annual revenue generation budgets that are aggressive yet attainable. If current staff is unable to function in this entrepreneurial and accountable environment, an infusion of outside talent may be required.

Cost containment similarly requires constant focus, tough-minded leadership, meticulous study of data, and creativity in order to be effective over the medium term. Many financially significant reengineering of processes require persons with skill sets in project management to head up the effort. If in-house experience in project management is insufficient, then external consultants should be contracted to facilitate the design and implementation of such complex initiatives. Short-term "fixes" such as freezing salary, hiring, and travel are unsustainable over time. Certain actions should be strategically driven. For example, why not exit from workforce development programs in low demand occupational categories or where regional overcapacity is in evidence? If, for instance, employment prospects for graduates of a certain program are dim and unlikely to improve anytime soon, is sustaining such a program truly a benefit for the students? On the other hand, closing down or reducing funding for specialized student support services such as math, reading, and writing labs or child care centers may undermine persistence by at-risk students. In summation, cost containment requires adaptation of surgical and thoughtful actions rather than shotgun methodology.

Management of Objectives and Performance Evaluations

Management by objectives (MBO) offers an evaluation process by which individuals define measurable and time-sensitive objectives and plans of action consistent with college priorities. This approach provides a basis for defining a relationship between administrators and college-wide annual operating plans and goals. Although certain goals may take years to realize, annual performance objectives and action plans should note what progress can be expected during each school year. Facilities planning and construction are illustrative of this point. Phase one/year one goals may call for completion of a facilities master plan and priority identification. Phase two/year two may call for architectural design, vetting, budget setting, and approval processes. Phase three/years three and four may allow for construction to meet college priorities, quality standards, and approved budget. Responsibilities are assigned at each stage and offer ways to measure success or lack of same. The same would hold true for educational, student services, or any enduring goal approved by the board of trustees. The contention that multiyear goals are not subject to performance evaluation calibrated to the school year does not hold up under closer inspection. Application of multiyear planning and accountability processes are fundamental preconditions for meaningful improvements of revenue generation and cost containment in an improved financial model.

Key indicators, or a "dashboard," of institutional effectiveness as reported annually to the board of trustees must reflect the quantitative results of revenue generation and cost containment initiatives, as well as quality controls needed to support the academic mission of the college. The durability and institutional impact of an improved financial model are more likely when embedded in a college's strategic plan, annual operating goals, and budgets. Transparency is assured by posting the results on the community college website, and issuing periodic report cards on progress to the board of trustees. Certain goals, such as improvement in graduation rates and persistence of students in developmental education, require multiyear planning and trend analysis. The same is true of the college's financial model. Public accountability plays an important role in sustaining institutional focus and assuring stakeholders that "results do matter."

Conclusion

Our chapter describes an on-going process whereby leaders make a difference in creating an improved financial model. The processes to realize institutional systemic change vary. They include alignment of multiyear strategic and annual operating plans with budgeted financial resources and efficient organization structures. Key administrative positions are held by change agents who are evaluated based upon attainment of objectives and demonstrative adherence to accepted behaviors. Processes are adopted that require evaluating data, rethinking assumptions, identifying ways to influence revenues and expenditures, reviewing the effectiveness of academic and student support services, improving operational efficiencies, streamlining organizational structures, setting priorities, and adjusting budgets to better meet student and community needs. Federal and state governments demand accountability, and reporting of data to authenticate the same. Colleges able to evidence generation of revenues from nontraditional businesses and containment of costs are more likely to be well received. Ongoing efforts toward institutional improvement and integration of an improved financial model into the college fabric are imperative. No matter the level of achievements to date, there are always opportunities for further gain. William Faulkner once cautioned in an interview with Jean Stein vanden Heuvel (1956), "Don't bother just to be better than your contemporaries or predecessors. Try to be better than yourself."

References

Collins, Jim C. 2001. *Good to Great.* New York: Harper Collins Publishers.

Giuliani, Rudolph W. 2002. *Leadership.* New York: Miramax Books.

Heuvel, Jean Stein vanden. 1956. "Interviews—William Faulkner, the Art of Fiction." *The Paris Review* Spring (12): 1–8. Available online at http://www.theparisreview.org.

Baldrige National Quality Program. 2010. *National Institute of Standards and Technology, U.S. Department of Commerce.* Gaithersburg, MD: National Institute of Standards and Technology. Available online at: http://www.baldrige.nist.gov.

Peters, Thomas J., and Robert H. Waterman, Jr. 1982. *In Search of Excellence.* New York: Warner Books.

Pohlman, Randolph A., Gareth S. Gardiner, and Ellen M. Heffes. 2000. *Value Driven Management: How to Create and Maximize Value over Time for Organizational Success.* New York: American Management Association.

Roueche, John E., George A. Baker III, and Robert R. Rose. 1989. *Vision: Transformational Leadership in American Community Colleges.* Washington, DC: The Community College Press.

Roueche, John E, Eileen E. Ely, and Susanne D. Roueche. 2001. *In Pursuit of Excellence: The Community College of Denver.* Washington, DC: Community College Press.

Chapter 6

Linking Strategic Planning, Priorities, Resource Allocation, and Assessment

Brenda S. Trettel and John L. Yeager

Introduction

During the second half of the twentieth century, community college missions have expanded and changed. Today's community college missions require its leaders to understand the changes in their complex work environment, including the symbiotic relationship that exists between the college and the community that it serves. Such an understanding allows leaders to continuously change and adapt to external and internal challenges (American Association of Community Colleges [AACC] 2009). At the same time, the state and sometimes local government have direct influence and interest in the colleges' financing and an indirect influence on governance structures and operations. It is this consortium of interests of state, local community, and business and industry that contribute to uniqueness, strength, and challenges of these institutions.

This chapter examines strategic and financial management best practices while offering insights that may help community colleges to better align their missions, programs, and resources through the integration of select management functions. It should be noted that many community colleges operate under various organizational and governance systems. We recognize that no single model that fits all situations, and there is a need for modification of our approach to fit each college's realities.

Community College Management

As these institutions grew in size and complexity, they required an increased administrative sophistication in order to successfully manage their operations. This represented an additional challenge at the outset. Many colleges were initially under the leadership of administrators and faculty who were not specifically trained to lead or operate these new organizations. Many of the professional staff came from public schools, two-year institutions, four-year institutions, the public sector, and business and industry. Naturally, they used tools and skills they found to work in their previous positions and to the degree possible, and modified them to fit the challenges encountered in the community college setting. This presented a situation where some of the major institutional decision-makers had a mixture of management training and many different individual perspectives as to how a community college should be administered. Finally, each institution was embedded in the culture of its immediate community and operated under the legal and political systems in the state that they resided.

The Institutional Planning and Budget Management Process

Institutional management partially links the five components of the management process: (1) strategic planning, (2) resource allocation, (3) implementation, (4) assessment, and (5) dissemination of information. In many cases, these functions have been treated as separate and almost discrete functions or *silos*. For some leaders the silos mentality is an intentional choice but nonetheless represents a lack of conceptual integration that has led institutions to develop inefficient and ineffective management practices resulting in suboptimization of their resources in support of program activities.

Silo orientation of management functions often inhibit an institution from achieving its desired outcomes and prohibiting the transparency of operations. While conceptually it is a relatively simplistic task to link the several functions in practice, in reality, it is a major challenge. The evolution of enterprise financial management software systems create opportunities to integrate partially connected silos. Under conditions of restricted resources, competition for resources becomes a major distracter in the procurement and allocation of program funds.

Institutional Strategic Planning

Strategic planning provides the foundation and direction for other organizational activities. Mintzenberg (1994, 109) states: "strategic thinking is about synthesis." The outcome of strategic thinking is an integrated perspective of the enterprise, and vision of direction. It does not happen just because a meeting was held titled with that label. To the contrary, designing a strategy is a process interwoven with all the pieces needed to manage an organization. Strategy-making offers exceptional potential as a silo buster at the enterprise level. It is essential that the strategic planning be successfully completed as a basis for all functional areas to design their goals and implementation plans.

The strategic plan does not represent a blueprint cast in concrete but rather an interactive baseline that can respond to both external and internal changes through clarifying institutional priorities and as a foundation for ascertaining and measuring the degree of success in meeting intended outcomes. The development of a community college strategic plan represents three particular institutional challenges. First, strategic plans usually cover a multiyear time period ranging from three to five years. This time period does not coincide with the many community college programs that are a mixture of diplomas, certificates, and two-year programs, resulting in shorter planning periods and implementation. Hence, it is important that faculty be involved in the planning process. This is a difficult proposition since a large number of community college faculty and students are part-time, reducing available planning time and causing possible interruptions in faculty input year on year. The second challenge is that due to the multiplicity of sponsorships and stakeholders, consensus at the program level is often difficult to achieve although collegial efforts help reconcile divergent perspectives. Finally, communications and buy-in of the strategic plan is important especially in multicampus community colleges because of logistics, culture, busy schedules, and faculty governance systems.

Organization

Most institutional strategic planning, while conducted under the direction of the president with the approval of the board of directors, involves an active steering committee that includes key faculty, staff, and administrators. This offers an additional dimension of involvement. The steering committee is responsible for the oversight of the planning process including the appointment of working committees, such as student affairs, workforce development, facilities, finance emphasis, among others, which approve timeframes, components of the plan and make recommendations to the president. Often the planning forums are open to the public and actively engage a variety of stakeholders.

Size

These committees typically range in size from between 10 and 20 individuals. While the size of these committees often reflects the desire of the institution's leadership to insure a sufficient degree of institutional representation, we recommend that committees consist of approximately 15 members (Rowley and Sherman 2001). Larger committees are often difficult to manage and the representation of a multiplicity of agendas makes it difficult to reach consensus. The literature, however, does not have consensus on this issue as illustrated by the Planning Advisory Council at Carroll Community College, which had 27 members and was able to successfully lead their planning process (Clagett 2004, 114).

Plan-to-Plan

The plan-to-plan remains the primary function and is a roadmap for the development of specific timelines and directives for plan coordination. This includes the rationale for developing the plan, planning assumptions, organizational units to be included, timeframe, and tasks of the roles and responsibilities of institutional participants, committee structure, a communication plan, and specification of resources for developing the plan. At a minimum, this plan contains a number of components such as (1) background/context for planning; (2) situational analysis that includes external scan, internal analysis, and competitor analysis; (3) vision and mission statements; (4) goals and objectives; (5) strategic initiatives; (6) resource availability; (7) implementation guidelines; and (8) plan assessment. The plan-to-plan can be developed at both the institutional and suborganizational levels such as departments or administrative units. The resulting plan therefore consists of a set of interrelated planning and processing components with each level contributing to the total plan.

Key resources such as past accreditation studies, college reports to the board of directors, and specialized academic and management reports from the institutional research offices inform the plan-to-plan. Further, both the institutional research and the budget offices have detailed longitudinal enrollment, student, and financial information available that is important for development of the plan. Finally, previous strategic plans as well as plans from leading community colleges should be examined.

Positions the Institution within Its Operating Environment

The strategic plan identifies and evaluates external and internal events and trends that might impact the institution within "situational analysis." Environmental scans, internal reviews and competitor analysis should include assessments of probability and the degree of impact that each trend or perception of reality might have on the institution's mission and operations. This process is usually conducted within a framework that permits each trend or event to be categorized into predetermined groups. A typical system is referred to by the acronym, political, economic, social, and technology or in an expanded version, social, technical, economic, educational, and political and assists the college in organizing trends and events that are identified in the external environment.

Of high importance is the review of the college's vision, mission, goals, and values and when appropriate to update them to reflect the information obtained from the situational analysis where there is agreement and support among the stakeholders since missions change due to limited or decreasing resources. The American Productivity and Quality Center (1996) recommends several best practices that are important for community colleges to consider when developing strategic plans. The following six best practices have provided guidance in the development of institutional strategic plans for almost 15 years, and remain relevant: (1) stretch goals that drive strategic out-of-the-box thinking, (2) keep planning processes flexibility to reflect a continuous improvement philosophy, (3) formalize the communication process, (4) emphasize action plans and strategic thinking, (5) explicitly recognize strategic planning as a key element in the management system, and (6) document the strategic thinking process.

Therefore, the strategic planning process can serve as a framework for several specialized institutional subplans such as technology, facilities, enrollment, human resources, financial, and development plans. An important aspect of this process is to have the strategic plan be aligned with the budget.

The Resource Allocation Process

The strategic plan identifies priorities that are required to implement an appropriate resource allocation program based upon the institution's vision and mission. This becomes a key connection between the institution's strategic plan and the allocation process. The specification of a hierarchy of priorities offers a basis upon which to embark upon a resource allocation process.

Institutions that do not systematically define these important priorities, except in general terms, leave room for misinterpretations or misallocation of resources. Community colleges may elect to place programs or activities in general categories such as imperative, important, and highly desirable rather than in specific rank order. These assessments and assignments are determined based on perceived institutional mission relevance, previous or continuing commitment, current outcome attainment, and contribution to institutional prestige. This process is important in assisting to differentiate for funding purposes between the various program activities. It is typical that departments are requested to submit resource requests to the central administration in terms of the programs to be supported and their intended outcomes as well as a justification of the amount of funds requested. Too often the amount of funds requested are not in close alignment with the activities to be supported or the intended outcomes are approximations of the department head's or dean's requirements, which can be overly ambitious. In too many instances, little effort is made to examine program need requests in a comprehensive manner in terms of costs and relative outcomes.

Regular and periodic program review information can be used to augment or inform resource allocation decision. The resource decision process becomes even more complicated when both new programs and existing programs are considered in the same mix. While in many cases, institutions have made decisions concerning the relative merits of existing programs utilizing separate executive committees or specially appointed faculty/administrative resource allocation program committees. A more inclusive process to such decisions should be considered when choosing program trade-offs among new and existing programs.

One such process would apply a type of a decision tree model to assist in establishing relative program trade-offs considering program characteristics such as mission alignment, perceived program quality, costs, and competitive advantage. One example is the multiple attribute decision model, which proposes a methodology of assessing programs through the use of both qualitative and quantitative measures and provides a mechanism for comparing programs based on a framework of predetermined dimensions and weightings (Lasher and Greene 1993). This process assists the institution in determining the relative priorities of programs to serve as a basis for resource assignment. With this information, it is then possible to consider program allocation of funds.

Most institutions of higher education focus the majority of their "budgetary" attention on the distribution of funds among the several activities of the institution that may not be linked to the strategic plan or reflect institutional priorities. Hence, focus on "fund distribution" can actively distract from the important consideration of how the institution should maintain each of its major assets such as the faculty and staff, facilities, grounds, equipment, libraries, and image and reputation (Jones 1993, 8). Several of the most common methodologies for institutional resource allocation are incremental, formula, cost/revenue center, zero-base budgeting, and performance budgeting (Lasher and Greene 1993). In most cases, these methodologies have been borrowed from the business and industry sector, and are not usually applied in isolation but in combination with other methods and characteristics attempting to meet specific institutional needs. Of these approaches, the incremental process is the most widely used. This method in general assumes that the previous base budget of the entities is an appropriate allocation and adjustments are made incrementally to that base budget. For example, an institution might increase all budgets by a fixed amount or percentage. The focus of this process is on the increment or decrement and not on the unit's base budget. Colleges often reduce the previous year's expenditures by a fixed percentage that is used to establish a reserve fund to support new initiatives or to provide for areas of extraordinary need after which budgets are then adjusted on an incremental basis. A major advantage of this process is that it is easily understood and provides a significant amount of flexibility and discretion to the administrative decision process. A major disadvantage is that almost all the attention is focused on the size of the increment and not on the total amount being allocated. Oftentimes once the budget increment has been announced, there is a tendency to give the increment without a careful analysis of exactly how the increment will be spent. In addition and most important, there is often only little attention given to how the base budget will be expended and the degree to which it is needed and to support the institution's mission.

Zero-based budgeting is an alternative process that requires the annual rebuilding and justification of each aspect of a specific unit budget. While this is an appropriate procedure, it is a difficult and time-consuming process since each section of the budget requires justification. Because of the potential benefits that can be derived by using zero-based budgeting, many colleges only examine selected areas on alternate years or the documentation process is truncated and not all costing and outcome estimates are provided in detail. Although not perfect, other factors such as tenure make the application of zero-based budgeting more difficult. These modifications provide important information in terms of the resource allocation process.

While many states distribute funding to community colleges based on various types of formulas, such as the number of students or credit hours generated, faculty positions, among others, community colleges do not internally disburse funds in a similar manner unless stipulated to do so by specific regulations. Internal allocation decisions are typically done based on demonstrated need for activities such as number of classes and sections to be offered, support services to be offered, previous commitments, and program continuations. These decisions consider previous plans and agreed upon initiatives as well as the feedback of performance information. While many states use formula-based budget allocation practices, formulas are used as method of distributing funding and not as a method of determining the amount of program funding required by a community college. While the stated needs of the institution, funding line item weightings, and the availability of state funds drive the format, there are many others that are unique to each state.

The college operating budget allocation process is done on an annual basis and represents a carefully orchestrated process since multiple revenue streams and changing expenditures must be comingled and integrated into an overall institutional budget plan within a specified time frame. While the process is usually annual, many institutions develop multiyear budget plans to more adequately assess current and future years of budget commitment although those budgets after the first year are for planning purposes only. Institutions have a number of revenue streams such as tuition, awarded contracts and grant allocations, state support, and local support from municipal governments, local businesses, alumni, and foundations. While many of the funding streams have restrictions, in total they provide a significant degree of latitude in terms of expenditures to permit management flexibility. Therefore to maximize allocations and program flexibility to any specific budget unit, the allocation must carefully consider and specify not only the amount of funds but the source of funding in terms of restricted and unrestricted funds.

While tuition is a critical source of funding, it is subject to the variability associated with enrollment levels. Some institutions have attempted to stabilize the estimated tuition portion of the budget through the implementation of a deregistration process. This process requires students to pay their tuition by a predetermined date before the semester starts to hold their class selections. The payment can be made through cash or a credit card by a student signing up for a payment plan and applying for financial aid and grants. If a student does not arrange some type of payment plan, they lose their class schedule after a date predetermined by the college. This permits the institution to monitor enrollments and tuition income immediately prior to the beginning of classes. The Community College of Allegheny County (CCAC) employs such a practice (CCAC 2009).

Plan Implementation and Monitoring

It is critical that the faculty and staff must be actively engaged in the development of the strategic plan and its implementation. To ensure faculty and staff input, community colleges should establish advisory committees with representation from faculty, staff, and administration to assist in the planning and allocation processes. This input is valuable in providing user feedback on decisions and to obtain information to assess the impact that various decisions might have on schools, departments, and individuals. Often frontline managers, faculty, and staff have a much clearer understanding of where the application of additional resources may have the greatest benefits or where reductions can be made without adversely affecting operations. This makes it imperative that the college administration, in order to make the best possible decisions, involves institutional-wide participation in the budget and plan implementation process. Therefore, it is important the institution members have a substantial understanding of why certain decisions were made. It is only through participation in the budget development process that individuals can gain understanding of both the decision process supporting budget development and program plan implementation.

Administrators and faculty are key planners and implementers of any program plan and have intimate knowledge as to the potential relative success and failure of programs. This information is particularly valuable when a college is confronted with fiscal difficulties and must reduce or eliminate programs.

Once program and resource decisions have been implemented, the monitoring process becomes critical to achieving key institutional outcomes. This requires the operating unit conducting the purposed activity to provide a monitoring system to assess progress and monitor program outcomes. One tool that has been found to be of assistance in performing this function is the creation of an institutional *performance dashboard*, which provides senior management with frequent timely snapshots of institutional performance data. These systems can be institutionally developed or commercially purchased. One partial shortcoming for the implementation of an assessment system is the fact that many community colleges do not have operational institutional research offices and college staff are often not trained to develop and maintain monitoring programs.

In a similar manner, monitoring processes have to be established for the institution's various financial income and expenditures. The institution's various income streams must be carefully estimated and charted throughout the course of the budget year and based on new information adjusted in terms of budget availability and program expenditures. One difficulty in establishing a monitoring process is that readily available operational data is not collected in a timely manner. Additionally, information support of identifying program performance and executive decision-making are often not available. It is important that most monitoring data show planned status versus operating status. For example, it is important that the college carefully projects and monitors its end-of-year fund balance. Colleges must be aware both as to potential budget surpluses as well as deficits since to only through such actions can sustain its short-term and long-term fiscal viability. Institutions should monitor planned revenue and expenditures on a monthly or quarterly basis using percentage estimates as benchmarks while a few use a composite of past year averages to develop benchmarks of patterns of revenues and expenditures. The purpose of these actions is to determine the amount of variances that are occurring between planned fiscal projections and actual expenditure (Capone 1991). The monitoring process can be done both at the college level as well as the department level. Finally, many colleges use the annual budget process, which oftentimes commences approximately half way through the fiscal year to collect monitoring data on program performance. It becomes essential information in the preparation of next year's budget.

Plan Assessment

A final function of the financial management process is evaluation/assessment. There are a variety of forms, each with their own unique characteristics. While this is a critical function, it is often not performed in a rigorous manner, and it is also not practiced by all community colleges. Hence, this section will identify processes to strengthen this element and to connect program outcomes to mission and goals. Measurement at this level is often difficult to formulate and successfully complete. The information that can be obtained from this process is essential for determining the degree the strategic plan is being successfully implemented. If the plan is not appropriately implemented, there is little chance that it can be successful. Once the strategic plan has been completed but before it is implemented, it is important to development an assessment plan. The assessment plan should include the frequency of assessment, what is to be assessed, who will conduct the assessment, the type of information to be collected, and what will be done with the result. Since strategic plans are multiyear in construction, assessments need not be conducted on an annual basis. These assessments are summative in nature since the organization has other processes in place to obtain formative assessment information such as budget reviews, accreditations, and specialized studies.

Outcome measures, as defined by key performance indicators (KPIs), represent one approach that could provide both quantitative and qualitative information, thereby providing critical information concerning the achievement of several of the most important institutional areas. Too often the resources required to obtain this information are considered low priority in relationships to other institutional needs and oftentimes unorganized subjective information substitutes for formal evaluation. This information is collected only when a major review is conducted such as an accreditation or a program review to determine whether or not a program should be discontinued (Aloi 2005).

Since the 1970s, all institutions of higher education are facing increased scrutiny in terms of program outcomes and fiscal accountability. Community colleges have not escaped this accountability. In fact, because of their multiple missions and funding, programs and all of their activities have increasingly been questioned in terms of their financial stewardship and their program effectiveness and efficiency. There is a great deal of interest by the general public, state and regional governments, business and accreditation agencies in community college accountability. Programs are being reviewed and evidence sought as to the degree they achieve their stated mission particularly in terms of student access, retention, and graduation rates.

Dissemination of Information

Dissemination of information is critical to the success of the institutional strategic management process. This provides a holistic interpretation that we profile as important for all future management plans. All institutional members, faculty, staff, and administrators need to be fully aware and informed of the mission and direction of the community college for the college to be successful. It is essential that the resulting outcomes be widely disseminated and discussed—the pursuit of the college's mission is everyone's responsibility. There are many ways to disseminate information. Mailings, email, posters, newsletters, presentations, and other formal and informal means of communication are all appropriate to provide information to faculty and staff.

Further at the end of the fiscal year and/or the planning period, the results should be reviewed and disseminated and where necessary plans should be revised. This is also an appropriate time to review planned goals and activities. These results should then be directed back into the fiscal and program management system and where necessary appropriate revisions made. As a final step, the results of the previous planning period and the revised plans should be discussed with institutional constituents and a revised strategic plan prepared.

Examples of Fiscal Management Systems

There are numerous examples of effective community college management systems that have been developed and implemented. One such institution, the Collin County Community College District located in North Texas, was able to successfully address several fiscal challenges through a disciplined implementation of an integrated management system (Tambrino 2001). Its strategic planning scanning process permitted them to identify potential fiscal problems in time to make adjustments and to develop a multiyear response plan. This awareness was accomplished through the addition of tracking such new factors as the volume of food stamps being distributed in the county along with home foreclosures, appraised property tax growth, and indigent health care claims. This new scanning information was then used to inform resource planning activities, which led to analysis and changes in instructional costs and reductions in a timely manner that permitted the college to make appropriate budgetary reductions. In addition to reducing costs, scanning assisted the institution in developing new funding streams such as charging for the use of college facilities by outside organizations. Also the college as a result of its revised planning process reexamined its budgeting process and decided that its previous incremental process needed to be replaced, one that clearly placed greater responsibility on budget managers. To that end, a form of zero-based budgeting was implemented coupled with open hearings that assisted in breaking down the silo effect through the sharing of budgetary information. This revised process helped to identify duplication of funding support that permitted greater institutional flexibility of program funding and provided broader and better information to the budget managers, a valuable educational process. A major lesson learned was the power of communication and the importance of focusing on the college's mission, goals, and strategic plan were of high importance in the financial and program management of the institution. The Collin Community College financial and program management system is an excellent example of an institution gaining greater efficiency and effectiveness through the integration of key management functions.

Another example is Iowa Valley Community College District, which consists of three separate operating units—two colleges, a continuing education unit, and a central office (Israel and Kihl 2006). This institution had previously experienced near fiscal bankruptcy in the early 1990s and implemented a contribution margin budget (CMB) system, which is a modification of a more generic responsibility central budgeting process. Under the CMB system, an institution empowers a unit budget manager to more actively manage institutional and program matters by making them responsible for all income and expenditures for their units. As a result of using a CMB system, the deans, division chairs, and faculty members of the colleges and schools are vested with fiscal responsibility in line with their academic authority. Each unit is responsible for developing and establishing their own budget. As a result of these efforts, Iowa Valley Community College ranks first in the state's community colleges with regards to fund balance as a percentage of operating expenditures (Israel and Kihl 2006).

Conclusion

Community college performance can be enhanced and assets maintained through the implementation of a comprehensive planning and management system that links strategic planning, resource allocation, plan implementation, and assessment. Each of these processes plays a significant role in the effective management of the institution. Strategic planning sets the baseline, describes the future directions of the institution, compares resource allocation trade-offs, and enables community colleges to evaluate progress towards mission achievement. However, to maximize the benefits of this process, it is important that all community college stakeholders—trustees, administrators, faculty, staff, students, and the general public they serve—be included in the planning and development of the process. All aspects of the four major functions and their associate linkages must be public and transparent, since it is only with such inclusion that the community college can achieve its mission. It is through the coupling of these processes a college has the ability to better understand and manage its various programs and resources through a comprehensive linking and selective integration of its management functions. This chapter has offered an enhanced model that is supportive of a rational system for aligning financial and other resources with college priorities embedded in the plan.

References

Aloi, Susan L. 2005. "Best Practices in Linking Assessment and Planning." *Assessment Update* 17 (3): 4–6.

American Association of Community Colleges (AACC). 2009. *Community College Past to Present*. Washington, DC: AACC. Available online at: http://www.aacc.nche.edu.

AACC. 2009. *Fast Facts*. Washington, DC: AACC. Available online at: http://www.aacc.nche.edu/AboutCC/Pages/fastfacts.aspx

American Productivity and Quality Center. 1996. *Strategic Planning: Final Report*. Houston: American Productivity and Quality Center.

Capone, F. W. Hendricks, and Ray Pohlman. 1991. *Building Budget Skills*, ed. rev. Shawnee Mission, KS: National Press Publications.

Clagett, Craig A. 2004. "Strategic Planning Carroll Community College." *New Directions for Institutional Research* 123: 114–120.

Community College of Allegheny County (CCAC). 2009. *Payment Due Dates for Credit Courses*. Pittsburgh: CCAC. Available online at: http://www.ccac.edu.

Israel, Cary A., and Brenda Kihl. 2006. "Using Strategic Planning to Transform a Budgeting Process." *New Directions for Community Colleges* 2006 (132): 77–86.

Jones, Dennis P. 1993. "Strategic Budgeting." In *Financial Management: Progress and Challenges (No. 83)*, ed. W. E. Vandament and D. P. Jones. San Francisco, CA: Jossey-Bass.

Lasher, William F., and Deborah L. Greene. 1993. "College and University Budgeting; What Do We Know? What Do We Need to Know?" In *Higher Education Handbook of Theory and Research (No. 9)*, ed. J. Smart. New York: Agathon Press.

Mitzenberg, Henry. 1994. "The Rise and Fall of Strategic Planning." *Harvard Business Review* 72 (1): 107–114.

Rowley, Daniel J., and Herbert Sherman. 2001. *From Strategy to Change: Implementing the Plan in Higher Education*. San Francisco, CA: Jossey-Bass.

Tambrino, Paul A. 2001. "Contribution Margin Budgeting." *Community College Journal of Research and Practice* 25 (1): 29–36.

Chapter 7

Budget Development Process for Community Colleges

Daniel Derrico

Introduction: An Experience-Based Pragmatic Approach

This chapter is intended to describe a practical approach for the practitioner—community college chief executive officer (CEO), or chief financial officer (CFO), and other administrators who have major responsibilities for creating and monitoring operating budgets and financial operations. Properly deployed, budget development and management is an indispensable component of an improved financial model. These ideas are being presented for now, and for the future, as colleges are increasingly challenged to balance their operating budgets while serving the needs of their students and community. It is also written for many others who are involved in, or are interested in budget and financial decisions. It presents common errors of current budget planning models, with a practical approach of how to avoid these mistakes, and what is required for a new model. An attempt is made to answer questions of what to do, when, by whom, how it should be done, and why. This approach emphasizes annual and multiyear budget planning models, multiyear revenue and expenditure forecasting, assumptions that lead to decisions, and the need to monitor revenues and expenses, evaluate results, and reexamine the accuracy of your assumptions on which your financial projections are based. The chapter is presented in a manner that would be applicable to any public community college of any size or location.

This method will require integrity, transparency, competence, planning, projecting and analyzing data, measuring results, accountability for results, and for the administration to work cooperatively with the board of trustees and the faculty and staff to achieve stated goals. Primary goals are to balance the annual operating budget, preferably to include an end-of-year budget surplus to add to the unencumbered fund balance, while maintaining or increasing quality, and achieving stated priority goals of the college's strategic plan. This chapter is not based upon research or a literature review. Rather, my observations and recommendations come from extensive experience with community college budget planning and implementation, as well as from lessons learned from other community college CEOs and CFOs with whom I have communicated over many years.

This chapter deals with the operating budget, consisting of all revenues and expenses except for grants, student scholarships and financial aid, foundation accounts, construction bonds, or other separately funded capital improvement projects. Operating budgets include revenues from state and local governments, student tuition and fees, contract for services rendered income, investment interest income, and auxiliary income from services such as cafeteria and bookstore operations. The budget plan is a summary of all projected operating revenues and expenses.

In these increasingly difficult financial circumstances that all public colleges and community colleges are now experiencing, it is more important than ever to supplement declining tax support with other revenues, to contain operating expenses, and to align the budget with the institutional mission, strategic plan, and priority goals. The budget should be aligned to the community college's mission statement, multiyear strategic plan, stated values, and priority goals. The main driver for all of this planning should be higher levels of student success, as measured by such factors as graduation and program completion rates, demonstrated skills, and job placements. Annual and multiyear budget planning should be done, reviewed, monitored, and revised as necessary, based on budget assumptions and projections of enrollment, student fees, state and local tax revenues, and auxiliary income. The budget development process is not an accounting tool. It should be used as a management tool to promote the mission and priority goals, and to create an improved financial model for the community college.

Common Operating Errors in Budget Development and Implementation

Some of the current community college budget development models do not have consistent, rational, or well-defined processes for developing their operating budgets. In this context, there are 14 common errors that have been made by community colleges. These errors must be avoided to develop and implement realistic operating budgets in order to support institutional mission and goals.

Planning

There may be little or no planning of projected revenues, expenses, or unit appropriations beyond the next single fiscal year budget. Longer-term enrollment projections and fee revenue must be projected, monitored, and revised every year, and budget allocations revised accordingly. Specific expense projections should be done for projected enrollment, new facilities, inflation, and proposed salary and fringe benefit increases. Planning should include improved purchasing processes such as bulk purchasing, obtaining bids for products and services, negotiated state-wide purchasing discount prices with venders for computers and other equipment, and energy-efficient systems.

Incremental Appropriations and Zero-Based Budgeting Models

In incremental models, staffing and funding resource allocation planning processes for the coming fiscal year start with the same base budget appropriation as the current year, and consider only marginal modifications with whatever total revenue increases or decreases are projected for only the coming fiscal year. This is often done with little or no regard to shifting enrollments, revenues, and costs among the various campuses or programs throughout the entire institution. On the other extreme is the zero-based budgeting concept that has been borrowed from the private sector. Our experience is that this model, which is further discussed in other chapters (chapters 6 and 9), is not well suited for community colleges, except in the limited application of cost and revenue projections for entirely new academic and support programs.

Inflation Impact

Does the college project the annual and the multiyear impact of general inflation, or for above average specific cost increases such as energy or health care employee benefits? This requires constant revenue increases, improved operational efficiencies, and priority adjustments.

New Facilities

Budget allocations do not adequately account for the immediate impact of new facilities expenses or new academic or support programs, and the lag time to achieve the later revenue that results from the enrollment increases in student fees, and the even later revenue increases that come from state support that these new facilities or academic programs may generate. Costs and revenues must be projected for new facilities, locations, or campuses. For example, a new academic building will require additional faculty, support staff, administration, furniture, equipment, utilities, and custodial and other facilities maintenance. How will this be funded?

Strategic Planning

Budgets tend to be appropriation driven, with no apparent alignment with the priority institutional goals, and with insufficient accountability for results. These priority goals should be stipulated in the institution's strategic plan, which should place an emphasis on student success as measured by retention and completion. They may include new academic or workforce programs, and new facilities or campus locations.

Stakeholder Needs

Budget development does not always adequately reflect the various roles and differing needs of the board, the administration, the faculty, the staff, the students, and the external constituents such as the community, local political leaders, and local business community.

Evaluation and Consequences

The budget planning process often has inadequate year-to-year evaluation of the cost–benefit analysis of academic and support programs for which there is a declining enrollment or need, and there is extreme reluctance to eliminate low-enrollment or cost-ineffective programs. The administration often has inadequate mechanisms for rewarding program or departmental effectiveness and efficiency, or for addressing program ineffectiveness and inefficiency.

Budget Monitoring

Budget data analysis and monitoring during the fiscal year is often inadequate, which does not allow the administration to identify fiscal problems and make in-year budget adjustments in a timely manner.

Communication

Budget planning details and rationale are not well communicated, nor well understood within or outside of the institution.

Instructional Costs

Though direct instruction is the largest expense, there is insufficient or even nonexistent planning and modeling of class size, faculty staffing formulas based on department and course enrollment projections, and faculty ratios for the numbers of class sections to be taught by full-time faculty, and class sections to be taught by less expensive adjunct faculty.

Special Fees

Specific "special fees" for student support services or for high-cost academic programs, and lab fees for specific courses, are often not adequately cost examined, projected, monitored, or allocated to the impacted departments to balance budget appropriations with expenses. They should be charged at real cost levels and monitored for accuracy each year. The process for charging and allocating special fees should be clearly written, well justified, and specifically audited.

Staffing Levels

There are often no staffing formulas, or peer institution staffing comparison data, for nonfaculty staff and administrative positions, complicating the decision and approval process for creating new positions in the budget, or for filling existing position vacancies when they occur, or for the next operating budget planning cycle.

Auxiliary Revenue

Operating budget revenues consist almost entirely of a combination of tuition and student fees, and state funding in all states, and local tax revenues in some states, with very little other revenue from either auxiliary enterprises such as bookstore, cafeteria, among others, private or publicly funded grants, donations from alumni, and other private donors.

Redundancy of Services

In large multicampus colleges or multicollege districts, there is duplication and overlap of operations and staff responsibilities that is cost-ineffective and even counterproductive. This duplication may also occur in smaller community colleges. Examples of this tendency for duplication include: information technology, research, promotions, media contact and public relations, academic program planning, data collection and reporting, fund-raising, business contacts, and workforce development. Miami Dade College centralized each of these functions at the district level many years ago, with very good results.

Successful Budget Planning: Who, When, What, and How

Who (Major Players)

The planning, development, monitoring, and adjusting (when appropriate) of the community college's operating budget is a team effort, requiring the involvement of many people. The CEO must initiate and lead this process, and establish the roles of others. Various guidelines have been delineated for the role and authority of the board of trustees, whether elected or appointed, by the regional accrediting associations, and by some state departments of education. See also chapter 3 by Valeau and Peterson on the role of the board, which is very important but must be limited. We maintain that the board should set policy; provide direction for long-term priorities; set goals for unencumbered fund balances; hire and evaluate the CEO; set the example for integrity, service, and transparency; lobby for the college with public officials and the private sector to increase revenues; and help with fund-raising and with business partnerships. The board and the CEO should have ongoing dialogue concerning long-range strategic planning, and the need for new facilities and new service locations, to serve community needs. These matters will impact budget planning and development. The board should provide input, and then should review and approve (not initiate or determine in detail) the annual operating budget. The board should never "manage" much less try to "micromanage" the budget. They should avoid directing or interfering with the work of staff.

The budget development process should start with a discussion between the chancellor and the board, based on established priorities, current institutional mission statement and goals, and the considerations of the long-range strategic plan of the institution. All of these things are dynamic concepts, the current versions of which should all be in written form, and communicated widely throughout the institution, and on the college's website. The mission and goals of a comprehensive community college, with a large and diverse service area, must be broad enough to encompass transfer education, workforce development, adult education, and remedial education. However, it must be remembered that the institutional scope and mission must have limits. It cannot aspire to be "all things to all people" and difficult priority choices must be made due to the very real budgetary restraints of limitations of available resources (people, financial revenues, physical facilities, human energy, equipment, and expertise). These realities must be reflected in the budget development process, and priorities have to be established as to what can be funded in any budget cycle. The successful budget development process at the Alamo Community College District (ACCD) in San Antonio, a five-college district now with over 60,000 fall term credit students and an annual operating budget now in excess of $270 million was made possible by recent chancellors, and by a board of trustees that understood and observed these concepts.

Each community college should have a CFO, reporting directly to the CEO, and as a member of the college's executive committee, which should also include the campus presidents and other high-level district administrators. The role of these and other major administrators are further described in the Derrico-Sutin (chapter 5). This group should meet regularly, with special meetings on budget development, under the direction of the CEO. The CFO should have the major responsibility for budget development, recommending staffing and resource allocation formulas, projecting revenues from student fees and state, local, and other sources, developing and presenting data comparisons for past years and for peer institutions, and leading the effort to identify and project expenditures for a list of nondiscretionary items (examples: utilities, mandated employee benefits, debt service) that must be funded before any discretionary budget allocations can be made.

While not always included in the traditional model, there is a trend for a role for the faculty to play in a shared governance decision-making model, which is now practiced by many community colleges. We strongly endorse this concept. Faculty unions or faculty senates should be involved in meetings and discussions, directly with the CEO and the CFO, and as members of or participants in executive committee discussions. Everyone throughout the organization should have the opportunity to receive information and to provide input. Student input concerning their priority needs and budget concerns are best channeled through student government organizations, recommending at the campus level, for consideration and response from the campus president.

External expert consultants should be used to provide input and analysis and peer institution comparisons into the budget development process. This is a very cost-effective way to get valuable expertise, a different set of experiences and viewpoints, and external advice by those with no internal biases to affect their observations and recommendations. These external consultants should include individuals from other community colleges, but also those from the world of business or public sector agencies that may have relevant perspectives to share. While a public community college has important differences from a private business, it can and should adapt suitable and sound business budgeting concepts including setting priorities, determining cost–benefit analysis of all operations and programs, projecting short- and long-term revenues and expenses, emphasizing positive results, rewarding effectiveness and efficiency, and holding budget managers and others accountable for performance.

A useful role for the public in general should be exercised through the process of open board meetings, with announced agendas, inviting comments, observations, and recommendations from the public to the board, which may be taken under advisement by the board and the CEO. The CEO should be a member of local chambers of commerce, and other appropriate community groups. The CEO should arrange meetings with local business, community, and political leaders to obtain their input, educate them as to what the college is doing and what it needs to better serve their community. This level of communication and cooperation can have a very positive impact on the budget.

Most community colleges will have an internal auditor, probably reporting directly to the board of trustees. This should be the only person, other than the CEO who reports directly to the board, for purposes of fiscal checks and balances, and due to the board's special responsibility for the institution's finances. Ideally, the internal auditor will also communicate directly with the CEO and with the CFO. He or she can be an additional pair of eyes for the CEO and the CFO to monitor financial data and the efficiency of internal procedures and processes, and for compliance with board policies. The internal auditor, in coordination with an external auditing firm contracted by the community college, will audit the budget after the fact each fiscal year. After consultation with the CEO and the CFO, the internal auditor should report his or her findings and recommendations to the board. However, the internal auditor should not play a direct role in the budget preparation process, unless in response to specific technical questions from the chancellor or the CFO.

In summary, the board of trustees, the CEO, the CFO, the campus presidents, the faculty organization, staff, and external expert consultants should be involved in the budget development process. The internal auditor reviews (audits) the budget after the fact, and reports his or her findings to the board.

As with any important endeavor in a large organization, budget planning and administration is indeed a team effort, requiring the skills, knowledge, talents, and hard work of many individuals. Such efforts best succeed if we care more about achieving a good result than we care about who gets the credit. There will be ample credit to share if all goes well. To sustain this success over time, the CEO and the CFO must distribute this credit widely and very publicly.

When

At a special board meeting, there should be a budget presentation by the CEO and the CFO. A report should be prepared to include data, comparisons, graphs, and charts. This budget report should be widely distributed to all board members and major college administrators, and to faculty and staff group leaders, in advance of this meeting. This budget report should include the proposed annual operating budget for the next fiscal year. For example, do a June board meeting presentation for the fiscal year that would start on September 1. This presentation, additional support data and peer institution comparisons, data comparisons to recent previous years, the college's mission statement, core values, and strategic plan documents, and a five-year model of annual budget projections should also be placed on the college's website for anyone to see. Working backward from this date of the June board meeting, a calendar should be developed for the annual budget planning process.

Assuming a September 1 start to your fiscal year (or adjust accordingly), you will need to start the initial data gathering during the preceding fall term. Start in October with a discussion at a board budget workshop to discuss any possible modifications or additions to board policy, priorities, mission statement, core values, and the long-range strategic plan. Draft an initial outline of the next year's revenues and unavoidable expense increases, such as utilities cost increases, health care cost increases, commitments already made, funding trends, and the like. Schedule the discussion, and input meetings first with administrators, and then with faculty and staff leaders. Have continuous presentations and discussions at the executive committee meetings. Hold open presentations, with questions and answers, for faculty and staff at each of your college campuses. Use the external consultants alluded to earlier. Update your five-year revenue and expense model in March, but revise this dynamic document (a one-page spreadsheet) as needed as new information becomes available on enrollment, and receipt of state and local funding.

The first draft prepared should be prepared of the next fiscal year operating budget for an executive committee presentation, and then for a board workshop. Finalize the budget for a board presentation and approval for the June board meeting. If necessary, as a result of the board's direction at the June board meeting, revise the budget for a special meeting of the board by late June or early July to get final board approval of the annual operating budget that will begin on September 1. Adjust these dates accordingly if your fiscal year is on a different calendar than my example of September 1 through August 31 each year.

What and How

A useful starting point to annual operating budget preparation is the development of a five-year budget model that is based on certain relevant assumptions, to project revenues and expense estimates each year. The assumptions should start with enrollment projections, followed by an annual assumption of cost inflation, tuition and fee increases, state funding support, local tax collections where applicable for tax base, rate, and yield, cost impact of new planned facilities or campuses, and other revenue sources such as auxiliary income, interest income, and contract for services rendered income from business or other clients. During the budget planning process each year, you should review the most recent five-year budget model, confirm or modify the actual data for the current year compared to the projected totals, and reconsider each one of the assumptions that were made, as specified in the preceding sentence above. Make whatever changes to the assumptions and to the data that are appropriate.

Convert the first-year projections to the actual numbers, or to updated projections prior to the final actual numbers being available, modify each of the next years' projections as may be required by new information, and project out the next year at the end of the five-year model. While there can be much backup data, the model can and should be printed and widely distributed on a one-page data spreadsheet with the criteria as the

Table 7.1 Alamo Community Colleges: District Operating Budget Projection

	2006–2007	2007–2008	2008–2009	2009–2010	2010–2011
Square footage	2,747,930	3,648,712	4,058,879	4,058,879	4,058,879
Enrollment[a]	51,672	54,252	61,934	63,112	64,.292
Operating budget[b]	220,121,423	238,896,933	275,483,884	284,928,284	295,927,817
Tuition & fees[c]	73,670,796	81,216,663	97,352,659	104,164,548	111,417,709
Continuing education	6,926,452	7,293,043	8,387,687	8,556,795	8,726,380
Tax revenue[d]	67,520,210	72,823,377	78,469,475	84,478,206	90,870,618
State funding[e]	65,368,636	72,814,547	73,962,054	86,040,941	86,040,941
Other[f]	10,232,501	11,049,960	13,553,412	13,965,875	14,383,665
Total projected revenue	223,718,595	245,197,590	271,725,287	297,206,365	311,439,313
Net revenue	3,597,172	6,300,657	(3,758,597)	12,278,081	15,511,496

a. Enrollment is for the fall term credit hour headcount and includes exempted/waived enrollment. Enrollment information provided by the office of Student Outcomes Assessment and Research as of 20 February 2007.

b. Operating budget will increase based on enrollment growth rate, annual inflation of 2.0 percent, and a surcharge of 20 percent of US$6.00 per square foot on new construction. Construction management and accounting costs for the CIP is included at a fixed annual amount of US$680,000.

c. Tuition and fees will increase with enrollment plus an anticipated annual Tuition & Fees increase of 5.0 percent in FY06/07 through FY10/11.

d. Tax revenue projections are based on an increase in net taxable value of 6.0 percent annually. No tax rate increases are projected. Tax revenue projections have been adjusted for the impact of Proposition 13.

e. State funding is projected on biennial increases in enrollment and an increase in the funding rate of 6.0 percent per biennial for each full-time student equivalent (FTSE).

f Other funding is projected to grow at 60.0 percent of the enrollment growth rate.

left column showing projections for enrollment, facilities capacity, total expenditures, and projected revenues from the various sources of tuition and student fees, state funding, local tax support, and other revenue. The next five columns of numbers from left to right would be the current fiscal year, followed by the next four fiscal years. The footnotes at the bottom of the page should be your assumptions, such as annual enrollment growth of X percent, an annual general cost percentage inflation factor, facilities growth of X square feet and associated costs, tuition and fee increases, state funding support projections, local tax collections, and other funding revenues. An actual example of this five-year budget development projection model is shown as Table 7.1, and is described below.

The 2007–2008 opening fiscal year operating budget for the ACCD was $245.2 million. An assumption of a 4 percent per year general cost inflation would add approximately $10 million dollars per year, each year, to a budget of that size. This inflation increase alone would add over $50 million of expenses to the fifth budget year ahead, just to pay for the same items at inflated prices and salaries in the operating budget. Inflation will require periodic increases in tuition and student fee schedules. Local tax revenue increases will be required to cover inflation expenses, and must come from either increases in the local tax base, or the tax rate, or both. When the tax base is expanding tax rate increases will probably not be necessary. When tax bases are static or decreasing, tax rate increases must be considered to increase revenues. Future year state funding is difficult to project. In all states, state funding as a proportion of the total community college operating budget has decreased dramatically over the past 20 years or more. In Texas, that percentage decreased over that period of time from approximately 60 percent to approximately 30 percent. This decline is similar for Florida and many other states. This has required community college administrators and boards to significantly increase tuition and student fees, and in Texas to shift much more of the funding burden to the local taxpayers, requiring greater revenues from property taxes. Community colleges in most of the larger states, including Texas, California, New York, and Illinois, receive significant local funding, but many, including in Florida, receive little or no local tax support. In the current economic recession, when both state and local tax revenues are in decline, it is especially important to create additional auxiliary revenue from sources such as grants, interest income, and food service and bookstore income.

Nondiscretionary Items

Nondiscretionary items should be listed in your current budget, which should be reviewed again, with estimated costs of what you regard as nondiscretionary items that must be funded in the budget. These items, and their estimated cost increases, include debt service on capital bonds and other debt items, utilities, board elections (where applicable), employee health care and other mandated fringe benefits, insurance premiums, vehicle replacement, computer and technology replacements, and other multiyear replacement programs, which should be in place and funded in annual operating budgets at a fixed dollar amount or percentage of inventory value each year. This list, with expenses, should be published and distributed, and subject to continuous review.

Historical Data

Leaders need to use college historical data on enrollment, revenues, and expenses, and charts and graphs of peer community college comparisons should include past year actual and coming year proposed category summaries of how much funding is allocated to the different functional categories that are required for state reporting. While varying somewhat from state to state, they are very similar, consisting in Texas of eight functional categories: direct instruction, academic support, student services, public service, institutional support, plant operations and maintenance, scholarships and exemptions, and auxiliary expenses. Direct instruction should be the largest expense category.

Staffing and Dollar Appropriation Formulas

Staffing and functionally targeted dollar appropriation formulas can be helpful guides in the budget development process. There are a wide variety of such allocation formulas that have been implemented by different colleges, and others suggested in the literature on community colleges. Miami Dade College had staffing formulas for offices based on general enrollment, and some specific to function, such as the number of financial aid awards for their various campus financial aid offices, or to the number of custodians per square footage of buildings. Miami Dade, a very large multicampus college, has an excellent formula for budgeting the number of faculty positions and the cost of faculty salaries. It is based on average class size targets for different courses, then a ratio of sections to be taught in-load, overload, and by part-time adjunct faculty. In-load faculty salaries are at the highest rate, faculty overload (set rate per class) is less expensive than in-load, and the adjunct faculty rate (set at two-third of the per-course overload rate) is the least expensive per class. Their departmental enrollment projections, in combination with class size goals, calculate the staffing formulas that tell them how many full-time faculty they need, and the dollar amount that they expect to spend on full-time faculty salaries and overloads and on adjunct faculty.

In multicampus colleges or districts you could have such staffing formulas. You might also use an allocation model to each campus that includes all of the tuition and student fee revenue and the state student contact hour funding. The college presidents, with input from each of their administration, faculty, and staff, could have much discretion in allocating these appropriations to their departments and to meet their internal priority needs and goals.

Unencumbered Fund Balance

Most states allow for an annual end-of-year unencumbered fund balance after the annual budget has been balanced. This fund balance is an excellent thing to have as a contingency fund to balance annual budgets in tough economic years, to support new programs, facilities, or campuses until they can become self-sufficient, and for special "one-time" expenses, such as purchasing land for future college growth. At ACCD, we had a board policy to maintain a minimum fund balance of 15 percent of the last year's operating budget, which for 2007 was a target fund balance of $36,000,000. We exceeded that target. That is a good place to be, and it also allows you to obtain substantial interest revenue for the operating budget each year.

CEO's Contingency Reserve Account

The CEO's contingency reserve account should be budgeted, which is not always specified in traditional budget models. From my experience, 1 percent of the operating budget should be so set aside in the CEO's contingency account of the operating budget. At ACCD this was US$2.5 million. We called this account the Chancellor's Reserve Account, which was to be allocated as the year progressed. No money should be spent directly from this account. Budget transfers should be done after the start of the fiscal year. They may be requested by the college or campus presidents or the district vice chancellors, and reviewed by the CFO. However, they should require the approval of the CEO, to meet emergencies, underfunded priorities, and other one-time needs. They are budget allocation transfers for the current year only, with the new annual appropriation starting again in the chancellor's contingency account at the start of the next fiscal year. Another method of funding this contingency account is to start the year with a smaller appropriation, and then to accrue monies from salary residuals from open (vacant) positions during the fiscal year. The CEO must have some method to access funds for such contingencies, to meet the unanticipated or underbudgeted needs of either the district offices or of the college or campus presidents. This contingency chancellor's reserve is in effect a reserve for the priority needs of the entire institution. To demonstrate transparency and accountability, a specific list should be maintained of all budget transfers funded from the chancellor's reserve account. This list (when, what, amount) should be revised and dated with each appropriation, with a running free balance, and made available to high-level administrators and others.

Salary Residuals

Salary residuals need a method for accumulating and distributing the unpaid salaries of positions that become temporarily or permanently vacant during the fiscal year. Each and every approved position in the budget should be assigned a unique position control number, and should be fully funded in the budget. Salary residuals are created as a result of vacant lines after termination salaries have been fully paid. These budgeted salary residuals can be left to accumulate for the year-end fund balance, or they may be budget-transferred for other purposes, either where they are, or preferably to a central salary residual account where they can be reprogrammed for other high-priority needs, or for new positions elsewhere that were not in the initial budget, but have now been approved.

Direct Instruction and Other Functional Categories

Direct instruction, consisting mainly of the salaries and overloads (for teaching additional courses beyond their base workload) of full-time faculty, and for the salaries of adjunct faculty, is generally about 50 percent of the entire operating budget expense of a community college. This has been consistently confirmed by various national studies, and by data comparisons of peer institutions in recent years, including for the ACCD and the other five largest community colleges in Texas in 2006. The ACCD spent another 10 percent or so on academic support, another 10 percent or so on student services, and most of the remaining 30 percent of the operating budget on the categories of institutional support and plant operation and maintenance.

It is therefore very important to have a staffing and budget plan for this expense, based on average class size targets for different courses. Cost ratios can be computed and budgeted for average faculty costs per class for faculty overload and adjunct faculty instruction. Develop faculty staffing formulas based on those class sizes and the departmental enrollment projections, and a ratio of the numbers of class sections to be taught by full-time faculty in-load, faculty overloads, and by part-time adjunct faculty. While some community colleges have had higher percentages of full-time faculty in the past, there is a clear trend toward more use of part-time adjunct faculty, who are less expensive to employ. Some colleges have gone below 50 percent for full-time faculty, but many faculty and administrators believe that lower levels would compromise the quality of instruction. My recommendation for the mix of teaching (by percentage of classes) that is cost-effective while maintaining quality instruction is as follows: Full-time faculty in-load, 50 percent; faculty overload, 10 percent; and part-time adjunct faculty, 40 percent.

Ratio of Compensation to Total Budget

Many community colleges target a ratio that is an appropriate guide for community colleges today. The total expenditures for all compensation costs for salaries and fringe benefits, including health care premiums, FICA (Federal Insurance Contributions Act), etc., should not be allowed to exceed 80 percent of your total operating expenses. This remaining 20 percent of budget appropriations is about the minimum required to purchase supplies and equipment, pay utilities bills, and all other noncompensation expenses. Before new staff can be approved, or salary increases can be provided, or fringe benefits increases can be funded, your annual and long-range budget planning models must take into account projected cost increases in all noncompensation expenses, and attempt to maintain this 20 percent noncompensation ratio. There is always pressure from faculty and staff for most or even for all of revenue increases to go for higher salaries or fringe benefits. There is always pressure from administrators for more staffing. These requests must be balanced against budget constraints and limited fiscal resources. Adhering to the 80 percent/20 percent ratio is a good guideline to follow in budget planning and preparation.

Lessons Learned Concerning the Budget Planning Process

The five-year budget model does allow us to plan and project revenues and expenses for the coming budget year and in outline for the next three years, while updating the data for the current fiscal year. While reviewing the current year budget, we do not simply add or subtract *incrementally* around the margins to prepare the next budget. We would revisit assumptions, projections, and priorities, and annually calculate staffing and allocation formulas based on new realities. We would account for *inflation,* and for the cost and impact of new facilities and programs. A "CEO's Contingency" account is created, funded, and monitored. A healthy unrestricted fund balance is maintained, as a matter of board policy. All of the key *stakeholders* are given a meaningful role to play. Information is gathered, compared with peers, discussed, and widely distributed. External expert *consultants* are used. A budget preparation *calendar* is developed and implemented. New programs are subject to *cost–benefit analysis* before they are approved and implemented. Academic or support programs of declining enrollment, or with significantly increasing costs, are similarly analyzed as part of each fiscal year's resource allocation process.

Class Size and Faculty Staffing Models

Class size and faculty staffing models should be continuously analyzed, refined as necessary, implemented, and monitored in an open and accountable process of enrollment management. As a reward mechanism, an academic department that exceeds their budgeted class size average is allowed to keep, to reallocate, and to spend the savings in adjunct faculty salaries for the lower number of courses required for their student enrollment, as they are allowed to keep and to spend the course student lab fees and other generated revenues. Budget-projected enrollments, revenues, and expenses are monitored throughout the year and are compared to the actual enrollment and revenue data to make the necessary plus or minus adjustments. If at the end of the fall term, enrollment and therefore student tuition and fee revenue is above projections on any campus, then they will be allocated that additional student fees revenue generated by that enrollment in order to offset the additional delivery expenses that are related to those same enrollment increases. Many people underestimate the large cost savings that can be realized by even moderate increases to average class size. When enrollment increases moderately, there is an opportunity to increase class size, thus increasing revenue while not increasing faculty cost. Conversely, when enrollment declines, it is very important to reduce the numbers of class sections, so that you do not have the same instructional expense with less offsetting revenue from student tuition and fees. If the target average class size is 20 students in each of 20 English classes, then a 10 percent enrollment decrease from projection should not result in 20 English classes of 18 students each. Two classes should be cancelled during registration and have 18 classes of 20 students each. At the ACCD, we had more than 15,000 individual credit course class sections each year. An increase in average class size of one student, from 20 to 21, was a 5 percent increase in faculty productivity, producing 750 fewer class sections (5 percent of 15,000), and a cost savings of more than $1,700,000 (750 sections at the average adjunct faculty rate of $2,300 per section). Academic deans and department chairpersons must add, cancel, or combine class sections to meet their assigned class size targets. This requires decisions as to which classes can be increased by one, two, or more students, and which classes cannot be increased for academic or facilities limitation reasons. These decisions are best made at the campus and academic department level by academic administrators.

Budget Committees

There should be academic committees who review and recommend budget-related decisions including class size, student lab fees, potential new academic and student support programs, and the possible elimination of low enrollment programs. However, budget preparation should be initiated each year by a budget preparation team, under the direction of the CEO and chaired by the CFO, including business office staff. This committee should do the data collection and analysis, past history, peer community college comparisons, revenue and expense projections, and staffing and allocation formula data runs to prepare the initial draft of the next annual operating budget. The enrollment projections are best provided by a district office of institutional research, with input from, but not directed by, the campus presidents and their staffs. The budget committee to review the work of this budget preparation team should be the executive committee of the community college, chaired by the CEO, and consisting of the campus presidents, district vice chancellors, and other high-level district administrators, and perhaps one representative of the faculty union or senate. For a board that has board subcommittees, one of those subcommittees could be the board committee on audit, budget, and finance. Reports can be made to, and workshops can be held with this subcommittee, and then with the entire board of trustees. This can be done prior to the final presentation to the board for their review and final approval of the annual operating budget, which must be done at an announced open meeting of the full board of trustees.

Funding Anticipated Future Enrollment Growth

There has been a decades-long trend of community college enrollment growth, which is expected to continue. How can community colleges project and plan for their budget growth to accommodate their enrollment growth over time? The general answer to that increasing annual expense problem is as follows.

Fund Enrollment Growth Expenses

Fund enrollment growth expenses with the corresponding enrollment growth revenue of the increase in student tuition and other fees that generates an immediate increase in total collections from the greater volume of student credits at the same per-credit rates, and the increase in state funding for the greater volume of student contact hours that comes later in the next state funding cycle. It must be remembered that community college boards mostly have control over student tuition and fee rates, control (with voter support) over local tax rates, but no control (hopefully some influence) over their state funding support.

Fund Inflation

Fund inflation (annual consumer price index [CPI] increases for goods, services, and salaries) from the inflation-created larger sales tax and local property tax revenues at the same tax rates, during those economic growth periods in the business cycle.

Partially Fund Annual Movement through Salary Schedules

Partially fund annual movement through salary schedules and periodic general salary increases with the differences between the higher salaries of retiring and otherwise terminating faculty and staff with the lower salaries of their entry-level replacements. All jobs should have a salary schedule with minimums and maximums for each pay level. Employees should be allowed to progress through their pay ranges toward the maximum, but not beyond, unless they are promoted into a higher pay level (or faculty academic rank) position, with a higher salary maximum. There are many such community college salary schedules available for review. Consider implementing a model that has a 50 percent spread for each pay level, except for faculty positions, for which there could be a 100 percent spread for the four commonly used academic rank pay "levels" of instructor, assistant professor, associate professor, and full professor. One full professor retirement at the top of that pay schedule, at say $80,000, who is replaced by an entry level instructor at say $40,000, will provide for a reasonable salary increase for each of the remaining faculty in that department. The same is generally true of staff turnover throughout the institution. The remaining part of your annual salary increases comes from the same inflation factors that in most years will provide additional state and local sales and property tax base growth, and tax revenue growth, without the need to increase tax rates.

Conclusion

The proposed approach for an effective budget and planning model will be of use to practitioners seeking to improve upon budget creation, while avoiding common errors of traditional models. The planning, developing, implementing, monitoring, and adjusting of the annual and longer-term operational budget is a critical piece of the success of any community college. Community colleges are vital to the success of the United States, and to the education of our people. They are in the forefront of the United States' commitment to the concept of quality education for the many, not just for the few.

It is now many years ago, in his seminal work *The Outline of History*, H. G. Wells wisely observed that: "History becomes more and more a race between education and catastrophe." It is the job of the community colleges, and of America's other educational institutions, to make certain that catastrophe does not win!

Reference

Wells, Herbert G. 1920. *The Outline of History.* New York: Doubleday and Company, Inc.

Chapter 8

Facilities Management Operations
Chris Moran

Introduction

The objectives of this chapter are to place facilities management in its context within the community college environment, sharing insights into effective operating practices and identifying ways to best manage and measure the performance of this function. Sound planning, budgeting, and management of facilities maintenance, including renovation and new construction, are essential to an improved financial model because facilities related costs are the second largest component of the operating budget of community colleges and the allocation of resources impact the entire college community. A dedicated senior administrator is normally charged with responsibilities for operational management of facilities, even if certain services are outsourced. These individuals need to demonstrate technical knowledge of the field, including basic maintenance and custodial operations, while anticipating barriers to progress and creating ways to succeed. This chapter reflects insights gained during 30 years of experience in senior leadership positions in facilities management at the Miami Dade College and Miami Dade County Public Schools in Florida.

Technical Knowledge of the Field

Maintenance encompasses a wide range of activities including preventative maintenance, repair, operation, and servicing equipment and buildings.

Maintenance departments also undertake landscaping, valet services such as hanging pictures and installing furniture, renovations, minor capital projects, and custodial services. These tasks may be funded through capital outlay funds, discretionary funds within an operating budget, or a charge-back system that allows purchase of services at predetermined cost bases allocated to departments. Thus, planning and budgeting of maintenance operations must be aligned with college priorities and agreed upon operating goals and responsibilities for this function. Overall, maintenance effectiveness is then evaluated through successfully meetings goals and responsibilities.

Organization

An organizational structure normally allows managers and supervisors the authority and accountability to ensure work is completed in a timely manner and within quality expectations. Single-function or multidisciplinary units are measured on completed operations and meeting predetermined performance expectations. Each unit or function should have quantitative measures, developed by administrators and staff, and reviewed several times a month to document among other things progress on work orders, aging of work, and funds expended.

Evaluation of Performance

The most important measure of performance is work completed in conformity with quality standards and predetermined goals. It is often difficult for administrators, whose role it is to deliver education, to evaluate skilled trade performances in an increasingly technical field. Two problems are most common. First, maintenance personnel often describe their budget and workforce needs using technical jargon unfamiliar to educational leaders. This is a by-product of the differences in training and career experiences. It is important to cut through the technical jargon by discussing with the maintenance staff how their needs connect to the overall college functions. The second problem involves bias that maintenance operations can be completed more economically. Some administrators gauge the cost of repairs or renovation with those of their personal residence. Well-managed operations are not easily measured and are rarely the same as home improvements. Understanding these differences is central in the evaluation process.

Work Orders

Maintenance activities are either conducted on a scheduled, preventative basis or as a response to emergencies, and documented in work orders.

This permits tracking progress of work completed and the cost expended in the current year. The managerial tools in these processes include backlog, aging reports, closed out work orders, open work orders, customer complaints, cost per square foot, and cost per work center. Using these basic measures, goals can be set by the facilities manager on a monthly, quarterly, or on an annual basis. Quarterly and annual goals, coupled with weekly monitoring, are an effective way for maintenance managers to help employees focus on productivity and priorities. Emergency work can be incorporated into the productivity evaluation using these measures. The primary goal should be to reduce the ratio and expense of emergency or breakdown maintenance to planned maintenance.

Problems sometimes occur when least expected. In such instances, tracking work orders becomes an indispensable tool. Sometimes new facilities managers discover that critical data and management reporting is hopelessly out of date or is lost in the system. I recall discovering one location containing backlogs of thousands of open work orders, some of which were five years old. Well-run operations complete work orders within 30 days or less, and maintain accurate data to document complete or pending work, all of which is subject to review by management. Clearly, work orders over 365 days should be examined to determine whether they should be incorporated into a capital project, cancelled, or reentered as a priority.

Performance Measurement and Management Information

Performance measurement is relatively new to facilities management and maintenance, and may be met with resistance. Performance management goals can be defined by workgroup discussions within the function and through alignment with a colleges' annual operating plan and budgeted priorities. College culture and expectations must be taken into consideration when defining these goals. While many departments have peak season activities, the maintenance budget to cover labor, parts, and materials are best projected at similar monthly levels. In doing so, it is important to understand that there are likely to be either positive or negative variances to a budget within the school year. The ultimate measure, therefore, is delivery of goals within budget, while meeting quality standards. It is prudent to include a contingent budget for unanticipated and emergency repairs.

Anticipating Barriers to Progress

Certain variables can hinder implementation of sound facilities management practices. They include (a) age of the buildings and equipment; (b) lack of understanding of the roles and responsibilities of a facilities manager; (c) lack of decision-making criteria regarding contracts for services rendered by outsiders and various forms of outsourcing; and (d) implementing green principles without understanding long-term cost/benefit to the institution.

Age of the Physical Environment

Budget and staffing affects the quality and reliability of the physical environment. Equipment and buildings have predictable service lives, yet budget constraints may cause utilization beyond those years. Old equipment, aging buildings, floors, and roofs are costly to maintain and often a source of frustration to faculty, staff, and students alike. A systematic approach to replacement of equipment that has outlived its useful life is apt to save money over time. This must be considered when planning and operating and capital budgets. Conversely, failure to address aging facility needs will result in work that is more expensive later on.

Clarity of Roles and Responsibilities

Barriers to productivity may stem from departments outside of facilities management who view their role as policing rather than providing services. As a consultant, I once interviewed an administrator in charge of procurement in a major community college. Through integration of services, a procurement unit did not respond well to emergencies nor have the special knowledge to determine which parts to acquire for campus repairs or when to do so. She stated that her primary goal was to avoid the scandal and problems that had occurred in the past as the result of "bad acts" of others.

Implications of Contract and Outsourcing Services

Contracts for services rendered by outsiders constitute a significant service of the maintenance department. Some colleges use a mix of in-house management and outsourced staff to maintain expenses. In-sourcing and outsourcing of these contracts have their own rules and regulations.

Service Contracts

There are many ways to contract for maintenance services. Term contracts provide services for a limited time or expenditure and are effective means of obtaining services without bidding each event separately. For construction and maintenance activities, the terms of the contract should provide the college with flexibility to set aside limits, dismiss those that are ineffective or that are disruptive to the college, and extend the contract in the case of an emergency.

Contracting requires application of art and science by management in order to be effective. Some states establish a limited pool of prequalified contractors who can bid for work or assigned contracts. Other states use "job order contracts contracting" where a price book is used as a catalog of common work and a contractor is selected based on low bid of a factor applied to the line items in the price book. A transparent policy procedure in which the highest quality is provided at the lowest price is imperative in either case. Except in egregious cases, prompt, regular payment builds a "partnership" between the community college and vendors and ensures a better performance. I frequently structured contracts allowing for two additional one-year periods, but staggered them so that the college was never left without at least two vendors. Contracts should contain language making them nonexclusive, with either defined or no minimum services. It should reserve the right for the college to assign similar work to in-house staff or other contractors. "Failure to perform" clauses may allow the college to terminate a contract prior to expiration in the event that services failure to improve despite warnings from management. If the college's staff are trained to implement the contracts effectively, they can minimize overtime. If additional supervision beyond the hours or capacity of college staff is needed, independent project management consultants can be assigned to review after hour's work and document performance. These contracts are most often used for discrete work that is often related to emergency or after-hour functions that internal staff are unable to conduct, such as hurricanes, blizzards, tornadoes, or the effect of the 2010 Gulf of Mexico oil spill.

Outsourcing

There is no magic bullet for effective outsourcing. Some colleges use a mix of in-house management and staff and outsourced staff. Outsourcing may involve work that is dangerous or involves high skills such as boiler/chiller, sprinkler systems, fire alarm repair, or elevator and escalator maintenance, or periodically needed, such as cleaning high exterior windows. In most cases, only the largest organizations can afford to perform these services with in-house staff. Work that requires frequent contact with faculty, staff, and students can be in-house. Decisions to outsource all of maintenance operations should be based on criteria that are not strictly financial.

Labor relations, local political considerations, the degree to which poor performance and inefficiency are entrenched in the organization, and the financial considerations play important roles in determining what choice to make.

There are certain benefits to outsourcing. Purchasing materials can become part of the contractor responsibility and very efficient procurement processes can be implemented. Costs are predictable. The scope of work and responsibility is easy to define, and can be tailored to meet the college needs within the contract. Moreover, a contractor's poorly performing staff can be discharged. Even when outsourcing, it is critical to retain expert internal management to monitor contractor performance including an external review of cost and quality of services provided.

Green Principles

The discussion of "green principles" is a very broad topic and includes energy, water, material, wildlife, and other resource conservation. Maintenance can take the lead in implementing "green principles" but custodial staff, administration, faculty, and students should play a role. Energy conservation is everyone's responsibility. Major cost savings can be realized by simply turning off unneeded systems. Expensive automated systems can have good paybacks, but turning the system off manually does not require any capital investment. In the original energy crisis of the late 1970s and again in current years, awareness campaigns resulted in major savings.

The energy consumption of lighting and computers is directly proportional to the number of hours of operation. When calculating the savings, it is important to add the benefit of reducing replacement and the environmental impacts of waste disposal. Some colleges have implemented a four-day work schedule, summer shut downs, and other means of energy savings. These can be very effective if the heating, ventilating, and air conditioning (HVAC) are turned off. Energy-efficient lighting and infrared motion sensing controls using its own funds will have a quick return on investment. Yet, systems other than lighting generate saving, but the calculation may not be as linear. Consideration should be given to climatic issues such as overheating of unair-conditioned spaces in the hot summers or freezing of pipes in cold winters in some areas. Additionally, if buildings are shut down it may impact the schedule of cleaning and renovation. A significant effect of hard shut downs of buildings can reduce staff costs because no straight-time, part-time, or overtime should be occurring in a closed building. Indeed, senior administrators need to understand and consider cost/benefit and qualitative standards when evaluating and budgeting the maintenance operation.

Many colleges have established aggressive recycling and energy conservation programs. However, little was known about the recycling of chemicals and materials in the motor pool, the very conservative limited use of chemicals for landscape and insect control, the attempts at wildlife and natural area restoration and conservation, water conservation, tree planting, and many other things maintenance did as a matter of routine until new laws and regulations went into effect governing their use on campuses.

While highly visible efforts such as planting trees should be considered, advisedly, institutions should plant trees that are compatible with the environment. Community colleges should design and implement landscaping plans with a long-term vision. For example, young trees will grow into the stately trees that reduce the urban heating effect, provide native cover and food for small mammals and birds, and beautify the campuses. Simultaneously, conservation efforts must take into consideration all mammals and birds, such as cats, pigeons, ducks, and squirrels that reproduce at a rate that causes health and sanitation issues for the institution as they can be aggressive in their pursuit of food. It is always best to enlist supporters of these animals for direction in creating feeding stations far from garbage and human interaction and to implement a trapping and neutering program where the animals are either adopted or re-released to the campus. It is important to point out those small mammals like rats, mice, and other animals that are undesirable, and plans to avoid infestations are implemented.

Key Elements for Success

Although the need for a qualified maintenance manager in a small college may seem different from a larger one, the basic skills needed to head up facilities management and maintenance are similar. The selection criteria may be subject to some variances and choices for senior leadership do vary somewhat, but effective managers share some common characteristics.

Technically Qualified

The larger the facility, the more important it is that the manager has a professional (business or engineering) background, very strong technical knowledge, and significant experience. Smaller organizations should supplement their in-house expertise with consultants.

Strong Communication and People Skills

The most important day-to-day function is effective communication with all stakeholders. The director of maintenance has to translate the operational needs of the educational and student services to the maintenance workers, while explaining the needs and priorities of the building systems and workers to senior management. Maximum effectiveness of the organization in meeting its educational goals requires nothing less. Finally, the manager must be able to convince others that the facilities and maintenance department is effective, well run, and deserving of the budget and support that it takes to operate effectively.

Nerves of Steel and Self-Confidence

Every day the head of a maintenance operation faces workforce challenges. Some workers, faculty, and administrators may overstate what they feel is an emergency. Sometimes calls for action are legitimate. It is critical to understand when and how to react to a perceived emergency. Care must be taken to avoid allowing maintenance workers to delegate their tasks and decisions to the manager. Emergencies may occur when individuals are aware of an issue for an extended period and fail to communicate to facilities management. Small and manageable problems have a way of expanding in the absence of calls for action.

Effective Multitask Management

Administrators responsible for maintenance need to be proficient in multitasking. Maintenance involves a variety of functions that are intertwined. Multiple stakeholders are part of the equation. Therefore, success depends on the ability to focus, prioritize, and implement decisions and move to the next item immediately.

Problem Resolution Oriented

Problem-solving maintenance is more exciting than preventative maintenance as it is more rewarding to fix the broken pipe than it is to change a belt even if it allows for uninterrupted service. Doing major capital projects is more fun than maintenance work. Installing new items and valet service is more fun than doing preventative maintenance. The key is to perform routine tasks well, yet have the ability to undertake work that is more complex.

Astute Contract Services Management

Success depends on an essential partnership between the community college and the resources (vendors and contractors) that provide its services. Such resources include people power, expertise, and abilities that the college needs to function. There is a need for maintenance administrators to be able to exert their power with contractors as well as with their colleagues. In cases of poor performance, the administrator should have the power to terminate services.

Pride of "Ownership"

In a community college setting, many people feel that they own the building. This is especially true of the maintenance departments. This may cause conflicting priorities. Facilities requiring time and focus by maintenance workers are often of little consequence to teachers and students, that is, until they fail! For example, if the air conditioning system or roof is working, those who use the building may prioritize certain tasks such as moving desks or accommodating the setup for special events as taking precedent over basic day-to-day operations.

Dedication to New Employee Training and Motivation

New employees require training, orientation, and integration into the workforce. Nonetheless, an understaffed operation has no resources to help with such orientation and can even reduce productivity by diverting worker's attention. My experience indicates that providing training, recognition, occasional rewards, and praise for work well done makes for a loyal workforce.

Skillful Use of Overtime

Overtime, if planned and utilized correctly, allows rapid augmentation of capacity in response to arising needs and needs to be planned for correct utilization. It can be authorized very quickly and does not require bidding or contracts. Even though overtime pay is 1.5 times base, it is not costly since base pay includes most overhead and benefit costs that are already absorbed. Maintenance ideally should be staffed so that major and disruptive operations (such as painting, stripping floors, installing new equipment) should take place after work hours. However, there is often an insufficient critical mass of employees to build a complete set of working crews on second and third shifts. There is also a need for sufficient number of daytime operations to run the college efficiently. Finally, it is less costly to authorize occasional overtime to meet peak or emergency requirements than to staff up to levels not required during most of the school year.

Contingency Plans for Emergency and Disaster Recovery

Unpredictable events occur, be they caused by weather, fire, floods, earthquakes, tornado, or acts of terrorism. The key is to create viable disaster recovery plan, accompanying communication plans, and train leadership and staff on action steps to follow. This often requires coordination with local authorities responsible for disaster recovery. In the Gulf Coast and Atlantic regions, hurricanes are expected. On the West Coast, the same is true about fires and earthquakes. Each event requires major resources to remove downed trees, waterproof buildings, clear debris, do safety inspections, and repair damaged buildings. In addition, documentation of expenditures and policy are required to make sure that all possible insurance and FEMA reimbursements are obtained. An office (usually risk management) in the college should be designated to maintain awareness of Foreign Exchange Management Act (FEMA) rules. Maintenance should work with the internal or external risk managers to understand these requirements. FEMA does not substitute for the institutions' own insurance. FEMA rarely or never fronts money to institutions. They perform an effective service, but this should be managed with extreme care if you wish to maximize your reimbursement.

For seasonal emergencies, an annual review several months before the season should start to make sure that contracts are in place, vendors are committed to clean-up and start-up of the college, there are stocked supplies, and a communication plan exists. This is the foundation for a culture of preparedness. In addition, a board-approved disaster recovery plan should be developed with input from the top down. It should be clearly stated who is in-charge, what authority they have, what the purchasing limits are, and who is to report to work. Rules regarding pay including overtime, compensatory time, and straight time should be outlined.

Dedication to Influencing and Controlling Entrenched Workforce Behaviors

It is common in community colleges that there are more personnel issues, grievances, disciplinary actions, and terminations in maintenance than in any other department. The workforce of facilities management and maintenance departments are often resistant to change. Some demonstrate passive resistance to change in the form of not reporting all information required, slowing down work, not answering radio calls, or ordering incorrect parts. More active resistance, by individuals or groups, are in the form of filing nuisance grievances, creating direct verbal, and sometimes physical confrontations. A clear set of rules and goals and a supportive chain of command are necessary to overcome the passive and active resistance in the long term. In the short term, breaking up cliques by using nondisciplinary transfers is a very powerful tool for exerting influence within the organization. The college human resource policies and procedures will provide managers with the authority to influence and prevent mundane or extreme behavior. Managers must be prepared to utilize progressive discipline, from oral and written warnings and discharge, if warranted. It is the administrator's job to apply procedures fairly, quickly, and efficiently. If the employees observe swift and consistent action, most issues can be averted. The key is to treat all within the college community with respect.

Conclusion

A well-managed facilities maintenance operation is critically important to the total effectiveness and cost-efficiency of the entire community college. A maintenance operation is not for faint hearted or mediocre administrators. It needs energy, focus, tact, a diverse technical knowledge, and exemplary leadership and financial skills. In my experience, it is much harder to find a good facilities management and maintenance administrator than it is for capital projects. The same person who handles direct communication with trades in the field must be capable of communication to the college president, planning for the long term, and reacting to emergencies as they arise. They must know personnel laws, technical information, and environmental laws; and they must protect the college from negative press. Sometimes they have to deal with multiple trades unions. A well-administered facilities unit saves the college money and plays an important role in assessing institutional effectiveness.

Chapter 9

Performance Metrics in a Results-Driven Environment: Use of Performance-Based Budgeting to Improve Accountability

Steven M. Kinsella, Edward J. Valeau,
and Rosalind Latiner Raby

Introduction

For the first time in history, there is an acute demand for higher education accountability spurred on by increased costs, student request for program relevancy, and accrediting agencies pressure from government to improve and monitor higher education. In the form of budget performance measures, it increasingly commands the attention of community college leaders. Recently, various performance metrics have been utilized as community colleges struggle with defining a transparent and accountable measurement of budget allocation that balances the various needs of each user group that relies on these resources to perform functions necessary for students to obtain quality education. This chapter will (a) define the limitations of traditional measurements, (b) describe new measurement metrics and their role in program development, (c) compare the two metrics, and (d) provide a model of how new metrics were applied in a two-college district in California.

The primary issue is how to allocate monies when tax or grant agency dollars are the source of the money and what type of oversight obligation is recognized during the allocation process. Many believe that taxpayers and granting agencies are entitled to see how their taxes are allocated and what administrators have accomplished with them. Hence, legislators, parents, students, and the public want to see concrete and understandable results from the money provided to community colleges. What those results are and how they are determined, measured, and assessed remains open for debate. Nonetheless, use of objective performance-based decisions can minimize external biases such as political pressures.

Complicating this process is that community colleges are service organizations that provide a wide range of comprehensive educational service organizations with no limit on the demand for those services. However, there is a limit on recourses available. Despite the need, there is no single budgetary theory that community colleges can use to make budgeting and resource allocation decisions. In 1940, Key called attention to the lack of budgetary theory that could assist in making important resource allocation decisions. Since budgeting is essentially a form of applied economics and requires the allocation of scarce resources among competing demands, Key urged that this question be explored from the point of view of economic theory. Lewis (1952) succinctly noted the question again in 1952 and suggested that budgeting "involves questions of value preferences, which must be based on philosophy rather than science or logic" (Lewis 1952, 44). The budgetary problems noted by Key in 1940 and Lewis in 1952 still face community college leaders today and likely future generations of administrators.

Contemporary administrators must develop appropriate ways to quantify results to provide meaningful answers to such things as student success rates, student learning outcomes, graduation rates, and for workforce training entities, and a student's ability to pass entrance exams of professions. Resulting measurement matrixes will then be used to demonstrate the prudent use of resources. The voices for reform are getting louder. The comparison of traditional measurement methodologies with newer methodologies will help to shift away from resource allocation decisions–based on political influence to an objective metric that demonstrates effective and measurable results to all stakeholders.

Defining Traditional Measurement Methodologies

The traditional measurement methodologies used by community colleges are based on a number of factors, but output is usually not one of them. A lack of objectivity has allowed easy manipulation by those with the most political influence. Two traditional resource allocation budget approaches are found to contain certain shortcomings.

Zero-Based Budgeting

Zero-based budgeting is the process of building a budget one line item at a time. Essentially, you start at zero and add items to the budget as each item is justified and those lacking support are deleted. In zero-based budgeting, there is no base budget for the starting point for the year's allocation of funds. Thus, comparisons based on longitudinal data across all sectors of the college environment are non-existent

Incremental Budgeting and Rollover

Incremental budgeting takes the previous fiscal year's budget and increases it by a specified percentage or dollar amount. Rollover budgeting uses the budget from a previous year and carries the same allocation forward into the new budget year. The disadvantage of using both these methods is that the actual expenditures from a prior year to the previous year's budget are difficult to compare. This practice is common despite the fact that comparing allocation to expenditures expended has little value since it only shows that funds are over allocated or under allocated. Once a budget is allocated, the department is free to move funds from the area where excess funds have been allocated to any other expense category. A main weakness is that the budget process does not reflect the realities of operational transactions that occur within cross-departments and since decisions of one department impact others, this will cause some departments to incur costs that they have no control over. This practice results in the use of resources for expenditures that may not be the highest and best use of resources from an organizational perspective. Over time, inconsistent practices and wasteful and inefficient spending occurs.

Contemporary Budget Approaches

Since traditional budgeting did not identify the costs that occur in multiple departments, a new construct emerged in the mid-1990s. The focus shifted from inputs to outputs that allowed an opening for new evaluation techniques to be used within the governmental sector called performance-based budgeting (PBB) (Melkers and Wiloughly 1998). Without a profit motive, governmental entities have few universal measures to judge their performance. Hence, the emphasis on maximizing outputs became a key means to evaluate performance. Taxpayers led the call for budget reform and demanded that budgets be determined by (a) citizen desires and needs, not government rules and regulations; (b) results, not efforts; and (c) better communication about progress toward goals and objectives (King 1995). As traditional models were unable to respond to these demands and the resulting emphasis on accountability and disclosure of results, PBB emerged as a key respondent and in recent years, and one of the PBB methodologies, activity-based costing (ABC), has received increasing attention.

Performance-Based Budgeting

A performance-based methodology sets an objective or series of objectives that show the public stakeholders that resources have been allocated to achieve the highest and best results for the students who enroll at the community college. It identifies a full range of activities that occur and the costs associated with these activities across the college. PBB is mostly restricted to connecting budget allocations to the institution's strategic plan, but it can be utilized for so much more.

The goals of each PBB system vary widely from college to college. Some goals may not require measurement of an outcome, but support strategic planning to assess the direction of the college. By linking strategic planning objectives to the budget process, resources are allocated to achieve stated objectives based on a fiscal year basis. Some objectives require several years of resource allocations while others do not. Planning efforts can be elaborate or simple. The objective of strategic planning is to identify what needs to occur in order to achieve the future vision. Integrating planning, resource allocation, and evaluation of outcomes resulting from planning efforts remains a difficult challenge for some community colleges to master. Standards applicable to the Western Association of Schools and Colleges (WASC) accreditation require colleges to demonstrate how resources are allocated to achieve strategic planning objectives and the simplest form of PBB is prominent.

Clearly, every unit within the college needs to identify appropriate performance measures. Some states have established laws that performance measures be "objective, quantifiable, and measurable." The language in such legislation encourages the use of PBB where a clear cause-and-effect relationship is visible between inputs and outputs. In the broadest sense, any resource allocation process that provides resources to achieve a specific result is performance-based budgeting. Demands for more public accountability and transparency has resulted in community colleges' use of more complex or at least more detailed approaches to establishing the amount of resources that are going to be allocated to a unit or department.

Administrators face numerous challenges when making decisions about resource allocations. The process is highly participatory and in some states like California legally mandated participation by the faculty is required. Such participation requires dialog and consensus on the use of funds and their intended results. From an accountant's standpoint, the process of allocating resources is an objective and mechanical process. For example, if classrooms are cleaned three times a day, the accountant in discussion with the lead custodian can quickly calculate the number of hours required. Adding travel time to and from each room multiplied by the number of hours used by the hourly cost of the employees to do the work is verifiable. Identifying projected cost for providing this level of service presents the problem since it is the point where the price appears considerably higher than anticipated and resistance to budgeting for the "desired" standard of cleanliness begins. If the classrooms are cleaned once a day, increasing the number of times the classrooms are cleaned will result in some additional cost. In all likelihood the cost will not increase threefold. On the other hand, there has to be recognition that unless something else is sacrificed, there will need to be additional resources added to the department to reach the higher standard of care. The administrator responsible for providing custodial services will tell you there has to be an increase in cost if the volume of work increases. This is when the conversation about supporting resource allocations begins to change character. It is this conflict between what the users want and what the users are willing to agree is the cost necessary to provide the stated level of service where performance metrics can be valuable.

PBB is very useful in controlling user expectations and in educating campus-wide user groups about how changes in performance standards impact resource decisions. Fewer surprises arise when these systems are used. With objective and verifiable data as found in the PBB model, users come to understand that any time there is a change in the performance standard or criteria, it is reasonable to expect a change in resources to achieve the revised standard. The challenge all administrators face lies in designing a resource allocation model that will provide useful performance metrics to assist in determining the amount allocated and methodology to measure its effective use. PBB is an important tool in maximizing the use of the limited resources available.

Activity-Based Costing

ABC can be used as part of the PBB methodology to map out all costs necessary to complete an activity. ABC is easily adapted to a wide range of situations and because it identifies cause-and-effect relationships, and helps to provide a context for students as they work their way through an educational objective. ABC is a management tool that is increasingly being used in governmental sectors along with total quality management, benchmarking, process engineering, and balanced scorecard (Kidwell et al. 2002). The goal is to be able to make a comparison at the end of the fiscal year with the budgeted performance results and to determine where model assumptions were inaccurate so changes are made for the following year.

Each institution will need to evaluate information useful for its own decision-making purposes. The accounting structure of the institution should record, summarize, and report financial results on a periodic basis. The ABC model does not alter the financial reporting model, but assists with managerial decision-making. Benefits from using ABC include streamlined processes, reduced costs, and competitively priced services (Goldsmith 1999; Kinsella 2002). For example, the city of Indianapolis used ABC to learn that vehicles and other pieces of equipment were purchased and charged to a department that had low utilization. Costs to maintain the equipment was wasted and increased prices charged for services (Meyer 1998). The model provided the city with a mechanism to isolate wasted costs and remove them. Despite examples of success, few community colleges have incorporated ABC into their budget methodology.

Granted, creating an ABC model for the first time is time-consuming because much of the required data to calculate costs and develop a realistic budget projection is not part of traditional budgeting methodologies. Moreover, objective data will not be readily available and may have to be extracted from other reports and assembled (Cokins 1999). The four objectives of this process are to (a) eliminate or minimize low-value-adding costs; (b) introduce efficiency and effectiveness and thus streamline the value-adding activities to improve the yield; (c) find the root cause of problems and correct them (remember, costs are a symptom); and (d) remove distortions caused by poor assumptions and bad cost allocations (Cokins 1996, 9). Hicks (1998, 28) states, "no matter how closely the activity-based distribution of costs to activities, products or services reflects actual cause and effect relationships, the final answers will be wrong if the process starts with inaccurate or irrelevant cost information." Indeed, the use of computers has increased ABC use and has greatly improved the ability of many organizations to benefit from ABC (Cooper and Slagmulder 2000a). However, once developed, the model is replicable. It can provide "aha" moments and a few outright shocks that could result in instant changes to processes or procedures.

Moreover, ABC is beneficial in the understanding and controlling indirect costs. It identifies the functions that generate or create costs by determining what really drives costs; it can attack and reduce, if necessary, the so-called fixed costs (O'Guin 1991). Also, it can determine how much to budget to ensure that adequate resources that are available to fully support an instructional function. Several studies concluded that ABC generated improved metrics upon which to base key management decisions and that these metrics proved especially valuable on issues of personnel allocation, space utilization, and deployment/allocation of support services staff (Geiger 1993/1994; LaPlante and Alter 1994; Evans and Bellamy 1995; Kaplan and Ridenor 1996; Richardson 2000). Cost avoidance and the ability to identify less costly means of producing the same product or delivering an equivalent service seems to be the common thread between these studies that examine both the governmental system and private sector applications of ABC.

Comparing Traditional to Contemporary Approaches

When resources are abundant, more traditional budgeting methods exist. However, in lean times, there is greater interest in PBB. Due in part to the economic crisis of 2009, and continued budget woes across the nation, there is widespread institutionalization of PBB. Below are four examples that highlight the weaknesses of traditional budgeting processes to support why PBB as a contemporary approach is gaining currency in community colleges.

The first weakness is that traditional budgeting lacks transdepartmental transactions. Specifically, traditional budget processes compare the same amount of resources each year to the prior year allocation. In good years, incremental increases allow all departments some additional funds. Yet, each department remains a silo with its own money to work with to accomplish goals. As such, this budget process does not reflect realities of operational transactions that occur across all departments within the institution. Transactions cross organizational silos and costs involved institutionally. PBB does a far better job of identifying the full range of activities and the costs associated with the activities regardless of the department that conducts the work. For example, the mathematics department has funding to purchase 24 computers to establish a computer laboratory. The department chair places an order, contacts the information systems department, and requests that the equipment be set up for the new semester. The director of information systems explains to the chairperson that the laboratory room has several problems. They include inadequate power, cooling, and ventilation to operate 24 computers, lighting that will cause a glare, and inadequate technical support due to a shortage of computer maintenance workers. In this scenario, a lack of transdepartmental transaction problems results in college-purchased computers that are not ready to be used in time for student learning.

Second, traditional cost accounting systems ignore the below-the-line expenses like sales, customer service, marketing, research and development, and administration. Yet, PBB assigns costs to services since it is more expensive to serve some customers than others. It is relevant to point out that community college vocational programs are generally more expensive and require different amounts of equipment and facility resources than liberal arts or general education programs. Recognizing the utilization differences of students enrolled in the various programs provides a foundation for isolating cost drivers and in determining an allocation methodology that recognizes the differences in student support demands.

Third, traditional cost management historically developed from our experience as an industrial nation that relied on labor hours, which rarely reflect the true cause-and-effect relationship that exists between indirect costs and individual products. When they are combined, confusion often arises. An average rate is calculated using a broadly defined activity measures in an attempt to redistribute costs to operating departments. Irrelevant factors, unrelated to actual usage data, can be used to allocate indirect costs. There is little consideration given to the fact that the functions of the academic departments are responsible for creating costs in the administrative service functions. However, a connection does exist and PBB highlights it. As an example, when a college receives $12 million for a new learning resource and high technology center, everyone is excited about all of the possibilities of what can occur with the new assets once construction is complete. Several years later, the building is complete and ready to open except no one budgeted for the additional faculty and staff to run it.

The final weakness related to traditional budgeting centers around politics and the participatory process involving numerous interest groups who bring their own interests, beliefs, and power into the allocation process. In the traditional construct, the emotional factors of each interest group collide and those with the most political influence maintain the surviving resource allocation decisions. Also in this construct, emotions, political power of departments, and sometimes empathy for students may overwhelmingly influence decision making. The result is a budget allocation compromise agreeable to internal users but may not sustain public criticism, as it may lack objective criteria. PBB seeks to minimize the political and emotional influence so that resource allocation decisions are developed to achieve a desired and quantifiable output. As an objective criteria, it is easily understood by external stakeholders who want validation for where, why, how, and which resources were allocated. For example, using student services, arguably, traditional budget allocation metrics often define support services in this area as overhead (nonvalue-adding processes). They are seen as luxuries that drains funds away from mission-critical activities. PBB instead identifies such services as critical to meeting operational objectives because they add value and make a significant contribution to overall output. Indeed, today, if support services such as libraries, computer infrastructure, language laboratories, computer laboratories, audiovisual/web technical support, and support systems are to comply with public agency reporting, purchasing-, contracting-, and finance-related activities, they must be factored into cost accounting.

In sum, administrators responsible for the final resource allocation are frequently unaware of how to identify useful criteria needed to determine appropriate levels of funding for the full spectrum of costs related to operating varied educational programs. As administrators get trained and more proficient at using PBB, it should expand to reach all segments of the community college. In addition, to shed further light on the use of the model, in this chapter and discussed below, we highlight its use in two community colleges located in California community colleges, the nation's largest system of community colleges.

The Performance-Based Budgeting Model

The PBB methodology was applied in a California two-college district. The West Valley-Mission Community College District has 17,000 full-time equivalent students (FTES) and an operating budget of $107 million for fiscal year 2010/2011. While unique to the district, the resulting workable model is replicable in any community college. PBB was used as a vehicle to provide sufficient data to illustrate the true costs of various programs that convince a political body to allocate resources appropriately.

The WASC standards for community and junior colleges require that colleges have a program for evaluating the effectiveness of the institution (Standard I, sub-section B). Program reviews, while designed separately for each college, largely adhere to these standards for accreditation. As a result, each college in the state has developed its own unique review process. Common to all program review processes is a focus on resource allocation and integrated planning.

The PBB model presented emphasize the service support structure and the five steps followed to help convert financial information to information that is useful for operating decisions. While other variations of the model can be used, this method was easily replicable in the West Valley-Mission Community College District given its organizational structure.

Define and Organize Activities

Since the district offers a broad range of services, selected activities were decompressed into activity groups. Each activity defined by its performed functions and processes, was grouped into categories (i.e., executive administration, instructional administration, student administration, student instruction, and student support and college operations). It helped to illustrate functional areas where the activities were performed. Fixed costs do not fluctuate with changes in volume measure or level of activity. Activity-driven costs are variable in nature. Such categorization showed that while each of the two colleges performed a number of functions to support the overall operation of the college, so too did the district central office. However, costs appeared in the individual college operations area and there were additional costs for similarly labeled cost objects for the district central office. The effect of centralization on the ABC model is that direct support services will need to be reported as college-level costs and not district-level costs.

Both colleges in the district use different processes to evaluate effectiveness of programs. West Valley College uses "Assessment and Planning for Instructional Programs and Services," which does not comment on the evaluation of the financial aspects of the program under review. In this action, nothing was done to determine the reasons why the program cost analysis was omitted from the program review process. Moreover, none of the reviews placed an emphasis on productivity or the resources consumed to generate FTES. This information does not appear to be of value in the review process. Mission College with a credit enrollment of approximately 9,000 uses a program review that refers to a need to consider the adequacy or inadequacy of support for staffing, facilities, offices, equipment, services, and supplies. This review process does not include an assessment of whether the resources allocated are in fact the best use of those funds.

Map Organizational Processes

This allows grouping of functions into primary activity areas. It identifies district central office costs and assigned appropriate costs to colleges.

These processes suggest the need to gather full-time equivalent student data by total operations processing system. In California community colleges, the designation of academic disciplines is called TOPS code. Costs are assigned to FTES using TOPS codes to determine cost per FTES. The total costs amounts are obtained from the California Community College District Fiscal Trend Analysis of the Unrestricted General Fund and Other Fiscal Data (CCSF-311), which is published in an *Annual Financial and Budget Report* each year. Direct cost per FTES is obtained by dividing total cost by total FTES.

Determine the Net Cost of Educational Course Offerings by Day

During the late 1990s and early 2000s, many students chose to work during the day and took classes in the evening and during the weekends. In an effort to reach an enrollment growth target, the Computer Applications Training Department offered Sunday classes in the main building. This caused the annual heating/cooling systems operations to increase by $44,000. The extra income did not show up in the budget accounts (which would have showed a loss) but instead became part of the facilities director's budget. Applying the techniques of ABC showed that only three courses on the Sunday schedule generated sufficient revenue to pay for the costs generated by instruction. Relocating the classes to a smaller building would have boosted new revenue to $39,434. After 2002, the enrollment situation changed and the college exceeded its state-funding levels for FTES, thus eliminating the need for the class and its revenue. In fact, it ended up costing the college money due to increases in utilities, police services, and custodial services.

Determining the Cost of Support Services

The student support service costs (counseling, admissions and records, instructional technology, library services) can be calculated using either the number of students served or the cost per FTES. Use of the number of students served provides a more accurate expenditure because the better indicator of volume is the number of individual students that receive services. FTES is a good volume indicator for determining the cost of academic services since the cost of instruction and the revenue received from instruction is expressed in terms of FTES. Support service costs are more accurately expressed in terms of the number of students receiving services. Using the FTES numbers by discipline, one can calculate the proportionate costs of student support services incurred to serve students in any academic discipline. For example, the English program generated 1,220 FTES. The costs to support students who took English on an FTES basis was $69,698 for admissions and records, $271,718 for counseling services, and $118,791 for library services. These costs use an FTES base to distribute the cost to the program. When completing a program review, the cost for support services may be added to the analysis in order to provide an understanding of how academic program activities influence costs incurred by other departments.

Determining the Cost of Providing Programs of Instruction

Community colleges balance the academic program mix to provide both vocational, which is more expensive, and academic transfer programs. To calculate the cost, first the requirements that students have to satisfy in order to complete a course of study must be identified followed by the cost elements of the class, student activities, and infrastructure-sustaining activities. The final cost driver includes all direct costs and all intermediate costs, such as counseling and student activity costs.

Utilize ABC data to Make Informed Decisions

Using information about the organizations' expenditure patterns helped to identify the variability of cost data for use in PBB applications. When selected components are chosen for decision analysis, it illustrates how to break down the accounting information and activity information into elements that can be arranged as needed to help the decision making process. Each decision will require use of different pieces of information. Because PBB is useful in determining all costs associated with the different operating activities of any organization, the model can be easily adapted to provide information for different types of decisions.

Arguably from the discussion above, a PBB model maximizes services by providing information about the true costs of all the various educational programs offered by the college. With this information, one can take steps to evaluate whether changes in operations of a college should be pursued in a way that may change the cost structure of the college. For example, cost per FTES as listed by TOPS code could be used in the program review process to compare program costs across the district. Student support costs can also be used.

Conclusion

Students arrive at our colleges with different educational goals and skills to achieve them. If colleges are to help them achieve their dreams and aspirations then they must become expert stewards at budgeting and planning since resources are becoming increasingly scarce, and public demand for effective use and accountability rising locally and nationally. Thus, college administrators must develop an arsenal of tools. This chapter maintains that PBB is an allocation methodology to assist administrators in designing, planning, and operationalizing how the college allocates its resources. It reveals the different costs that result from each major category of student served by the college. It is useful to colleges in expressing the true cost of educating each type of student. It can be used to help colleges develop strategic plans and determine the appropriate mix of programs to be offered. The needs of decision makers will ultimately determine the level of detail that is used to assist in developing the output-based performance metrics of an institution. Readers are encouraged to modify and adjust these techniques to meet the needs of the institution. There are some broader concerns that potential users of these types of systems should be aware of.

In public higher education, resistance to change is a common organizational characteristic. During periods of recession, resources provided to colleges start to decline. The resulting external pressure may be the catalyst to initiate implementation of creative processes, such as the PBB model. Many of the reasons for failure are manageable because of the widespread belief within the organization that a change is inevitable. Given current economic conditions, the time to introduce PBB, and possibly ABC may be right. Administrators regularly confront issues related to balancing the need to provide for instruction vs. support services. There are no easy solutions and institutions have to recognize and respect the constraints and regulations that may affect resource allocation decisions.

Solutions to operating in an environment of constraints are best identified when it is acknowledged that there are constraints and that there are interdependencies that exist between direct services and support system requirements. Improvements can be achieved in both areas by evaluating operating activities, recognizing and properly planning for support services as well as direct instructional activities, and concentrating on maximizing productivity in all areas. Developing performance metrics created from information learned using a performance-based budgeting approach, like ABC, can be a valuable tool in developing an objective standard from which performance is measurable. These methods are useful for highlighting the full impact of decisions on the cost structure of an institution.

There is a way to prevent such problems. PBB identifies processes performed as services they deliver. Each step in the process has a cost associated with it where money can be allocated to achieve the desired outcome with all of the costs appropriately accounted for. Additionally, the use of PBB methods may be used by community colleges to budget to achieve an outcome unlike traditional approaches that concentrated on getting more and more resources into the organizational unit with little concern for measuring outcomes achieved with the resources.

PBB is very different from rollover and incremental budgeting because budgets are created to achieve a specific outcome. It shifts the focus away from the input method where all emphasis is on the amount of money put into operating the organization and instead concentrates on what outputs or results can be achieved. We highly recommend that every institution of higher education go through a budget development process using the principles and procedures described in this chapter at least once every five years. It is amazing what you will learn about the cost structure of an institution when this approach is used.

References

Cokins, Gary. 1999. "Learning to Love ABC." *Journal of Accountancy* 188 (2): 37–49.

Cokins, Gary. 1996. *Activity Based Cost Management: Making it Work*. New York: McGraw Hill.

Cooper, Robin, and Regine Slagmulder. 2000a. "ABCM System Architecture-Part III." *Strategic Finance* 81(8): 63–72.

Cooper, Robin, and Regine Slagmulder. 2000b. "Activity Based Budgeting-Part 2." *Strategic Finance* 82(4): 26–36.

Evans, Patricia, and Sheila Bellamy. 1995. "Performance Evaluation in the Australian Public Sector: The Role of Management and Cost Accounting Control Systems." *International Journal of Public Sector Management* 8(6): 30–38.

Geiger, Donald R. 1993/1994. "An Experiment in Federal Cost Accounting and Performance Measurement." *Government Accountants Journal* 42(4): 39–52.

Goldsmith, Stephen. 1999. The Twenty-First Century City: Resurrecting urban America. Lanham, MD: Rowman & Littlefield Publishers, Inc.

Hicks, Douglas T. 1998. *Activity Based Costing: Making It Work for Small and Mid-Sized Companies*. Somerset, NJ: John Wiley and Sons.

Kaplan, Robert S. and Matt Ridenour. 1996. Indianapolis: Activity-Based Costing of City Services (A), HBS, 9–196–115. Rev. March 22, 1996.

Key, V.O. Jr.. 1940. "The Lack of a Budgetary Theory." *American Political Science Review* 34 (6): 1137–44.

Kidwell, Linda A., Shih-Jen Kathy Ho, John Blake, Philip Wraith, Raafat Roubi, and William Richardson. 2002. "New Management Techniques: An International Comparison." *The CPA Journal* 72 (2): 64–69.

King, Laura M.. 1995. "Operating and Capital Budget Reform in Minnesota: Managing public finances like the future matters." Government Finance Review 11 (1): 5–16.

Kinsella, Steven. 2002. "Activity-Based Costing: Does It Warrant Inclusion in a Guide to the Project Management Body of Knowledge (PMBOK Guide)?" *Project Management Journal* 33 (2): 49–56.

LaPlante, Alice, and Allen E. Alter. 1994. "U.S. Department of Defense: Activity Based Costing." *Computerworld* 28 (44): 84–92.

Lewis, Verne. 1952. "Toward a Theory of Budgeting." *Public Administration Review* 12 (4): 43–45.

Melkers, Julia E., and Katherine G. Willoughby. 1998. "The State of the States: Performance-Based Budgeting Requirements in 47 Out of 50." *Public Administration Review* 58 (1): 66–78.

Meyer, Harvey. 1998. "Indianapolis Speeds Away." *Journal of Business Strategy* 19 (3): 41–46.

O'Guin, Michael C. 1991. *The Complete Guide to Activity Based Costing.* Englewood Cliffs, NJ: Prentice Hall.

Richardson, Helen L. 2000. "The New Shape of ABC." *Transportation and Distribution* 41(5): 111–116.

Chapter 10

Reducing Reliance on Public Funding: The Place Where Creativity and Practicality Converge

Stewart E. Sutin

Introductory Remarks

This chapter comments on the economic and sociopolitical context that necessitates strategic and tactical responses by community colleges and leadership choices that can make a difference. Community colleges supply essential educational, workforce development, and community services to their regions. As such, public sector funding for operating and capital expenditures of a community college is warranted. Yet, the financial resources of the state and the local government are constrained. Funding for community college is increasingly unpredictable and insufficient to meet growing demands for their services. Systemic changes supportive of an improved financial model offer a way to sustain educational quality and maintain affordability and access for students. Although many community colleges already give practical application to certain suggestions made in this chapter, continuous and comprehensive improvement is now imperative. Byron McClenney, one of our nations' most successful community college leaders, observed in an interview with *The Chronicle of Higher Education* that economic recessions and funding crisis call for community colleges to decide which programs and services are higher priority, and, implicitly, to make choices accordingly (Bushong 2009).

Economic Realities

Government and households alike have been affected by our recent economic recession, which began as a financial crisis exacerbated by unsustainable levels of debt. Debt burdens underscore two troubling realities.
First, meaningful restoration of government appropriations for community colleges is unlikely in the near term. Second, students normally served
by community colleges cannot afford tuition and increased fees above the
level of inflation. As reported by the Center on Budget and Policy Priorities
on July 15, 2010, 48 states recorded accumulative budget deficits of $192
billion for 29 percent of their total state budgets. Accumulative federal
budget deficits are projected to reach $13.8 trillion in 2010, or about 94.3
percent of US gross domestic product (GDP) (US Office of Management
and Budget 2010, 134–135). Cities and state accumulate budget deficits
are high and will become more acute as underfunded pension liabilities
become payable. As reported by the Cato Institute in July 2006, total
state and municipal debt in 2005 accumulated $1.85 trillion. Consumer
debt equals 120 percent of disposable income at a national level, and the
bottom 40 percent of wage earners, a population largely served by community college, accounts for 0.2 percent of the nation's wealth (Federal
Reserve Board 2009). Double-digit unemployment exists in many states,
not to mention low-wage earners who are underemployed. Students are ill
positioned to rely upon loans to finance their educations. National data
collected by College Board (2007, 10), documents that tuition and fees
from two-year public institutions more than doubled in inflation-adjusted
dollars between 1977–1978 and 2007–2008 ($1,040 to $2,361). While it
is true that four-year public and private institutions increased tuition and
fees at comparable rates, community colleges largely serve students who
are from low- to middle-income families and are more severely affected by
tuition hikes.

Sociopolitical Realities

Notwithstanding declining appropriations for community college operating funds, public officials and other external stakeholders demand
accountability and an affordable education from community colleges.
Simultaneously, many underlying costs to service students are rising. According to data from the American Association of Community
Colleges, 60 percent of students attending community colleges are taking one or more remedial courses. Support for developmental or remedial

education constitutes a growing portion of operating budgets. In addition, community colleges educate an increasing percentage of nonnative English-speaking students. This adds to service costs. More students today rely upon distance education and instructional software, which adds still further expense. Many students requiring additional support are at-risk minority students from low-income minority families. It may well be that community colleges today face their most serious challenges since their inception. Conversely, community colleges are in the public consciousness more than ever. Effective, substantive, and timely responses to educational and affordability challenges are apt to be recognized and valued. The stakes associated with institutional performance have risen as emergent challenges pose risk and reward opportunities in tandem.

Many community colleges are already frugal, financially responsible, innovative, agile, and effective. What is the problem? Economic realities have changed. Performance expectations have risen. Public funding for community college is apt to get worse before it gets better. Consequently, the standards by which to evaluate effective institutional performance are changing and prevailing financial models need to adjust accordingly. Public constituents demand data as evidence of performance and are less disposed to be sympathetic toward advocacy in the absence of evidence of improved cost containment measures and efforts to increase revenues from nontraditional sources. They require proof statements of accomplishments from community colleges. Report cards with evidence of actions taken, and their consequences, enhance the credibility of community colleges leaders. The Delta Cost Project (2009, 6), observed that "every institution should be able to tell students, boards, and legislatures basic facts about where the money comes from, where it goes, and what it buys."

Financial Literacy

Community colleges are well-advised to make known their financial challenges and their potential consequences of failure to respond effectively. Leaders must communicate financial realities to their boards, faculty, administrators, and staff in ways that broaden institutional financial literacy. Full disclosure of financial information builds a case for reform. Internal and external stakeholders alike expect transparency. Data sources should include recent operating and capital budgets, audited annual financial statements, the adverse consequences of declines in revenues from public sources, and nondiscretionary expense increases. Special attention should be afforded to major expense categories such as cost of instruction, student support services, repair and maintenance of facilities, administration, health care, legal, technology, travel, energy, and office supplies. Revenue and expense trend lines and forecasts should be disclosed as well. Widespread support for institutional systemic reform and a new financial model is more likely when supported by the weight of evidence. Financial literacy among constituents is fundamental in this process.

A Culture of Financial Self-Reliance

An institutional culture may be viewed as the sum of prevailing individual behaviors, values, and beliefs by all employees and leaders who work there. In order to sustain change, institutions must adopt values and beliefs consistent with their priorities and strategic direction. If we agree that government appropriations for community colleges will be problematic for years to come, then increasing financial self-reliance is indispensable. Public funding for community colleges can be a mixed blessing. While essential to sustaining affordable tuition, excessive dependence on government financial support may dull competitive instincts and inhibit the application of sound practices in the enterprise. Application of financial analysis tools, creative thinking, collaborative planning, entrepreneurial behavior, and effective processes will reduce the impact of diminished funding from public sources.

Revenue-Generation Mindset

One consequential way of responding to shortfalls in government appropriations for community colleges is to adopt businesslike approaches to development of revenues from nontraditional sources. A pragmatic and entrepreneurial "mindset" must supplant thinking that it is somehow illegal or immoral for public institutions to engage in "for-profit" businesses. Tax and legal questions are best dealt with through consultation with outside legal and tax counsel. The ethics of launching "for-profit" activities need only consider the affordability of tuition as a reality check.

Noncredit ancillary enterprises such as workforce development and community education offer extraordinary opportunities where one can be imaginative, and responsive to the communities' educational needs. In noncredit education, restraints of shared governance or organized labor do not apply. Data-based decisions can be made and business plans can be put in place by asking the right questions such as: What have other community colleges done to generate meaningful revenues from nontraditional sources? What businesses or services have proven to be highly successful?

If certain services already generate profit for the community college, has a business plan been adopted for aggressive growth? If so, what are the revenue growth targets over the next five years? Is current staffing up to the challenge? If not, what plan is in place to recruit experienced and creative bottom-line-driven leaders? How will success be quantitatively defined? What additional revenue-generating services can be credibly and profitably offered by the community college?

Community colleges are known and respected by local residents, and thus can create or expand nontraditional educational enterprises to leverage brand or name recognition and local market awareness to deliver educational services. Corporate workforce training programs and community education should be developed as income-generating businesses rather than nonprofit services. The creation of new enterprises or aggressive growth of existing ones offers revenue-generating potential as exemplified by Central Piedmont Community College in Charlotte, North Carolina, and SAIT Polytechnic in Calgary, Canada. Both are very entrepreneurial. George C. Dehne, president of GOA Integrated Services, observed during the annual meeting of the National Association of Independent Colleges and Universities, "the first thing we recommend…is to seize the day." He proceeded to note that a severe economic recession creates duress along with opportunities for reforms and changes that might not otherwise be attainable (Hoover and Supiano 2009, 1).

Revenue Generation: Identify and Exploit Opportunities

Good ideas have arisen within higher education over the years as means of self-generating financial resources. The best examples demonstrate how improving financial self-reliance can be in harmony with a quality education. Some initiatives have come from community colleges, while others originated elsewhere in higher education. Opportunities for improved revenue generation abound. A look into a fascinating historical example of educational entrepreneurship in higher education reveals the extent to which necessity can facilitate invention.

Booker T. Washington launched Tuskegee Institute (now University) on July 4, 1881. A review of Washington's autobiography, *Up From Slavery* (1901), is germane. By 1884, Tuskegee had launched night school, and created its own brickworks as a supply source for constructing their buildings. Excess bricks were sold in the region. Tuskegee had enrolled 1,400 students, owned 2,300 acres of property, and manufactured 1,200,000 bricks by 1901. Most of its 67 buildings were designed and built by staff and students. Work skills and work/study programs were the focal points of the Tuskegee system. Booker T. Washington was an extraordinarily able fundraiser and entrepreneur. Under his direction, Tuskegee created revenue streams and contained costs that enabled low-income students to attend. Tuskegee graduates developed life and work skills that served them well after graduation. In certain ways, Tuskegee was the prototype of our modern community college.

Student retention and optimization of classroom capacity offer revenue generation and cost-containment opportunities. In Anglin's case study, we note how significant financial resources are gained through improving retention. Another example is the use of classroom facilities that are underutilized during afternoon, early morning, Friday evenings, Saturdays, and Sundays. Enrollment of students more likely to study full time or to study during off-peak hours may be a source of significant additive revenues from tuition. Adjunct faculty can teach these courses at comparatively little additional cost to the college. Another example is a new pilot program at Ivy Tech in Fort Wayne, Indiana, in health care support that will allow students to graduate in one year if they attend community college five days per week from 8:00 a.m. to 5:00 p.m. (Fuller 2010). While this initiative is funded with a grant from Lumina to provide tuition-free education, the model itself is worthy of consideration by community colleges with underutilized instructional capacity. Fast track, full-time, or off-peak hour study models benefit the college by using vacant classroom space and help students either move into the workforce more quickly or transfer to four-year colleges. Community colleges would also be more likely to improve graduation and persistence rates. If classroom space is already fully utilized, one can pursue low-cost lease opportunities by partnering with local school districts willing to rent classrooms during late afternoons, evenings, and weekends, or by offering full academic programs online. The U.S. Bureau of Labor Statistics projects material increases in baby boomers who will continue to work after the age of 65, often by training to enter new careers (Hoover 2009). Some may be interested in enrolling as students, while others can be trained to serve as adjunct faculty.

Community education is a core activity for most community colleges. Skills-based programs, adult learning, and leisure or recreational programs alike are often found within this function. Revenue generation from community education is not new to community colleges. What if community education were more aggressively developed as a revenue-producing enterprise, and generated income on a larger scale? What if this activity were treated as a business unit of the enterprise? What if new programs and courses were created to meet resident needs? What if fee schedules for all courses were revised to deliver acceptable profit margins, perhaps allowing for tuition scholarships for some on a financial needs basis? Community colleges can design and operate tutorial and supplemental instructional services in direct competition with for-profit organizations that serve primary and secondary school-age students. Reading, writing, math, and science workshops should attract primary, middle school, high school, and college students. Educational workshops are likely to improve their academic performance in college, while revenues generated in excess of expenses can be deployed to mitigate tuition increases. In summation, consequential revenue growth is attainable through any number of thoughtful initiatives that may include workforce training, improved retention, more complete use of classrooms, and community education.

Cost-Containment: No Pain No Gain

A cost-containment mindset is of paramount importance. Elimination, reduction, or containment of cost increases requires certain behaviors to include imagination, problem-solving skills, and a will to make difficult evidence-based decisions. Since the highest percent of any institutions' operating budget is human resource compensation and benefits, this suggests that changes can be painful. Many community colleges are collegial and familial. Therefore, changes of organizational structure, process reengineering, downsizing, and discharging unmotivated personnel can be uncomfortable. One needs to reflect upon institutional priorities. Does fidelity to students and a community college mission to sustain affordability and access trump pain associated with systemic reform? In the ultimate sense, progressive personnel management is a behavioral issue.

Cost-containment initiatives should be comprehensive. Adoptions of short-term emergency measures along with those that may take longer to implement are of equal importance. Asking the right questions will help stimulate productive discourse, analysis, and solution creation. Are administrative and "back shop" staffing levels appropriate relative to the size and overall staffing of the institution? Are operations and services efficient and effective? Can services be delivered at lower costs? Do certain approval processes require too many administrators, or can processes be both soundly controlled yet expedited by empowering middle management to make certain decisions? Are certain administrative and staffing positions redundant and compressible in multicampus and multicollege districts? Will peer group information sharing on staffing help identify cost saving opportunities? Simpler, less labor intensive, more technologically driven processes have ways of improving service quality while reducing costs. All other line item expenses should be studied with like rigor in an effort to control overhead. Done correctly, cost containment will support rather than erode an institutions' educational mission by controlling discretionary expenses and aligning limited financial and other resources with academic and student services priorities.

Short-Term Actions

Economic crises can create fertile ground for community colleges to think out of the box. For instance, highly qualified early retiree professionals from outside of education may need to supplement retirement income and remain professionally engaged. They offer a supply of highly experienced part-time labor to supplement permanent staff, often at a fraction of the costs, in career tracks that include accounting, human resource, procurement, marketing, public information, law, electricians, carpenters, plumbers and facilities management, not to mention adjunct faculty. Another opportunity may come from unleased commercial or retail space and may offer cost-effective alternatives to new construction. School districts share the same funding challenges, and may welcome the opportunity to lease classroom space during afternoons, evenings, and weekends to supplement revenues and may be productive educational partners. Many institutions find ways of saving money through collaborating in procurement in health care, energy, stationery, and supplies. A problem with cost containment and reduction approaches such as freezes on hiring, salary increases, and travel is that they are not sustainable. During good times, the resistance to creative and cost effective actions may prove insurmountable. But in our current environment, crisis can be the harbinger of opportunity.

Comprehensive Intervention

Attention to operating costs should be the first priority of leadership action. Revenue generation from ancillary enterprises, while extremely important, may require years to yield material results. However, institutions do "own" their operating expenses. An inclusive and collaborative approach may prove beneficial. One tactic is to convene a project task force to generate recommendations, in which case the credibility of participants is of paramount importance. Immediate actions and longer-term initiatives should all be studied. Sustainable reductions in costs and improvement of educational and service quality for students are worthy enduring goals for this team. College organizational structure, services, and processes are all open to inquiry. All line-item expenses such as travel and entertainment, marketing, institutional dues, and memberships should be subject to examination. Perhaps student governments should review student activity fees and consider opportunities to contract. The argument that costs covered by student activity fees do not represent a cost to the college does not hold up under closer inspection. Students who struggle to meet tuition payments may welcome fee reductions. Those who commute to community college by public transportation subsidize others who park free of charge, since repair and maintenance of college parking facilities are within college budgets.

Energy Costs

Energy costs are worthy of special attention, given their price volatility and generally upward trend. Some companies have hired energy consultants and made a conscious decision to buy a certain percent of their energy through long-term futures contracts during times when prices are down, leaving a lesser percent open to purchases on the spot market in the event that prices fall still further. Community colleges can do the same. For example, some college have conducted energy audits and made changes that are cost effective. Three- or five-year break-even analysis to recommended upgrades can help guide this study. Florida Gulf Coast Community College is reportedly 100 percent self-sufficient in energy through its installed solar energy facility, while Butte Community College in northern California is 30 percent photovoltaic solar-generated energy (Carlson 2009).

Open Bidding

Open bidding practices, outsourcing, and procurement collaboration may offer cost-savings opportunities. For example, Utica College, collaborated as partners with St. Luke's Healthcare in building a cogeneration plant. It now provides 70 percent of the college's energy needs at a cost savings of $200,000 per annum (Carlson 2008) to the Community College of Allegheny County, with active support from its local American Federation of Teacher's bargaining unit, was admitted to the health care consortium headed up by the Allegheny Intermediate Unit. Health care benefits and the percent employee contributions to the plan did not change, but the college saved money since it no longer pays for 100 percent of plan administration. The financial metrics of the agreement between Johns Hopkins, which provides library services to Excelsior College (a distance learning college), results in $1 million in revenue to Johns Hopkins annually, while Excelsior saves the cost of operating its own library (Moran 2008).

Interest Expenses

Interest expenses may offer fertile ground for cost savings, especially during periods of historically low interest rates. During these cycles, banks can help community colleges to consolidate and refinance from higher to fixed lower rate debt obligations. Community colleges with an investment grade credit rating may find opportunities worth exploring. Community colleges may elect to hire consultants to help identify opportunities to reduce interest expenses, or speak directly with their bankers to assess cost-effective ways to refinance their debt obligations.

Transformative Strategies

Transformative tactics should be given careful attention. Expense containment or growth of nontraditional revenues may motivate some, while being viewed as a threat by others. Prior discussion with the board and its ongoing support is essential. Staff reduction or reorganization may induce workplace insecurity. Employees resistant to change are not beyond passive/aggressive behavior to discredit leadership. Collaborative, transparent, and honest communications are essential. In the final analysis, those unable or unwilling to perform in a transforming environment are better off seeking employment elsewhere, or they should be encouraged to do so by their leaders.

Leadership by Example

Leadership by example sends a message throughout any institution. Executive compensation and spending behaviors will be under close scrutiny by board members, internal and external stakeholders alike—not to mention the media. Executive travel, entertainment, and club memberships offer opportunities to reduce expenses. Uses of college and educational foundation funds are subject to audit, legal, and compliance review. In short, executive behavior and spending patterns are subject to public disclosure and scrutiny. All spending habits of top leaders must be legal, ethical, in the best interests of the college, and be above reproach. Aligning expenses with an operating budget, being consistent with the educational mission of the college, and being within board-approved policies and practices remain important. Yet, how these choices are vetted by the media is equally critical. Fairly or unfairly, optics are a reality, and change resisters to institutional reform may leave few stones unturned in efforts to undermine reform-minded leadership.

Emergence of Nontraditional Competition

For-profit trade schools, colleges, and universities have grown rapidly during the past 30 years, and often compete head on with community colleges for student enrollment. By studying what makes these colleges successful from a financial and enrollment standpoint, one may learn which, if any, institutional behaviors are appropriate and adaptable by community colleges. For example, their processes to create new curriculum and programs reportedly consume a fraction of the time required of other segments of higher education. Rather than offering individual courses via distance education, for-profits offer entire programs. I suspect that a closer study of for-profits would reveal standardization of programs, curriculum, and syllabi throughout the institution. Faculty is neither tenured nor unionized. Significant attention is purportedly given to job placement. Some competitive advantages are neither transferable nor necessarily desirable, such as high advertising and sales expenses. This commentary does not purport to assess the educational quality of for-profit colleges and universities, much less make a case for wholesale shift to the for-profit business model. Indeed, increasing public attention has been afforded concern to relatively higher delinquency rates on loans to students enrolled in certain for-profits. Some offer a higher quality of education than others. I have not seen data on graduation rates, but it would also not be surprising to learn of different results here too—as with other segments of higher education. Nevertheless, having served as vice-chairman of the board of trustees and chair of the finance committee of one for-profit organization, I can testify to the quality of education and the profitability of that institution and its attention to containing cost.

Rene Champagne, former chief executive officer (CEO) of ITT Educational Services, reportedly informed colleagues in the for-profit segment of higher education, "if this is not our moment, I'm not sure when it will be" (Blumenstyk 2008). Displaced workers, coupled with capped enrollment in some community colleges, represents an exceptional growth opportunity to for-profit colleges. For-profits compete for students who might otherwise attend community colleges, some of whom have had difficulty sustaining student access due to lower state funding combined with direct or indirect controls over student tuition rates, and offer federal financial aid to students. What do we know about the size of the revenue/profit pie they own? A closer look at the financial statements of some publicly

Table 10.1   Key Statistics and Enrollment of Five For-Profit Colleges

	Fiscal Year	Total Revenue (US$ billions)	Net Income Continuing Operations (US$ millions)	Enrollment 2009	Enrollment 2008	Percent Increase (%)
Apollo Group Inc.	31 August 2009	3.97	598.3	420,700	345,300	22
Education Management Corp.	30 June 2010	2.51	121.3	112,700	91,600	23
Career Education Corp.	31 December 2009	1.84	145.4	93,100	83,300	12
DeVry Inc.	30 June 2010	1.92	279.9	90,365	74,765	21
Corinthian Colleges Inc.	30 June 2010	1.76	146.0	86,088	69,211	24

Sources: Author's tabulation based on data from Hendry (2009) and Yahoo!Finance.com (2010).

traded for-profits is revealing, using data sourced from Yahoofinance.com. For-profits appear to manage effectively the cost side of their enterprises. In all likelihood, they utilize basic financial analysis tools such as product costing, cost-benefit analysis, return on investment, marginal or incremental cost analysis, cost allocation, and break-even analysis. One cannot attribute their achievements solely to oversized marketing and aggressive sales budgets on the front end and reliance on adjunct faculty at the back end. It is what for-profits do in between that community colleges would do well to study. Data on for-profit enrollment growth and profitability reflects significant enrollment growth and income from operations as illustrated in Table 10.1.

Strategic Responses

Strategic plans are characterized by an institution's collaborative discourse and affirmation of priorities undertaken to realize one's mission and enduring goals. Resource-constrained institutions do not have the luxury of wide margins of error and need to make prudential staffing, facilities, financial, technological, structural, educational, personnel, and student services decisions in a strategic context as opposed to ad hoc or day-to-day actions. A comprehensive multiyear strategic plan, accompanied by financial plans, is a basic component of an improved financial model.

Strategically led community colleges are more likely to succeed if leaders adopt a nonhierarchical and collaborative approach to idea generation and constituency building. John Kotter (1996), a leading authority on organizational change and a member of the faculty of the Harvard Graduate School of Business Administration, advocates creating a "guiding coalition," one comprised of highly credible, thoughtful, team players and respected change agents to facilitate the process of change. The guiding coalition must embrace creation of an improved financial model as integral to systemic change. During times of crisis, one should not underestimate the willingness of faculty, students, staff, and administrators to generate valuable ideas and share in their sense of ownership. This approach is more likely to assure collective buy-in when seeking support for mission and goals later on.

Comprehensive strategic plans offer a foundation upon which community colleges determine their priorities. Sources of data that allow one to codify demographic, industrial, and workforce trends within community colleges' geographic footprint include census reports, and studies done by Workforce Investment Boards (WIB) and chambers of commerce. Hiring decisions should be supportive of aligning resources with priorities throughout a college, rather than simply filling vacated positions. Programs with minimal student enrollment in low occupational demand categories are candidates for closing or restructuring. Such action may be painful or subject to labor union contractual stipulations. Facility master plans must be aligned with the institutions' strategic plan and regional growth projections, changing demographics, business growth trends, and the shift toward distance education. Costly new construction should be considered as a last rather than a first resort. Science faculty may prefer virtual rather than real laboratories. Math and English faculty may wish to take advantage of learning software and function more as mentors than lecturers. If health care providers clamor for expansion of high-cost programs to provide more registered nurses or graduates of allied health fields, then it is appropriate to ask for financial, faculty, and/or technological support. The point is that strategic plans offer an evidence-based platform for decision-making, and an improvement over case-by-case "fixes" in safeguarding the educational and financial interests of the college.

Systemic Change

In a way, systemic reform is an end product of a well-executed strategic plan. A systematic approach to selecting choices upon which to act is preferable to intuition or reliance upon anecdotal information. One may think of four quadrants of financial reform, namely short-term revenue and cost savings and longer-term revenue generation and cost savings. Once data supports placement of options within each quadrant, then leaders can assess the trade-offs and resources saved or required by each initiative.

Issues of cost control and quality improvement may be addressed through applying certain proven methodologies—one of which is Six Sigma. William Deming provided much of the intellectual capital for institutional applications. Motorola and General Electric reportedly benefitted to a considerable degree by its rigorous use. In essence, Six Sigma is an evidence-based process applied to controlling quality and containing costs. Problems are defined, measured, analyzed, and processes improved and controlled. In certain ways, the Learning College and Achieving the Dream, which are well understood by community colleges, represent like combinations of evidenced-based planning, actions, data tracking, and creative solutions. These processes are productive, proven, and already understood by many community colleges. Why not apply like processes toward building an improved financial model? Systemic change of a community college financial model is best done within the framework of institutional strategy and not as a special project. While there is no shortage of sound and proven processes to drive change, leaders, middle management, and boards of trustees play key roles in assuring that plans are not only well-designed but acted upon. This alone assures the sustainability of an improved financial model.

Cost from a Student's Perspective: An Area of Opportunity?

The ultimate charge of the community college is to support its students through delivering an affordable education, and any opportunity to achieve that end is worthy of exploration. Affordability goes beyond tuition and fees, and includes textbooks, transportation, childcare, school supplies, and income lost while attending classes. Community colleges who design solutions for such expenses contribute to affordability. Amazon is currently funding an e-textbook experiment in collaboration with seven universities, while Flat World Knowledge Inc. is also collaborating with colleges for the purpose of delivering on-line texts at lower costs (Young 2009). Both models offer the potential to deliver textbooks to students at a lower cost per book than was available before. What if affordable childcare could be arranged, especially at nights and on weekends, perhaps by creating student cooperatives in which parents/students take turns in working at childcare centers on campus? What if a transit plan were mapped out with local public transportation companies, or through creating ride-sharing programs, to help students commute in ways more affordable than one-to-a-car driving? Some examples from other sectors of higher education are worthy of study. For example, Northeastern University in Boston operates a highly successful work-study program. They help students locate jobs with the same employer for six-month periods and students return to their studies for the remaining six months per year. This program affords students an opportunity to develop important workplace skills and behaviors while earning income that is applied to their educational expenses.

Where Do We Go from Here?

The revenue generation and cost-containment ideas presented are indicative of opportunities available to community college leaders seeking to alter their financial models. The idea generation, feasibility study, decision making, planning, and implementation process is complex and will take time to enact. This is precisely why three- to five-year timelines are needed to evidence material and sustainable change. But make no mistake, revamping community college culture and ways of doing business are fundamental to affordability of tuition in an era of crippling government budget deficits. Decisive actions on short-term cost savings initiatives are important as a way of indicating the serious intent of leadership. Those who successfully complete this journey are apt to undergo cultural change in which a more agile, creative, effective, and sustainable institution wedded to a more durable financial model is in place. Times have changed and so too must institutions. Stephen T. Goldbert, executive vice-president for finance and administration at Cornell University, championed change by stating: "In the current financial times... it is going to require a great deal of creative thinking and alternative ways of doing business in order to protect the cores of our institutions" (Shieh 2008, 1).

Conclusion

Community college leadership has long received high marks for creativity, student-centric planning, and community consciousness. If those tools can be applied in a more comprehensive and consistent way toward improving the financial model of community colleges, then we may approach the future with confidence. An improved financial model requires systemic reform, improved operating efficiencies, and a student-centric institutional culture supportive of continuous improvement. The passion to deliver high quality and affordable education is already present. By undertaking vigorous, sustainable, comprehensive, and documentable revenue generation and cost containment reforms, community colleges will manifest a more resilient financial model capable of supporting high quality, affordable and accessible education that might not otherwise have been achievable. To win the day, successful community colleges will need to shed the mindset of top heavy financial dependency upon government appropriations and tuition-based revenues, and manifest a culture of financial and educational self-reliance.

References

Blumenstyk, Goldie. 2008. "Economic Downturn is a Boon for For-Profit Colleges." Chronicle of Higher Education 55 (17): A13.

Bushong, Steven. 2009. "Community College Enrollments are up, but Institutions Struggle to Pay for Them." *Chronicle of Higher Education* 55 (20): A24.

Carlson, Scott. 2008. "Land-Rich Colleges Explore Opportunities to Create Alternative-Energy Solutions." *Chronicle of Higher Education* 54 (46): A10.

Carlson, Scott. 2009. "Big Costs, Little Cash, For Energy Efficiency." *Chronicle of Higher Education* 55 (2): A1-A16.

Center on Budget and Policy Priorities. 2010. *Recession Continues to Batter State Budgets: State Responses Could Slow Recovery.* Washington, DC: Center on Budget and Policy Priorities.

College Board. 2007. Trends in College Pricing. Homepage. Washington, DC: College Board. Available online at: http://www.collegeboard.com.

Delta Cost Project. 2009. Trends in College Spending. Homepage. Washington, DC: Lumina Foundation. Available online at: http://www.deltacostproject. org.

Federal Reserve Board. 2009. "Survey Reports 2007." In *New York Times Almanac 2009*, ed. John W. Wright. New York: Penguin Books.

Fuller, Andrea. 2010. "One Year Associate Degree: Will It Improve Graduation Rates and Lower Costs?" Chronicle of Higher Education, 56 (33): A16.

Hendry, Erica. 2009. "For-Profit Colleges See Large Increases in Enrollment and Revenue." *Chronicle of Higher Education,* August 25. Available online at: http://chronicle.com/article/For-Profit-Colleges-See-Large/48173/.

Hoover, Eric. 2009. "Community Colleges Anticipate Boom in Baby-Boomer Students." *Chronicle of Higher Education*, February 6. Available online at: http://chronicle.com/article/Community-Colleges-Anticipate/5184/

Hoover, Eric, and Beckie Supiano. 2009. "Marketing Consultants Offer Advice on Making the Most of the Recession." *Chronicle of Higher Education*, February 4. Available online at: http://chronicle.com/article/Marketing-Consultants -Offer/1499/

Kotter, John P. 1996. *Leading Change*. Boston, MA: Harvard Business School Press.

Moran, Cailtan. 2008. "Library for Hire: Johns Hopkins U. Sells Services to an Online College." *Chronicle of Higher Education*, December 10. Available online at: http://chronicle.com/article/Library-For-Hire-Johns/114862/.

Shieh, David. 2008. "Colleges Must Be Smarter About Money, Panel Says" *Chronicle of Higher Education*, 55 (16): A13

U.S. Office of Management and Budget. 2010. Federal Budget, Section 7. Washington, DC: US Office of Management and Budget. Available online at: http://www.budget.gov.

Washington, Booker T. 1901. *Up From Slavery: An Autobiography*. New York: Doubleday.

Yahoo!Finance.com. 2010. Key Statistics. SunnyVale, CA: Yahoo!Finance. Available online at: http://www.Yahoofinance.com.

Young, Jeffrey. 2009. "This Could be the Year of E-Textbooks." *Chronicle of Higher Education* 56 (3): A1.

Case Study 1

Maintaining an Agreement: The One-Third Funding Philosophy in Illinois and New York

Christopher M. Mullin and Robert A. Frost

Introduction

The economic state of affairs facing states of the twenty-first century posed substantial threat to the future availability of public funds for postsecondary education. The *American Recovery and Reinvestment Act* (Public Law 111-5 2009) provided temporary relief to state budgets through the State Fiscal Stabilization Fund to ensure that appropriate funding continues for education and government services.

The act of the federal government providing operating revenue extended the federal role in funding education beyond its traditional, grants-centered approach. This action touched on a question inherent in the financing of postsecondary education: to what degree is the state (or any other entity) fiscally responsible for funding education? The answer to this question remains unclear. The purpose of this case study is to understand how this question has been answered in two states that have clearly articulated defined roles for funding public community colleges. Accordingly, the events and arguments that led two states—Illinois and New York—to develop the same philosophy for funding public community college systems were examined to better understand the viability of philosophies that require maintenance of effort from responsible parties and the extent to whether the founding philosophies have been maintained.

A Philosophy of Funding

The funding philosophy in a state has both a practical and a policy dimension. In practical terms, it contributes to stability in the planning of institutional operations. If institutions know that a certain percentage of their budgets will come from reliable sources, they can work within the budgetary limits during long-term planning—an aspect critical to supporting student success and the efficient and effective operation of an institution. From a policy perspective, a funding philosophy espouses the degree to which the individual and society are expected to shoulder the fiscal burden on educational opportunity.

As it relates to community colleges, revenue sources vary greatly by state. In approximately 25 states they receive at least 10 percent of their revenue from local sources, whereas the other 25 states, community colleges do not receive local funding (Palmer & Franklin 2007). For those community colleges that have three public revenue streams—the student, the state, and the local government—there is not always a clear delineation between the various sponsors as to what proportional share they are responsible to provide at a maximum or minimum. However, in a few of these states there is a belief relative to funding community colleges that each partner in the postsecondary education process should carry an equal burden. In these states, there exists a "one-third" philosophy.

While the "one-third" ideal was discussed in seminal works on community college finance (Carnegie Commission on Higher Education 1973; Garms 1977; Breneman and Nelson 1981), it came into existence prior to these monographs. To date, funding philosophies have received little attention while the mechanisms for the allocation of funds (Medsker 1956; Wattenbarger and Starnes 1976; Mullin and Honeyman 2007), annual trends (Honeyman, Williamson, and Wattenbarger 1991; Palmer and Franklin 2007), and surveys relative to community college finance (Katsinas and Tollefson 2009) have continued.

The states selected for this study offer key historical, political, and taxation similarities. Illinois and New York also have similar demographic characteristics, state higher education contexts in terms of private institution influence in policy, and incorporate an explicit one-third philosophy.[1] In order to develop the contemporary case for each state, the study examined the events leading up to the formation of a "one-third" philosophy and the historical trends of revenue sources after the funding arrangement.

Illinois

The nation's first community college was established in Joliet, Illinois, in 1901. Over the next 49 years, public and private junior/community colleges were established throughout Illinois with little, and occasionally contradictory, state guidance (Hardin 1975; Krebs, Katsinas, and Johnson 1999).

Legal and Fiscal Evolution

In 1951, Governor Adlai Stevenson signed House Bill 472, which placed public community colleges under the purview of the state's common public school system (Hardin 1975). There was not, however, state funding for these institutions until 1955 when a flat grant of $100 per student was granted by the state. The inclusion of state-aid raised questions as to whether public junior colleges could charge tuition as the School Code in Illinois set forth that common schools should be free for those between the ages of 6 and 20 (Hardin 1975).

After much debate between the maintenance of a free junior college system and one that charged tuition, the matter was decided by the 71st General Assembly of 1959. House Bill 192 allowed the district board to "require each junior college student to pay a portion of the cost of his tuition not to exceed 33 one-third percent of the per capita cost of maintaining such college" (Hardin 1975, 177). The 71st General Assembly also passed a new formula to replace the flat grant per student to one which provided $7.60 for each semester hour completed by a student in a junior college (Hardin 1975). As such, it had become the case that, for the first time, funding for community colleges in Illinois was to come from state, local, and student sources, albeit specific "shares" had yet to be delineated.

A Master Plan

In 1961, the Illinois Board of Higher Education was formed and charged with the task to develop a master plan for postsecondary education in Illinois (Erickson 1969). Ten committees were created and charged with addressing a number of topics, with Committee F delegated the responsibility of studying the junior college and providing recommendations for their expansion and development. Committee F identified five issues facing the development and maintenance of a community college system in Illinois:

1. Establishing improved relationships between junior colleges and four-year colleges and universities
2. Organization and fiscal support of junior college education
3. Coordinating and supporting the study of the needs of junior colleges
4. Distributing junior colleges geographically
5. Organizing a state system of junior colleges (State of Illinois Board of Higher Education 1963, 16–23).

To address these issues, the committee developed and considered three plans: Plan A, development of a state-supported and state-controlled system of junior colleges under the jurisdiction of a state agency; Plan B, development and expansion of the present junior colleges by enlargement of regions served and by coordination of their operations; and Plan C, establishment of a system of two-year branch campuses of existing state universities to serve the junior college area and level of education (State of Illinois Board of Higher Education 1963, 24–26).

In its report, Committee F recommended Plan A be adopted, with full state support and oversight of the community college in Illinois. One member, Robert O. Birkhimer, who was the Community College Liaison for the office of the Superintendent of Public Instruction, suggested Plan B would provide a better option in a ten-word "minority report" (State of Illinois Board of Higher Education 1963, 30). The matter pertaining to tuition and responsibility for funding the community college had not yet been set as the 74th General Assembly met to consider the Master Plan recommendations and the dialogues following its release (State of Illinois Board of Higher Education 1964).

In the end, the *Junior College Act of 1965* (Public Act 1965) relied on the minority opinion of Birkhimer in adopting the principles of Plan B, in effect continuing the policies and practices of local governmental control while removing the junior college from the system of common (K-12) schools. The act put a ceiling on how much revenue could come from tuition—colleges could charge up to one-third of the cost of instruction—and on state revenue at 50 percent of operating expenses.

Defining Revenue Shares

Local revenues in Illinois originated from three sources: local taxes, charge-backs, and a corporate personal property replacement tax. Local taxes were determined utilizing the equalized assessed valuation for a community college district and an operating tax rate. Charge-back revenues originated from the practice of charging in-state students from outside the community college district a rate that included the local effort contributed in the institution attended. For example, if Quantel resided in the Black Hawk Community College District (near the quad-cities) and wanted to pursue a curriculum track not offered by Black Hawk, he could attend a community college that offered the program such as Sauk Valley Community College. Black Hawk would then have to pay Sauk Valley the difference in cost to Quantel between tuition and fees for in-district students and the rate charged out-of-district students (Public Act 1992). The corporate personal property replacement tax revenues originated from taxes on corporations, utilities, and partnerships (Illinois State Constitution Article IX 1973).

Public community colleges in Illinois were supported by the state via grants distributed by the Illinois Community College Board and from other state sources for Adult Education, Vocational Education, and the State Board of Education. Illinois employed a tiered funding formula to distribute the grants, with considerations of program costs and degree/certification type (Mullin and Honeyman 2007; Illinois Community College Board 2007). Other state revenue came in the form of categorical grants for veterans, small colleges, and workforce preparation to list a few (Illinois Board of Higher Education 2009).

Revenue from students came in the form of tuition and fees. By statute, tuition was not to exceed one-third of per capita costs at the institution utilizing accounting practices approved by the state board (Public Act 1992).

Historical Balance of Revenue Trends

The historical record of the percentage share of operating revenue for public community colleges is depicted in figure CS1.1. An examination of the data indicated that the three revenue sources have had differentiated contributions over a 41 year period.

Only recently has the student share approach the 33.3 percent limit imposed by statute. The upward trend was most noticeable between the years from 2000 to 2007. The local governments have consistently supported their community colleges at levels in excess of the 33.3 percent as expected in a one-third agreement. The state never reached its 50 percent share ceiling, having decreased support of community colleges from 40 percent in 1979–1980 to less than 20 percent in 2006–2007.

Thus, in the case of Illinois, even as the state produced legislation to support up to 50 percent of the funding toward community colleges as

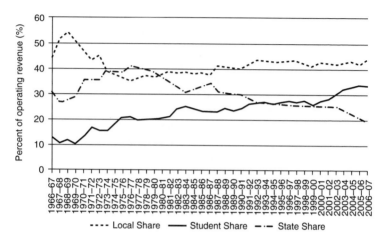

Figure CS1.1   Percent of operating revenue for Illinois community colleges.
Source: Fiscal Year 1967 to 2007.

higher education institutions, the monies never, for nearly 60 years followed the public perception of even partnership.

New York

New York was a latecomer to the provision of public education as its heritage lies firmly grounded in private educational entities (Carmichael 1955). It was not until the middle of the twentieth century that the state ventured to provide a coordinated system of public higher education. The actions and political actors of this age set forth the umbrella under which all educational institutions continue to operate.

Legal and Fiscal Evolution

In 1784, the New York legislature established an educational entity entitled the "Regents of the University of the State of New York" to oversee and control all higher education in the state as well as museums and other cultural entities. For their purpose, "university" was in the manner of the French, referring to the "idea of a universal education with centralized control and unified administration" (Carmichael 1955, 2). The historical record bears that the Regents were primarily concerned with protecting and forwarding the interests of private institutions, as such the provision of public postsecondary education would have to be created by state leadership.

The lack of a public postsecondary education system in New York resulted in increased political and societal pressure to provide such services. In 1946, Governor Thomas A. Dewey established a Temporary Commission on the Need for a State University to "examine into the need for a state university, including professional and graduate schools, to be established in the state" (Temporary Commission on the Need for a State University 1948, 7).

Initially, the focus of the new public system of higher education, as conceptualized by the commission, was on developing community colleges as the foundation of public education in New York. As it related to community colleges, early drafts of the plan advocated for by the Chancellor of the University of the State of New York William J. Wallin advocated that community colleges within the state system be state supported institutions [50 percent of operating costs] with local and student contributions [the other 50 percent]. Other members of the committee, including John E. Burton, then director of budget for New York state, shared this position. In a December 1947 meeting of the commission, a majority vote was cast in favor of Wallin's plan of state supported institutions (Carmichael 1955).

During a heated debate amongst commission members one month later in January 1948, Burton and accompanying advocates were able to persuade the commission to change direction in their perspective on community colleges in the final recommendations. The plan set forth by Burton shifted community colleges from the main focus to but one part of a comprehensive system. Simultaneously it cemented his proposal for financing community colleges under the guise of state-aided as opposed to state-supported—a line of distinction placing community colleges as local educational entities with aid from the state, rather than state institutions with aid from local governmental entities. Specifically, Burton stated,

> While recognizing that there was a place in our system for community colleges, I could not quite see why community colleges should be placed, as proposed, at the very core of our system of higher education. The community college would thus become the major recipient of the state's higher education funds...such a foundation would pull down the standards of our entire system...we should strengthen the state's private universities and colleges through an expanded scholarship program and extend financial aid. (as cited in Carmichael 1955, 170)

The commission presented its final report, which addressed all facets of education beyond the high school from community college to medical school, in February of 1948 (Temporary Commission on the Need for a State

University 1948). As it related to community colleges, the commission recommended their establishment with financing of the manner such that "one-third of the current costs should be financed by local contributions, one-third by student fees, and one-third by state aid under a long range master plan" (Temporary Commission 1948, 16). In further commenting on this recommendation, the commission placed the fiscal burden primarily on the shoulder of the local sponsor by (a) suggesting the one-third share from the state be the maximum amount and (b) suggesting the maximum share contributed by the student should be one-third of the operating costs. As such, if either student or state revenue sources failed to provide the maximum amount, local governments would have to bear the fiscal burden of the shortfall.

The Master Plan

In continuing its historic advocacy of advancing private and public institutions, the focus of the Master Plans of New York relied heavily upon the inclusion of aid as a funding source. The 1964 master plan was broad, reading more as a collection of general ideas than as a specific course of action. Of the ten goals set forth in the plan, only one addressed financing. It specifically stated a "program of financial support both to public institutions and to individual students which will enable each qualified student to choose an institution appropriate to his needs and interests rather than on the basis of costs" (State University of New York 1965, 31). The Regents justified the reliance on high-tuition–high-aid policy in the community college as they saw the student benefiting from their education and as a means to offset rising costs at postsecondary education institutions (State University of New York 1965).

Already discussed extensively in previous debates, there was scarce mention as to how the state, or local governments, would contribute to financing community colleges. Again reinforcing the diminished focus on community colleges in the State University of New York (SUNY) system, the Regents appended a statement on the comprehensive community college in New York to the Master Plan touting how important they were while also outlining seven propositions for the institutions, none addressing how these institutions should be financed (State University of New York 1965). Thus, the one-third philosophy had been cemented.

Defining Revenue Shares

Operating costs for the community colleges of the SUNY were split between the local sponsor,[2] state, and student. Local revenue in New York was a function of local sponsor contributions, charge-back revenues, and out-of-state tuition revenues. Sponsor contributions were funds derived from general revenues, tax levies, gifts, and/or the provision of services. Charge-back revenues were reimbursements between community college districts for students who were residents of New York, but not of the attending community college district (Laws of New York 2009). Out-of-state tuition revenues were those funds charged to students whose residence was outside of New York (Laws of New York 2009).

Initially the amount of state aid for operating costs was to be one-third. A provision for 40 percent of operating revenue from state sources was added in the early 1970s. Both provisions were subject to the state's funding formula for community colleges. Specifically, it stated "[s]uch formula or the amended version thereof, upon enactment into law, shall replace any limitations and regulations then in existence concerning the financing of community colleges" (Laws of New York 2007). The inclusion of the funding formula as final arbiter of revenue share from the state relegated the percentage philosophy and as it applied to the state share, a goal of the funding formula (Martens 1985). Starting in 1972 and dating to the present, the funding formula employed two calculations to determine the state share, whereas the calculation resulting in the lowest amount was utilized for the fiscal year. One calculation set a maximum (ceiling) amount equal to 40 percent of operating costs, and has only been applied once (1975–1976). The other calculation varied somewhat over the time span investigated for this study, at one time or another including but not limited to considerations for curricular choices among students, disadvantaged students, rental costs for physical space, small college funding, high needs funding, and dollars per full-time equivalent student.

Revenue from students came in the form of resident tuition. By law, the amount charged to a student was not to exceed one-third of operating costs. The local sponsor was charged with providing the difference when charges were less than the one-third amount.

Historical Balance of Revenue Trends

The historical record indicated that the balance of revenue responsibility in New York has shifted over time, with the 1992–1993 academic year serving as the point of discontinuity (figure CS1.2). It was at this time that the state took a less supportive role, by suspended the funding limits set on the student share.

The result was a substantial increase in revenue from the student share and a proportional decrease in the state share. These actions contradict the

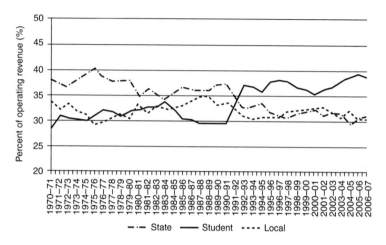

Figure CS1.2   Percent of operating revenue for the State University of New York community colleges.

Source: Fiscal year 1971 to 2007.

SUNY statement on tuition and fees in 1963, which regulated tuition and fee levels across all institution types for the first time when it stated, "[t] o emphasize the University's future needs does not imply that the Board of Trustees favors the imposition of tuition as a substitute for legislative appropriations. Increased appropriations, sufficient to meet the costs of the university's expanding obligations, must continue to be enacted" (State University of New York 1963, 10).

Implications

The historical record in Illinois and New York provide unique perspectives for not only considerations of "one-third" funding philosophies in their respective state, but also for the way public funding of community colleges is addressed in the future. As suggested at the outset, there exists a fundamental question that needs to be continually examined: to what degree is the state (or any other entity) fiscally responsible for funding education?

The case studies of Illinois and New York have shown two outcomes for a similar state policy over an extended period. In light of these findings, it may be that there are those perspectives to take moving forward.

An Agreement Maintained

First, as exemplified in Illinois, a philosophy may serve as a viable model over time and have staying power beyond cyclical shifts in social and economic conditions. While the information examined in this case study cannot decipher the exact reasons for the maintenance of the funding arrangement, it is instructive.

Local entities established Illinois colleges and fought hard to maintain their control over these institutions as they developed. This is evidenced by the fact that a ten-word minority report could overturn a state-appointed committee. Such an outcome suggests the power of local politics in Illinois to the provision of public services. Further, it suggests the importance of sustained local involvement in the activities of the community college.

Second, it may be the case that in Illinois, state funds were used to equalize disparities in local ability to finance public community colleges. This may suggest that, given an explicit rationale for the state funds, state policymakers had a more challenging time ignoring their commitment. This resulting positive interdependence—a concept that team members depend on each other to succeed—amongst stakeholders may be instructive in thinking about future approaches to developing sustainable funding relationships.

Clearly, the results found in Illinois are instructive and provide the foundation for further examination. These initial results suggest the importance of local leadership and the enactment of positive interdependence.

An Expectation Discarded

State fiscal policy in New York has not supported the community college to levels expected. While the state share is capped at 40 percent, there is no floor. However, by extending a cap from one-third to 40 percent, one may argue the expectation for substantial state aid. It also foretells of future policy driven by the lure of substantial state aid. As the historical record showed, community colleges of the SUNY have not been a fiscal priority for the state. At this juncture, it is relevant to add a couple of things that may be instructive.

If states continue to defund public community colleges there may be an increase in the solicitation of private sources to fund a public service. This trend, already emerging in the areas of public-private investments, expansion of college foundations, and tuition support for industry-specific programs, could add a new ingredient to the current "mix of three" funding model. In the area of private investments in community colleges, Central Oregon Community College recently announced development of an academic village through a real estate development partnership. Lone

Star Community College district has sought private tuition support for allied health programs, allowing the district to quadruple the number of enrollees in these programs. Another example of the nascent importance of private investment is observed in the growth of college foundations over the past two decades, which portends a future with considerable more student financial aid arriving through private contributions.

The last consideration that may result from a shift away from stable funding amongst state sources is the adaptation of a strategy widely utilized in the K-12 subsector: adequacy. The concept of adequacy, as applied in educational finance, refers to a level of resources required to provide an adequate education. "Adequate" education is defined on a state-by-state basis and grounded in levels of performance required by legislative decree. This strategy is obviously a complex one, but with an increase in calls for accountability as measured by student learning outcomes, the future of its application as a funding strategy in states with dismal state aid may not be that far in the future.

While this chapter described the cases of two states, New York and Illinois, the common history of funding community allows for a few general, concluding statements. In the second decade of the twenty-first century, the economic state of affairs facing states and community college districts is difficult at best, and dire at worst. Given the ballooning US and state government debt, and current cost obligations home and abroad, the future availability of public funds for postsecondary education is in question.

However, there is a variety of assertions that can be made, which this case study suggests should begin with questions of adequacy in undergraduate education. Second, college and local leaders alongside state legislators will need to consider the drawbacks and benefits of defining statutorily what types of public-private partnerships will be appropriate to the public education models they wish to maintain into the future. Perhaps through this debate the one-third philosophy can evolve toward a one-fourth philosophy that allows increased entrepreneurship within colleges, and the student affordability, even while promoting enhanced relationships with private sector or other partners who can gain a reasonable profit on a public investment, wish to serve as benefactors, or otherwise stand the most to gain from a community college graduate.

Notes

1. An attempt was made to include Pennsylvania in the study, as it also matched up with Illinois and New York fairly well, but a lack of requisite data eliminated it from the study.

2. Local sponsor was defined as "[a]ny city, county, intermediate school district, school district approved by the state university trustees, or community college region approved by the state university trustees, sponsoring or participating in the establishment or operation of a community college." 7 NY Cons. Laws 126 § 6301 (3).

References

Breneman, David W., and Susan C. Nelson. 1981. *Financing Community Colleges: An Economic Perspective*. Washington, DC: The Brookings Institution.

Carmichael, Oliver C. Jr. 1955. *New York Establishes a State University: A Case Study in the Processes of Policy Formation*. Nashville, TN: Vanderbilt University Press.

Carnegie Commission on Higher Education. 1973. *Higher Education: Who Pays? Who Benefits? Who Should Pay?* New York: McGraw-Hill Book Company.

Erickson, Clifford G. 1969. "Rebirth in Illinois." In *Junior Colleges: 50 States/ 50 Years*, ed. R. Yarrington. Washington, DC: American Association of Junior Colleges Press.

Garms, Walter I. 1977. *Financing Community Colleges*. New York: Teacher College Press.

Hardin, Thomas L. 1975. *A History of the Community Junior College in Illinois: 1901–1972*. PhD diss., University of Illinois at Urbana-Champaign, Illinois.

Honeyman, David, Mary L. Williamson, and James L. Wattenbarger. 1991. *Community College Financing 1990: Challenges for a New Decade*. Washington, DC: American Association of Community and Junior Colleges Press.

Hurlbert, Allan S. 1969. *State Master Plans for Community Colleges*. Washington, DC: American Association of Junior Colleges Press.

Illinois Community College Board (ICCB). 1967 to 2008. *Data and Characteristics of the Illinois Public Community College System* (Annual Reports). Springfield, IL: ICCB.

ICCB. 2007. *Operating Budget Appropriation and Supporting Technical Data for the Illinois Public Community College System, Fiscal Year 2008*. Springfield, IL: ICCB.

Illinois Board of Higher Education (IBHE). 2009. *Data Book on Illinois Higher Education*. Springfield, IL: IBHE. Available online at: http://www.ibhe.state.il.us.

Illinois State Constitution of 1970, art. IX § 3(a) and 5(c). Available online at: http://www.ilga.gov.

Katsinas, Stephen G., and Terrence A. Tollefson. 2009. *Funding and Access Issues in Public Higher Education: A Community College Perspective*. Tuscaloosa, AL: Education Policy Center, University of Alabama.

Krebs, Phil, Stephen G. Katsinas, and J. LeLand Johnson. 1999. Illinois Community Colleges: Their History and System. *Community College Journal of Research and Practice* (23): 19–41.

Laws of New York. 2007. NY Consolidated Laws, Education Title 7, art. 126. Available online at: http://public.leginfo.state.ny.us.

Majchrzak, Ann. 1984. *Methods for Policy Research* (Applied Social Research Methods Series, Vol. 3). Newbury Park, CA: SAGE Publications, Inc.

Martens, Freda R. H. 1985. *The Evolution of the State University of New York Community College Funding Formula* (Topical Paper No. 4). Albany, NY: Office of Community Colleges, State University of New York.

Medsker, Leland L. 1956. Financing Public Junior College Operation. In *The Public Junior College. The Fifty-fifth Yearbook of the National Society for the Study of Education, Part 1*, ed. N. B. Henry. Chicago, IL: University of Chicago Press.

Mullin, Christopher M., and David S. Honeyman. 2007. The Funding of Community Colleges: A Typology of State Funding Formulas. *Community College Review 35* (2): 113–127.

Palmer, James C., and Doug Franklin. 2007. *Grapevine Compilation of State Higher Education Tax Appropriations Data for Fiscal Year 2007*. Normal, IL: Center for the Study of Education Policy, Illinois State University.

Public Act. 1965. *Junior College Act*. 110 Illinois Compiled Statutes (ILCS) 805. Available online at: http://www.ilga.gov.

Public Act. 1992. *Public Community College Act*. 110 ILCS 805, art. VI § 2. Available online at: http://www.ilga.gov.

Public Law 111-5. 2009. *American Recovery and Reinvestment Act of 2009*. Washington, DC: Government Printing Office. Available online at: http://www.gpo.gov/fdsys/browse/collection.action?collectionCode=PLAW

State of Illinois Board of Higher Education. 1964, July. *A Master Plan for Higher Education in Illinois*. Springfield, IL: Illinois Board of Higher Education.

State of Illinois Board of Higher Education. 1963. *Two-year Colleges: Report of Master Plan Committee F*. Springfield, IL: Illinois Board of Higher Education.

State University of New York. 2008. *Community College Funding History 101: Partnerships Shares, Student, State and Local*. Paper presented at a meeting of the Community College Business Officers Association, Saratoga Springs, NY, October 2008.

State University of New York. 1965, January. *The Regents Tentative Statewide Plan for the Expansion and Development of Higher Education*. Albany, NY: The New York State Education Department.

State University of New York. 1963, January. *Revised Policy on Tuition and Fees: A Report by the Board of Trustees*. Albany, NY: The New York State Education Department.

Temporary Commission on the Need for a State University. 1948. *Report of the Temporary Commission on the Need for a State University* (Legislative Document No. 30). Albany, NY: Williams Press Inc.

Wattenbarger, James L., and Dale Tillery. 1985. State Power in a New Era: Threats to Local Authority. *New Directions in Community Colleges* 1985 (49): 5–23.

Wattenbarger, James L., and Paul M. Starnes. 1976. *Financial Support Patterns for Community Colleges*. Gainesville, FL: Institute of Higher Education.

Case Study 2

Financing Community Polytechnics in Uganda

Christopher B. Mugimu and Jenna Cullinane

Community college model institutions in Uganda seek to improve access for underserved students and better align training with the economic and social realities of this developing country. The Government of Uganda (GoU) has begun establishing and funding community college model institutions on a limited basis but needs more information about the value of this form of education to determine plans for expansion.

Improved political stability in the last two decades has helped Uganda emerge as one of the fastest growing economies in Africa; however, it continues to face significant challenges including infrastructure gaps, internal budgetary pressures, and high birth rates (World Bank 2009). Uganda has a total population of approximately 33.4 million, 50 percent of which is less than 15 years old (UBOS 2004). Currently, more than 80 percent of Ugandans earn a living through agriculture and related activities (Jacob et al. 2009). Forty-six percent of the labor force is employed by the informal sector, while the public sector employs 43 percent and the private sector employs 11 percent (Ministry of Education and Sports [MOES] 2001).

Workforce indicators reveal that there is an inadequate supply of highly skilled workers to support economic development, and the country suffers from low labor productivity. Forty-seven percent of the firms in Uganda identify the deficiency of skilled workers as a significant constraint to business (AfDB/OECD 2008). Perpetual skill deficits cause the country to import labor from neighboring nations. Despite Uganda's high levels of underemployment and unemployment, there are an insufficient number of trained technicians to help develop basic infrastructure, work in manufacturing, and support the tourism industry (Wirak et al. 2003).

The GoU believes the pace of the country's progress depends heavily on the education of its young population. Education is key to attaining its social and economic development goals and the GoU has made tremendous investments in the sector. Enacted in 1997, Universal Primary Education (UPE) policies have helped increase primary enrollment from 2.6 million students in 1995 to 7.2 million in 2007 (World Bank 2009). In 2007, Universal Secondary Education policies started in selected schools and now, more students are accessing secondary schooling than ever before (MOES 2008). The so-called bulge of matriculating primary and secondary school completers has created excess demand for higher education.

In response, new public and private community college model institutions have been established including business colleges, technical schools, farm schools, and community polytechnics. Enrollment in these types of institutions has been rising slowly, yet the bulk of demand for higher education continues to be concentrated at more traditional university-type institutions. Community college model institutions reach only a very limited portion of the unmet demand for postprimary and postsecondary students at this time (AfDB/OECD 2008).

The purpose of this case study is to examine closely the services and operations of one type of Ugandan college, known as the community polytechnic. The study will pay special attention to the financing structures of community polytechnics.

The Emergence of Community Polytechnics

Community polytechnics (CPs) are public, low-cost, vocational institutions that provide education and training for students completing primary or secondary school and other targeted groups such as out-of-school children, unemployed, and underemployed persons. CPs are intended to offer flexible, market-driven courses that enable students to join the workforce rapidly and begin contributing to high-need occupations in the local communities (Raby 2009). CPs are also meant to be widely accessible to low-income students and those with low levels of academic preparation. CPs offer programs that usually last one to three years, and award a certificate or diploma upon completion.

Cross-cutting coursework in math, English, entrepreneurship, and computers is meant to support specialized technical training in carpentry and joinery, brick laying and concrete practice, tailoring and cutting garments, motor vehicle mechanics, electrical installation, agriculture, welding and metal fabrication, plumbing, home economics, and other specializations (MOES 2001). The motor vehicle mechanics program is particularly popular among men, and the tailoring program is most popular among women. Agriculture programs are significantly underenrolled because students do not believe the level of training surpasses traditional, low-tech methods. Most CPs are not equipped with the modern tools that would enhance agricultural productivity and require specialized training.

At the conclusion of a CP program, students can sit for the Ugandan National Examination Board exam. Student failure rates are rather high. English language, mathematics, and science content are seen as the primary barriers to students' success. The acquired technical skills are usually quite adequate. Some CPs also encourage students to sit for the Directorate of Industrial Training examinations, which certify technical skills only, not academic performance. Proficient achievement on these examinations suggests that CPs are adequately training students in the technical fields, though they are relatively ineffective in teaching traditional academic subjects.

MOES outlined its goal to establish and finance CPs in each of the 850 subcounties in Uganda in the *1992 Government White Paper on Education* (Kajubi 1992). To date, only 16 CPs have been established, plus one institution for instructor training. The CPs were established in 2003 to pilot the concept. The MOES intended to evaluate whether CPs should be replicated in additional subcounties. As of 2009, these programs have not been evaluated for the purposes of replication. The Business Technical Vocational Education and Training (BTVET)—the division of MOES that oversees CPs—cites the lack of funding as the primary reason so few CPs have opened their doors so far. It is believed that low enrollment and social stigma have also undermined the motivation for expansion.

Interviews with instructors, students, and other local stakeholders substantiated claims about negative social stigma. Because CPs accept primary and secondary school completers with the very lowest possible achievement levels, the perception is that all students who attend CPs are failures. Despite the relevance of the knowledge and skills students receive and the employability of its graduates, CPs are seen as education institutions of last resort.

The belief that institutions are underenrolled, however, appears to be false. CPs were designed to support only 150 students, often in rural or otherwise underserved areas of Uganda. MOES intended these institutions to be small day centers targeted to students for whom transportation would be challenging and those who could afford to attend school or live away from their families. Site visits suggest CPs often train many more than 150 students. Enrollment numbers culled by the MOES do not seem to reflect total enrollment on the ground. In some cases record keeping is inaccurate or imprecise. In others, CPs may only be reporting the number of students eligible for government funding. This example is symptomatic of a larger finding, that the value of CPs is not fully known or understood by the public or the central government.

Direct benefits of CP education primarily consist of increased earnings for students after graduation. Student, administrator, and employer interviews at Gombe CP revealed that $2.41 is a realistic, but conservative daily wage for students upon completion of their training. The Uganda National Household Survey from 2002/2003 substantiates that an average employee with primary education earns about $0.64 per day, $1.59 for secondary education, and $3.82 for specialized training or tertiary education.

The surrounding community is also a beneficiary of CPs. The community enjoys many social benefits that are not quantified in this analysis but are worth noting, such as improved access to education, poverty alleviation, economic development, improved productivity, enhanced quality of life and confidence, and reduced unemployment (Yizengaw 2008). Improved access to education also typically leads to improved measures of health and reduced crime, although no studies have tested these assumptions specifically in the Ugandan context. Because these additional social benefits are not reflected in typical evaluation metrics, including enrollment and examination scores, the value of CP education is not recognized.

Financing

Wherever short-cycle colleges are found, financing is a primary dilemma (Woodhall 2007). CPs are no exception. Financing CPs is considered very expensive compared to traditional academic offerings in Uganda because of the specialized tools and equipment needed for technical training (MOES 2001). CPs are highly subsidized public institutions, financed primarily by the GoU, with contributions from external donors, the community, and student fees as reflected in Table CS2.1. Government resources support approximately 40 percent of costs for CPs. Contributions from external donors, the community, and the institution itself make up another 27 percent of costs. Student contributions make up the remaining 33 percent of total costs.

Government Activities

The government provides three forms of financial support, which include (1) capital development funding (CDF), (2) wages, and (3) student capitation grants. CDF provides for initial construction, equipment for workshops and classrooms, and ongoing maintenance of facilities and equipment. CDF is a generic model espoused by the United Nations to promote millennium development goals, particularly in least developed countries. However, the amount of funding and the specifics involved are county-specific. CP facilities should include five classrooms, four workshops, instructor houses, an administrative block, water, and sewage facilities. Necessary equipment consists of furniture, workshop tools, and office equipment for at least seven programs. In reality, most CPs do not have the recommended number of workshops and many lack needed access to water and sewage facilities (MOES 2007). Informants at two of the CPs reported that the actual levels of funding for initial establishment was less than a third of the estimates required to establish and outfit the institution. Although ongoing CDF continues to improve the infrastructure at CPs, significant needs remain.

The government also provides funding for CPs in the form of direct wages for staff. Wage funding supports both instructional and noninstructional staff (Namuli-Tamale 2009; Gombe Community Polytechnic 2009). Most institutions report the need to hire staff in addition to those paid for by the government. For example, in 2008, Rutunku CP had a staff of 30, including 23 instructional staff and 7 support staff. 18 instructional staff and 3 support staff were supported by the government, and the remaining

Table CS2.1   Source and Type of Funding for CPs in Uganda (2010)

Source	Type of Funding	Percent of Costs	Description
Government with support from external donors	Construction/ equipment	33%	Initial construction or refurbishment, equipment for workshops
	Capital development funding	10%	Ongoing maintenance of facilities and equipment
	Wages	16%	Staff remunerations
	Capitation grants (per student formula funding)	6%	Purchase of supplies, training, materials, and stationary; support co-curricular activities, examination administration, school-based staff development and security
Student/Parent	Cost of attendance	23%	Tuition, fees, room and board, tools, and supplies
	Opportunity cost	11%	Student earnings given up to obtain education
Community	Land	1%	The equivalent value of land donated to CPs by the community

nine staff members were paid directly by the institution using other funding streams (Byaruhanga 2008). Supplemental staffing needs often exceed institutional budgets and many CPs report unfilled staff positions.

Student capitation grants are formula grants provided to CPs on per student, per term basis. The student capitation grants are provided by the government to purchase supplies, training materials and stationery, lunch, and support cocurricular activities, maintain security, conduct examinations, and provide continuous school-based staff development (Byaruhanga 2008). Capitation grants are awarded only to CPs for their eligible student population. Eligible students include those who have completed, but not matriculated beyond primary school with minimum levels of achievement. The cumulative performance assessment scale for primary school ranges where 4 is the best and 36 indicates failure in the four examined subjects (i.e., mathematics, English, science, and social studies). Students must have achieved at least 28 points aggregate to receive government capitation funding at CPs. The students who score in the 29–36 range must pay for their own tuition fees independently (Namuli-Tamale 2009). The intent of this MOES policy is to increase access to skills training for students with significant financial and academic barriers to education. The eligibility requirement rewards basic educational proficiency, while still permitting students with very low achievement to access training by paying for their own tuition and fees.

Government capitation grants and CDF are insufficient to meet the minimum institutional revenues required of CPs. CPs rely on financial resources from a variety of other sources. Student fees and labor, community contributions, income-generating activities, and NGOs supplement the day-to-day operations, equipment maintenance, and upgrading facilities.

Student Support

CPs establish payment structures for students ineligible for government support, including low-performing primary school completers, all secondary school completers, and other adults, unemployed or underemployed persons. Tuition levels increase as courses become more advanced. Students may also pay fees for a range of items including an identification card, registration, and water. All students, even those eligible for free tuition, will typically pay these additional fees. Many CPs also offer lodging for an additional fee. CPs have begun recruiting students from somewhat further afield for whom it is impractical to travel from home to the institution each day.

Even though costs to students are much lower than universities, many self-pay students at CPs find it difficult to pay the requisite tuition and fees.

CPs are not typically perceived as a more economical substitute for other types of tertiary education because CPs tend to serve students who would likely receive no advanced training beyond secondary school had a CP not been established in close proximity. Traditional universities are often inaccessible due to financial and academic barriers. Therefore, it is likely that the perception of expense reflects a comparison against tuition and fees charged for secondary schools, rather than university education. It also reflects the economic conditions of the villages or towns where CPs have been built.

Community Involvement

The role of the community was designed to be central to the education and operations of CPs. To help build community buy-in from the start, the MOES requires the community to satisfy a set of requirements before a CP can be established. The requirements include land, access to utilities, a technical proposal, and development plan. CPs require at least ten acres of land upon which the facilities can be built. The land represents a significant financial contribution from the community. Land prices in the various subcounties of Uganda vary considerably.

The community may also donate labor on a periodic basis to help construct facilities. The labor of students, parents, and instructors is used to reduce the cost of construction to the expense of materials only. Cost sharing of this variety allows government CDF to be stretched further. At the same time, students gain experience in the production of goods and economic activities (Lubwama 2009). For example, at the time of this research, students at Gombe CP were constructing their dormitories under supervision of their tutors.

The community also plays a role in the leadership of the CP. At least six members of the community may serve on a board of governors (BOG) committee, which guides the management of the CP and ensures the institution is meeting the needs of the community. When access to water reached the village of Gombe village, parents and other members of the community worked with the BOG. They asked for a new training program in plumbing to satisfy the new market demand. The BOG also plays an important role in establishing tuition and fees charged to students.

Outside of the administrative participation by the BOGs, community support remains a struggle. Negative stigma has hindered community mobilization and participation, not to mention financial support (Raby 2009). The MOES originally estimated community contributions would finance 10 to 15 percent of the recurring budget for CPs. In practice, most community contributions are limited to in-kind services. Rarely does the community provide direct financial support beyond providing land and paying for the students' fees. Many members of the community lack the means, the desire to contribute, or both.

Income-Generating Activities

Income-generating activities (IGAs) are a form of training with production where students gain practical work experience as part of their learning program. IGAs serve as financing mechanisms, which help students and/ or institutions offset the cost of training (AfDB/OECD 2008). Training with production can benefit education outcomes by helping increase the market relevance of training, provide hands-on work experiences linked to employment, integrate theory with practice, and enhance student motivation. In theory the economic benefits of training with production may extend to the community at large, private industry, training institutions, and students. Although MOES planning documents suggests IGAs could be an important source of revenue for CPs there was no evidence of formal IGAs arrangements between CPs and industry. Instructors report occasionally there will be informal arrangements made between students and local business owners. In the Ugandan context, the primary benefactors of student work in professional settings are the students themselves. Income from student production may serve as a primary source of revenue to cover the individual tuition and fees (Singh 1998).

Little research has been done to assess the benefits IGAs may be conveying or could convey to businesses in Uganda. Additionally, the extent to which IGAs could be organized on a more formal basis remains unexplored. The general public does not seem aware of CPs or their students and skills.

Nongovernmental Organizations

Nongovernmental organizations (NGOs) help finance CPs at the system and individual institution level. A number of German development agencies and the Japanese government support a range of BTVET institutions, which include the 16 CPs (ADEA 2008). Funding from external donors is primarily dedicated to financing capital developments at BTVET institutions, although NGOs like GTZ-Uganda have helped pilot low-cost modular coursework to support income generation in rural areas (AfDB/OECD 2008).

At the institutional level, NGOs have helped to provide equipment and supported the fees of attending students. For example, Care for Uganda, a local NGO, partnered with Bbowa CP to provide tools for carpentry, metalwork, vehicle mechanics, and building. Similarly, Plan International sponsors individual children to attend Bbowa CP by paying their tuition, fees, and lodging.

Conclusion

CPs face many challenges related to financing, insufficient or inconsistent information about enrollment, lack of reliable labor data to inform curriculum, community (dis)engagement, gender disparities, and relatively high expense compared to academic training. However, many students see CPs as sites that can offer valuable skills to enable them compete in the world of work. Further research should be done to study the range of challenges CPs face because despite these many challenges, CP are economically beneficial for students and socially beneficial for communities. CPs deliver accessible skills training to students who might otherwise receive no advanced education. They improve the future earnings of students and are positioned to make valuable contributions to the workforce needs of Uganda. As one employer said during an interview:

> The polytechnic has helped also the [Gombe] area because there are so many people who may not be able to go through the normal system of education. They can't access university. Usually, they end up there [at the community polytechnic]. It helps them get some skills. It helps the rural [people].

The public and education stakeholders in Uganda would benefit from additional information about the training CPs offer. Rather than institutions of last resort, CPs could be seen as a viable educational opportunity that is well-suited to employment opportunities. The favorable findings of this analysis could support further expansion of CPs to the subcounties of Uganda. Priority should be given to those regions without private-sector educational facilities of similar quality.

References

Association for the Development of Education in Africa (ADEA). 2008. *Enhancing Equity Access to BTVT Through Coherent Governance, Public-Private Partnerships and Multimedia Campaigns Development.* Paris: ADEA.
African Development Bank (AfDB), and Organization for Economic Co-operation and Developmet (OECD). 2008. *African Economic Outlook.* Accra, Ghana: AfDB, OECD.

Byaruhanga, Rose Kaisiki 2008. *Rutunku Community Polytechnic Sembabule District.* Kampala: Ministry of Education and Sports of Uganda (MOES).

Gombe Community Polytechnic. 2009. *School Profile.* Kampala: MOES.

Jacob, W. James, Yusuf K. Nsubuga, and Christopher B. Mugimu. 2009. "Higher Education in Uganda: The Role Community Colleges in Educational Delivery and Reform." In *Community College Models: Globalization and Higher Education Reform,* ed. Rosalind Latiner Raby and Edward J. Valeau. Dordrecht, The Netherlands: Springer.

Kajubi, William. 1992. *The Government White Paper on Implementation of the Recommendations of the Report of Education Policy Review Entitled "Education for National Integration and Development."* Kampala: Ministry of Education.

Lubwama, Everlyne. 2009. Email/phone conversation with Christopher B. Mugimu, Kampala to Gombe, 12 August 2009. Lubwama is the Head Instructor, Gombe Community Polytechnic.

MOES. 2001. *Status Report on Implementation of the Community Polytechnic Programme (Department of Business, Technical, Vocational Education and Training.* Kampala: BTVET, MOES.

MOES. 2007. *Needs Assessment Draft Report for the Page Seven Enrolling Institutions in Uganda.* Kampala: BTVET Section, MOES.

MOES. 2008. *Universal Secondary Education Headcount Report for 2008.* Kamapala: MOES.

Namuli-Tamale, Sarah. 2009. Personal communication with Christopher B. Mugimu in Kampala. Namuli-Tamale was the Assistant Commissioner BTVET at the MOES.

Raby, Rosalind Latiner. 2009. "Defining the Community College Model." In *Community College Models: Globalizaiton and Higher Education Reform,* ed. Rosalind Latiner Raby and Edward J. Valeau. Dordrecht, The Netherlands: Springer.

Singh, Madhu. 1998. *School Enterprises: Combining Vocational Learning with Production.* Berlin: UNESCO/ENEVOC.

UBOS. 2004. *2004 Statistical Abstracts.* Kampala: Uganda Bureau of Statistics Available online at: http://www.ubos.org.

Wirak, Anders, Besty Heen, Eli Moen, and Santa Vusia. 2003. *Business, Technical and Vocational Education and Training (BTVET) for Employment and Private Sector Development in Uganda.* Kampala: Royal Norwegian Embassy, Norwegian Agency for Development Cooperation (NORAD).

Woodhall, Maureen. 2007. *Funding of higher education: the contribution of economic thinking to debate and policy development.* Washington, DC: World Bank.

World Bank. 2009. *Country Brief: Uganda.* Washington, DC: World Bank.

Yizengaw, Teshome. 2008. *Challenges of Higher Education in Africa and Lessons of Experience for the Africa-U.S. Higher Education Collaboration Initiative.* Washington, DC: National Association of State Universities and Land Grant Colleges (NASULGC).

Case Study 3

Applying Financial Analysis to Student Retention

Pamela D. Anglin

This case study focuses on how a rural community college with limited resources used break-even and return on investment (ROI) calculations to estimate the potential benefit of self-funding the cost to participate in the Achieving the Dream initiative and to gain Board of Regent support. Retention rates were analyzed and the lost revenue calculations for each student not retained were used in preparing a recommendation to participate in the Achieving the Dream student success initiative.

The Achieving the Dream initiative began in 2004 and by 2006 there were 57 community colleges participating throughout the United States. These colleges represented institutions of all sizes including large urban multicollege districts (such as Houston Community College system) and small rural colleges (such as Mountain Empire Community College).

The goal of Achieving the Dream is to help community college students succeed, with a special focus on students of color and low-income students (Jenkins and McClenney 2009). For the first three years, Achieving the Dream participation was limited to college serving primarily minority students. Project funding came from the Lumina Foundation and Houston Endowment. Paris Junior College had not been considered for the initiative because the student population was 81 percent Anglo, 12 percent African American, and 6 percent Latino. In 2007, during the Round IV Achieving the Dream cycle, requirements for participation broadened to allow nonminority majority colleges access to the project. However, those that adopted Achieving the Dream needed to self-fund the cost of

participation. Because of the success of Achieving the Dream and identified needs of the college, Paris Junior College submitted a proposal based
on the college serving a majority of low-income students.

Achieving the Dream student-centered model of institutional improvement is focused on creating a culture of evidence in which data and
inquiry drive broad-based institutional efforts to close achievement gaps
and improve student outcomes overall. Colleges participating in Achieving
the Dream agree to engage faculty, staff, and administrators in a process
of using data to identify gaps in student achievement and to implement
and improve strategies for closing those gaps. A specific interest is placed
on low-income students and students of color because research shows that
they are most at risk of not achieving success. At the same time, by improving outcomes for these students, colleges will be able to increase success
rates for students overall.

Achieving the Dream seeks to help more students earn postsecondary
credentials, including occupational certificates and degrees. Recognizing
that community college students often take a long time to earn certificates or degrees, Achieving the Dream works with institutions to improve
student progression through intermediate milestones, including the rates
at which students (a) successfully complete remedial or developmental
instruction and advance to credit-bearing courses, (b) enroll in and successfully complete the initial college-level or gatekeeper courses in subjects
such as math and English, (c) complete the courses they take with a grade
of C or better, (d) persist from one term to the next, and (e) earn a certificate or associate degree.

Community colleges that join Achieving the Dream receive expert help
from a coach and a data facilitator. The colleges provide cohort data to a
central database and can compare their data to peer colleges involved in
the initiative. They help transform the institutional culture into one that
effectively uses data and other evidence to make decisions and to evaluate
effectiveness, and institutions become a participant in a national network
of community colleges.

Paris Junior College

Paris Junior College is a two-year community college in Paris, Texas, a
small, rural town in the northeast part of the state, with additional locations in Greenville and Sulphur Springs. The college was established
in 1924 as an extension of the local high school and was accredited as
a member of the Southern Association of Colleges and Schools in 1932.

The college serves a five-county area in northeast Texas, of which nearly 20 percent of the population lives below the poverty line. Two of the counties served are among the poorest, based on per capita income, in the State of Texas. In addition to serving a very large number of economically disadvantaged students, over 90 percent of the college enrollment is first-generation college students. Paris Junior College has an annual operating budget of approximately $21 million and enrolls 5,600 students, 18 percent of which are African American and Latino. The enrollment of the college mirrors the population of the service area.

The college's revenue comes from three primary sources. State appropriations make up 37 percent of the revenue while tuition and fees account for 34 percent and local tax revenue is 12 percent. The remainder of the revenue comes from federal grant funds, auxiliary enterprises, and other income. In Texas, local tax revenues are used for maintenance and operations of the physical facilities and state appropriations and tuition and fee revenue cover instructional costs, institutional support, student services, and academic support. Paris Junior College is at a disadvantage compared to other Texas community colleges because it has a very limited tax base made up of the city limits of the City of Paris, whose population is 26,000. Even though the college serves a state-designated five-county area its voter approved taxing district is limited to the City of Paris. Therefore, increased tuition and fees is the only possibility for additional revenue.

Due to the college being small and rural, data gathering and institutional research capabilities were limited. There was not a culture of using data for decision-making purposes. A very basic review of available retention data and student completion rates revealed a need for improvement. The college routinely looked at fall-to-fall and fall-to-spring retention data and graduation rates. Also, the college was required to show annual unduplicated headcount in the supplementary information provided with the annual financial audit. The college looked at retention and completion rates on a routine basis but had not looked at root causes of the lack of retention of the students nor poor completion rates in certain courses or student failure to complete a certificate or associate degree.

Decision to Submit an Achieving the Dream Proposal

Since 2004, a cost versus benefit analysis has been conducted at Paris before any commitment of resources is made. Likewise, the college asked what it would cost to participate in Achieving the Dream and found that it was a $730,000 commitment over the five-year period of the program. Of the approximate $146,000 per year, almost $100,000 per year would go toward implementing the strategies and interventions and the remainder would pay for the fees to participate in the initiative. There could also be costs above the $730,000 depending on the strategies identified to be implemented to improve student success rates and the interventions needed to increase retention and completion rates. It would be necessary to increase the operating budget by almost $146,000 per year or the college could reallocate some dollars already allocated for student services.

Prior to submitting the proposal, the college administration needed to receive a commitment from the board of regents for $730,000 spread over a five-year period. Each of the 50 community college districts in Texas is governed by a seven-to-nine member locally elected board. The Paris Junior College Board of Regents has nine members elected and they reside within the college's taxing district. In preparation to ask for a $730,000 commitment from the board of regents, the college administration began to list the benefits of participating in Achieving the Dream. In a typical cost–benefit analysis, the emphasis was on answering the question: what does the college get from its financial commitment?

Achieving the Dream benefit Paris College with experts assigned as a coach and a data facilitator. Coaches are typically former community college presidents or others with much experience in institutional leadership and transformation. Data facilitators have working knowledge on using data and institutional research to identify areas of weakness and opportunities for improvement. Access to expert consultants brings a broader and unbiased perspective to aid in institutional transformation. Systemic institutional transformation would facilitate the college becoming one that used data to evaluate and determine needed changes. The college would also have access to software managed by the American Association of Community Colleges that would help with data analysis and provide the opportunity for benchmarking with other Achieving the Dream institutions. Being a small rural community college, access to sophisticated data collection and analysis software and the ability to capture and present the data in a format for use, decision-making would be a tremendous benefit. In addition, the college would be invited to attend annual conferences and institutes that could provide valuable professional development to faculty and staff. Achieving the Dream institutions participate in a national network of community colleges whereby effective practices and implementation strategies are shared. Learned processes could help colleges transform their cultures into ones that effectively use data and other evidence to make decisions and evaluate institutional effectiveness. Finally, the college would receive benefits during the accreditation process since not it will have a means of demonstrating to the Southern Association of Colleges and Schools how student outcomes are being met.

Enrollment and Retention Realities

Being a small, rural community college with a limited tax base, the college has historically operated with a limited amount of resources. State funds are appropriated by the Texas Legislature based on a community and technical college funding formula. State appropriations to community colleges are used for instructional and administrative costs. The locally elected community college boards raise local funds through tuition and fees and property taxes to defray the expenses associated with construction and maintenance of the physical plant. The property tax rate for Paris Junior College was limited to 27 cents per $100 property valuation at the time the taxing district was established. The property tax rate in 2007 was 19 cents per $100 valuation and among the highest community college tax rate in the State of Texas. The board of each community college district sets the tuition and fee structure that varies from institution to institution. Tuition and fee revenues are considered institutional funds and are not appropriated by the state. Students residing within the taxing district pay a lower in-district tuition rate. Students living in Texas and outside the taxing district pay an out-of-district tuition rate and those students living outside Texas pay a nonresident tuition rate. Each locally elected board is required by state law to levy annual ad valorem taxes for the maintenance of the community college district.

A look at existing data in 2007, although limited, provided evidence of the need to improve student retention and student success rates. A review of unduplicated credit headcount enrollment compared to fall enrollment gave an indication of the number of students that entered the doors and enrolled but were not retained for various reasons during the year. Indeed, data from fall-to-spring and fall-to-fall indicated that students were not persisting. A review of the annual unduplicated headcount and the fall to spring retention rate indicated that 27 to 29 percent of the students did not persist past the first semester enrolled when less than 5 percent were enrolled in certificate programs one semester in length. The retention data, course completion rates and grade distributions, graduation data and couples with 48 percent of students enrolling needing some developmental course work identified the cornerstone for future changes.

To address the changes needed we sought to determine the lost revenue for each student not retained, estimate a break-even point and calculate an ROI. Break-even point is the level of activity where total revenues equal total costs (Ralser 2007). In this case, break-even point would be the number of students to be retained to equal the annual expenditure to participate in the Achieving the Dream initiative.

The *Dictionary of Finance and Investment Terms* defines return of investment as a return on invested capital. Usually termed ROI, it is a useful means of comparing companies, or corporate divisions, in terms of efficiency of management and viability of product lines (Ralser 2007). In its simplest form, ROI is return divided by investment. The unduplicated credit enrollment grew from 7,591 students in 2005 to 10,273 students in 2009. At the same time, fall-to-fall retention rates rose from 41.48% in 2005 to 44.62% in 2008 (Paris Junior College Institutional Research Department 2009).

Paris Junior College defines a full-time student as one taking 12 or more credit hours in a semester. Eighty-five percent of the college's enrolled students live outside the taxing district and for break-even calculation purposes the out-of-district tuition rate was used. The tuition and fee rate for an out-of-district student taking 12 hours is $930 per semester. The average state funding rate per contact hour is calculated at $3.79 per contact hour. A student taking 12 hours generates 192 contact hours per semester or an estimated state funding of $725 per semester. For every student lost, the loss in revenue to the institution is $1,655 per semester or $3,310 per year. The financial result from keeping 45 students enrolled full time on a fall-to-fall basis is retained revenue of $148,950 per year in the annual operating budget. A simplified break-even point and ROI was used to present to the Board of Regents for approval to participate in the Achieving the Dream initiative.

Break-Even Point and Return on Investment

The formula for break-even point for Paris Junior College on a semester basis is expressed as follows:

> Tuition Revenue per FTES + State Funding per FTES x Number of Students
> = Achieving the Dream Participation Cost

When the formula is applied in the case study, for 90 students, the result is $930 for the tuition revenue, which is added to the $725 for the state funding. The result of applying this formula reflected anticipated incremental revenues of $148,950, which equated with the estimated cost of participating in Achieving the Dream over a five-year period.

The break-even point will be the retention of 90 students from fall to spring. The college's investment in the program will be covered with the retention of 90 students from fall to spring or by retaining 45 students from fall to fall. The college will have a minimum positive ROI of $1,655 for every student retained above 90 students. The college is not currently operating at capacity; therefore, no additional full-time or adjunct faculty would be required.

The ROI for participation in Achieving the Dream is much greater than the dollar value calculated. As a culture of using data and evidence in making decisions is developed, the college will benefit by knowing that results are obtained as dollars are committed. The Texas counties served by Paris Junior College will benefit economically from the increased number of trained workers available to the local workforce and a better-educated citizenry.

Conclusion

The college entered Achieving the Dream as a Round IV institution. Priorities were identified during the first year of participation and strategies developed during year two. Strategies are in the process of being implemented and data collection has begun to determine the extent to which strategies and interventions are increasing student retention and success rates. Through this process, the college determined the success rates for developmental math students and found that an alarming 32.7 percent of students required to be remediated in three levels of developmental math had successfully completed College Algebra. Students beginning in the lowest level of development English produced a 35 percent success rate in college English. The college also identified gatekeeper courses and reviewed student performance in the identified courses. Gatekeeper courses are those entry-level general education courses that may keep students from persisting in their education due to the student being unsuccessful in the course. Gatekeeper courses identified were all levels of mathematics, English, history, and art appreciation.

The priorities established by Paris Junior College were to (1) help students gain a greater understanding of how college works while improving study skills and life management skills; (2) align student scheduling with preparation and technical skills and assure that students are working toward their educational objective; and (3) produce better student success results from the developmental studies sequence, and narrow the performance gap between various student groups.

As Paris Junior College completes three years of the five-year process, the college continues to review data and evaluate outcomes to improve student retention and success. The college has begun to see increases in student retention that are coupled with historical increases in enrollment.

Systemic change is taking place at the college and the culture is evolving into one of a culture of evidence or data-driven decision-making. Increased success of developmental students or those students enrolled in programs to remediate basic skill deficiencies helps the recruiting and marketing programs of the institution leading to additional enrollment and more student tuition and fee revenue along with reduced marketing and recruiting cost per student.

The simplified business calculations including break-even analysis and ROI can be used to express to boards and faculty groups the financial benefits of allocating funds for a new program. In this case study, the college would benefit not only from marketing and recruiting dollars being reduced per student enrolled, reducing the workload of admissions and recruiting staff due to greater retention of students already enrolled, but would benefit from the many benefits of the Achieving the Dream initiative and increased success of students. The institution could ultimately be transformed into an institution seeing greater success of students and a systemic change to a data-driven organization.

References

Jenkins, Davis, and Bryon McClenney. 2009. *Field Guide for Improving Student Success: Achieving the Dream*. Chapel Hill, NC: MDC Inc.

Paris Junior College Institutional Research Department. 2009. *College Fact Book*. Paris, TX: Paris Junior College Publishing.

Ralser, Tom. 2007. *ROI for Nonprofits: The New Key to Sustainability*. Hoboken, NJ: John Wiley and Sons.

Case Study 4

Financial Innovation:
The Iowa Case Study

Janice Nahra Friedel and Steve Ovel

Introduction

The agricultural recession of the 1980s witnessed the emergence of Iowa's community colleges as primary drivers in the diversification of the state's economy. Since 1983, with passage of the Iowa New Jobs Training Program Act (NJTP), 140,000 Iowans have been trained in new jobs through the sale of general obligation bonds issued and managed by the community colleges; the administrative fees from this customized job training program finance the ongoing provision of regional economic development coordination through the community colleges. The NJTP served as the model for comparable programs in Missouri and Kansas and may be useful as states respond to the current recession.

Iowa is in America's heartland, and is one of the states comprising the nation's "bread basket." Agriculturally, Iowa is one of the nation's top producers of corn, soybeans, and pork. For decades, as the United States industrialized, employment of Iowa's population shifted from the countryside to the cities. Jobs in the manufacturing sector, and specifically those in industries producing the farm implements so critical to the increased productivity of the agricultural sector, became a lifeline to the economic viability of the state and its people. State policy makers supported an educated citizenry and adult access to continuing education and training to acquire the skills and knowledge required of new industries and employers.

This case study utilizes Iowa's response to the agricultural recession of the 1980s to demonstrate the role that community colleges can play in creating a diversified economy and the skilled workforce to support these new employers. This case study describes the economic and political conditions, and the process by which Iowa's community colleges were enabled to deliver on their emerging economic development mission. General obligation bonds provide the community colleges and their region with an ongoing capability to develop a quality workforce necessary for the growth and diversification of the state's economy. The application of Iowa's community college use of the sale of general obligation bonds as a model for other states is discussed.

Iowa Community College Structure and Design

The enabling legislation for Iowa's system of publicly funded community colleges was passed in 1965. The Iowa Area Schools Act (Iowa Code Chapter 260C) created comprehensive community colleges and provided the authorization to local communities to merge the public junior colleges with the postsecondary vocational schools. Iowa is divided into 15 merged areas or community college districts; a locally elected board of directors (trustees) governs each community college. The Iowa Department of Education has statewide coordination, oversight, and regulatory responsibilities.

The merger of the public postsecondary vocational schools and the public junior colleges into comprehensive community colleges created a public system of community colleges devoid of mission duplication with other publicly funded state institutions. This created the foundation from which the community colleges would emerge as both the state's college transfer and the workforce development institutions.

Iowa's community colleges were built on three curricular pillars: (1) vocational education or career and technical education, (2) college parallel or college transfer (the first two years of the bachelors degree in liberal arts and sciences), and (3) noncredit/continuing education. All of the community colleges were required to provide vocational education; providing the first two years of the baccalaureate degree was permissive and not mandatory.

Since the 1965 Area Schools Act mandated that the community colleges offer vocational programs, this became their immediate priority. Workplace skills and technical knowledge were in high demand among the large numbers of veterans returning from military service in Vietnam. Community colleges formed partnerships with their local employers to develop, implement, and update vocational programs. The community colleges formed local advisory committees of employers for each of their vocational programs to advise on specific vocational program development, revision, job placement of graduates, and other issues important to the relevancy of the vocational programs and their students.

The community college outreach to both the citizens of the state and their employers led to four decades of steady enrollment growth. Iowa's community colleges are now the state's fastest growing sector of higher education. By 2008, almost one-fourth of all Iowans between the ages of 18 and 64 enrolled annually in a community college course (Department of Education 2008).

Beginning with their enabling legislation in 1965, funding for the Department of Education to provide statewide coordination, planning, and oversight for the state system of community colleges was inadequate. Understaffed and underfunded, the Department of Education's primary focus was K12 education; its functions with the community colleges were consultative and regulatory rather than coordination, strategic planning, or advocacy (Friedel 2009). While the Department of Education developed and advocated annual legislative proposals on behalf of K12 education statewide, generally the community colleges were left to fend for themselves in the state political process (Friedel 2009).

The absence of proactive and unifying state coordination resulted in the community colleges forming their own statewide organizations. In 1966, within one year of passage of the enabling legislation, the 15 community college presidents agreed to coordinate their legislative agenda and other statewide initiatives (Varner 2006). The presidents formalized their association as the Iowa Association of Community College Presidents (IACCP). They would attempt to develop and support a unified annual legislative agenda. That same year, a statewide association, the Iowa Council of Area School Boards (ICASB), comprising the representatives of the community college boards of directors was formed. In August 1971, the ICASB incorporated as the Iowa Association of Community College Trustees (IACCT) (Varner 2006). The significance of the IACCP and the IACCT would be acknowledged by state legislators as evidenced by their numerous requests for these groups to prepare reports for various legislative standing and ad hoc committees.

As the community colleges strived to fulfill their mission, funding was critical. The primary revenue streams for the general operating funds are state general aid (through an annual appropriation to the Department of Education, which specifies each community college's allocation), student tuition and fees, local property taxes, federal funds, and miscellaneous income. Minor miscellaneous income is available through earned interest, sales, services, and gifts. Both federal funds and local property taxes have shrunk over the years, the former dwindling from 11 percent to about 2.45 percent and the latter from about 12 percent to 4.75 percent of total general operating fund revenues from 1980 to 2009 (Department of Education 2010). From 1980 to 2005, the proportion of total generating funds generated by state general aid would shift from about 50 percent to 37 percent, and student tuition and fees would increase from 24 percent to about 49 percent. In 2001, student tuition and fees would become the principal source of operating funds for the community colleges (Department of Education 2010). The local board of trustees sets tuition and fees. In 2010, tuition and fees ranged from the low of $111/credit hour to a high of $153/credit hour.

With the inadequacy of state support and increasing operating costs, the colleges sought alternative and stable funding sources to meet the needs of their constituents. These constituents include local businesses and industries, and the employers for which the program graduates seek employment and job advancement. Employers serve on the advisory committees of every career and technical program, provide expertise in curriculum development and improvement, and assist the colleges in the acquisition of new technologies and equipment. Employers also provide program and technical expertise, equipment and updated technology, internships and on-the-job training opportunities, and sometimes even the instructional facilities.

By the early 1980s, Iowa's community colleges were developing and growing into institutions noted for their flexibility, responsiveness, resourcefulness, and partnerships with the public and private sectors (Friedel 2009). Through leadership committed to the "community" dimension of their mission, the community colleges had emerged "front and center" in local workforce and community development initiatives. Community colleges had become characterized by a positive, "can-do" attitude, capable of assisting local employers in navigating the red tape of government programs and incentives and in securing a qualified, well-trained workforce. In time, and with support from their local businesses and industries, the colleges built business and industry centers to provide training and retraining for workers in the knowledge and skills needed for the adoption of new technologies and processes, and in worker skills upgrading (Friedel 2009).

Context for Financial Innovation

The community college commitment to local employers and to service for all people, especially those most in need of educational opportunity, became highly visible during time of economic distress. The 1980s were particularly difficult for the nation's agricultural heartland. Record numbers of family farms went bankrupt and manufacturing plants closed production lines and laid off thousands of workers whose jobs were permanently eliminated.

The farm crisis reverberated throughout Iowa's manufacturing base: layoffs and plant closings struck the farm implement manufacturers of John Deere, J. I. Case, International Harvester, and Caterpillar, and their suppliers and transporters. The heavy manufacturing foundation of the state's economy was eroding along with the disappearance of family farms. The decline of the manufacturing sector had a domino effect on the construction and associated trades. Enrollments in the traditional associate degree vocational programs dropped as their curriculum relevancy and placement of program graduates into jobs declined. What had historically been a migration from the rural communities to the cities escalated into an exodus of Iowans to the Sunbelt.

As the recession of the early 1980s unfolded, the community colleges reduced or eliminated their noncredit nonvocational and adult leisure activity classes, and shifted the personnel and other resources supporting these programs and services to workforce and other short-term career preparatory classes (Anderson 2008). The drop in state tax and other revenues had a ripple effect across the public sector in the state. The drop in state revenues resulted in a midyear across-the-board cut mandated by the governor, declines in the annual general aid appropriations to the community colleges, and a drop in the local property tax revenues to the community colleges.

Community colleges responded with midyear tuition and fees increases. They deferred maintenance and reduced the number of personnel. This involved elimination of programs, outreach, and other student support services. They reduced and or eliminated developmental courses and programs; closed of off-campus sites, enacted early retirement incentives to replace seasoned and more highly paid faculty and staff with less-expensive and less-experienced personnel, and many full-time faculty were replaced with adjunct faculty to reduce instructional costs. The cuts in revenues and expenditures were deep and the colleges were faced with programs ill-matched to state economic development efforts to attract new businesses and industries to grow a more diversified, service-oriented state economy.

The community colleges provided programs for displaced homemakers who were entering the job market after years of absence from the workforce. The community colleges provided career and skills assessments, education, and training for the displaced farmers and other workers who had lost their jobs and livelihood, and whose skills were obsolete in the new and emerging industries and businesses (Friedel 2009). The community colleges partnered with their regional workforce development centers to form teams of "first responders" comprised of assessment experts and career counselors who entered places of employment immediately after an announcement of plant closure or layoffs.

Local and regional economic development efforts also recognized the criticality of job retraining for those displaced from farms and jobs, and the need to both attract a more diversified industry/employer base and to retrofit existing employers with a competitive advantage through increased productivity.

Another alarm was sounding: Iowa had long rested on its laurels as ranking first in the nation in education, with the highest state high-school graduation rate and high ACT scores for graduating high-school seniors. The increasing "brain drain" of its college graduates to the Sunbelt states was another signal that a nonpartisan, unified approach was necessary to create the educational and training programs necessary to develop and sustain a skilled workforce for new industry sector jobs. There was a growing realization that new employers would not be attracted to the state if there were not a qualified labor pool from which they could draw their workforce.

The urgency of the economic recession was the catalyst for consensus building and action. Up to this time, the community colleges had their own lobbyists; some had formed consortia amongst themselves to financially support lobbyists who worked on their behalf. If you liken state revenues to a pie, as one entity gained a small slice for its special project, the funds that were available to the community college state appropriation or to any other community college special interest became smaller. The pie was shrinking; the size of each slice and to what it was allocated was determined through the annual legislative appropriations process. Increasingly, the concern emerged that economic development should not be subject to the whims of partisan politics or the ups and downs of the economy.

The community college presidents and trustees seized the moment. They would unify in support of a common legislative agenda. They recognized, as did a majority of state legislators, the governor and the business community that the community colleges were the statewide entity with the capacity and credibility to initiate and sustain regional economic and workforce development initiatives. With a sustained funding source, the community colleges could work with employers in the development and delivery of customized education and training for their new Iowa workforce.

Through the IACCP and the IACCT, the community colleges were able to develop political alliances in support of a common statewide legislative agenda. "According to one state leader involved in the process, a team of creative legislators in Iowa worked with a bond attorney and a representative of a community college, who was also a former U.S. Congressman" (Prince 2006, 12). The institutional self-interests of the community colleges became secondary as the colleges worked with state legislators, industry and union leaders, state agencies' directors, and Governor Branstad to formulate a unified, coordinated approach to workforce and economic development. These state and local groups coalesced around the criticality for action. "Policy makers were motivated to address the outflow of jobs from Iowa and the rapidly expanding numbers of unemployed farmers" (Jobs for the Future 2005, 26). Policy designers worked to satisfy not only the state's needs for a cost neutral training program but also workers' needs for employment and advancement opportunities and employers' needs for a skilled workforce (Jobs for the Future 2005). Legislative action was sought to make the state more competitive in attracting new employers and businesses, and to diversify the base of the state's economy. Legislators sought financial incentives to first, attract new employers to the state, and second, to encourage the expansion of existing businesses in the state.

General Obligation Bonds as a Sustained Funding Source for Economic Development

In 1983, the legislature passed NJTP (Iowa Code Chapter 260E). NJTP was the "nation's first customized job training program to be funded through the sale of bonds rather than through state appropriations. The program is demand driven and self-funded" (Jobs for the Future 2005, 25–26). The bill was designed to both attract new employers to the state, and to encourage existing Iowa employers to expand in the state. NJTP is referred to as the 20E program.

Iowa's innovation is the funding mechanism of general obligation bonds issued by the community colleges to fund customized job training for new business startups and expanding basic sector industries locating or expanding in the state. The underlying premise of the bill is that "the sale of bonds for training would yield an economic return on a par with more traditional, bond-financed economic development efforts" (Prince 2007, 16).

[The NJTP] was created under several constraints: no new state funds could be appropriated and no state agencies could be created; the program would need to be free to participating businesses and workers; it would need to devolve decision-making authority down to local levels; and it would need to stipulate that no funds could be expended unless jobs were created. The NJTP also had a specific objective: to bring business to Iowa. (Jobs for the Future 2005, 25)

The NJTP is unique for no upfront funding was necessary. The community colleges issue tax-exempt or taxable bonds for up to ten years on behalf of the eligible businesses (Varner 2006). The proceeds of the bond sale are used to pay for the training and the related administrative costs. The training may be provided by community college staff or third parties contracted by the community college to provide the training. The community college reimburses the employer for the approved training courses. "The training may take two to three years to complete, necessitating a reserve to support the ongoing administrative costs of the program" (Prince 2006, 11). The community colleges are authorized to collect the administrative fees at the time of sale of the bonds, or spread them out over the repayment period of ten years. These administrative funds have enabled the community colleges to support to "a broad range of economic and workforce development activities, and special programs, in the community college regions for which other funds were not available" (Prince 2006, 11).

The community colleges finance the job-training program through the sale of bonds that are the obligations of the community college, and not of the employer. The principal and interest payments on the bonds are "repaid over a maximum of ten years through the diversion of 1.5 percent of gross payroll tax revenue, which is 50 percent of Iowa withholding tax revenue or 3.0 percent of gross payroll for jobs with wages exceeding the county or regional average" (Jobs for the Future 2005, 5). In other words, instead of the employee withholdings going into the state's general fund, the withholdings are diverted to the community colleges to pay off the bonds. When the bonds are retired, the employee withholdings are released directly into the state's general fund.

The general obligation bonds are issued by each community college. The bonds are secured through a stand by property tax levy that the community college board of trustees are authorized to levy in the event of a project default (if the state income tax repayments stream went away). The levy would generate the funding necessary to make the annual principal and interest payments on the defaulted bonds. This levy has been used in only a limited number of cases. There is no statutory limit on the amount of bonding a community college can issue in any given year. The bonds are issued for a ten- year period although the community colleges retire them on an average of eight years. The bonds do not have an annual approval provision. The 260E program is not part of the annual legislative appropriations process. The program is demand-driven and the funds are intended to support primarily noncredit customized training on a no cost basis for eligible employers creating new jobs. The availability of this program is not impacted by downturns in the economy and the resulting reductions in state general aid funding.

The 260E program is an economic development incentive designed to incent new job creation. The revenue from the state personal income tax revenue stream authorized and diverted to the community college by the program did not exist prior to the new jobs being created and therefore does not come from the state's existing revenue stream. This new revenue stream is shared between the 260E program and the state (50/50 in the enabling legislation).

It is important to note that bonding is the financial vehicle used to facilitate the program. Bonding provides a meaningful amount of funding to the employer, up front, to train the new employees hired to fill the new jobs creation. The financing vehicle is the state income tax withholding being generated by the new employees in the new jobs.

The local community colleges' board of directors approves the agreements with employers. The community colleges work with employers to develop the training programs and then monitor the training activities. Thus, the actual training that is provided is dependent on the needs of the new workers as determined by the employer in consultation with the community college, and within the limits of the legislation, program rules, and college policies. Examples of program services and training range from welding, blueprint reading, computer training, supervisory skills, stress and time management, principles of electronics, to total quality improvement processes, and computer-aided drafting (Jobs for the Future 2005).

Community colleges work in partnership with the employers to develop the training program. There are few limitations on the type of training delivered to the new employees. The amount of funding available for training is driven by the number of new jobs created and their salaries. These factors determine the state income tax withholding repayment system and through a financial modeling process, the net amount of funding available for training. There is no cost to the employer for this program.

In the 1986 federal tax reform, Iowa's Senator Chuck Grassley secured from Congress an exemption allowing Iowa's community colleges to continue issuing tax-exempt bonds in support of the New Jobs Training Program (Prince 2006).

The Iowa Department of Economic Development (IDED) is designated as the state agency to coordinate and provide oversight of the program. IDED has the responsibility to keep track of projects, monitor progress and to annually report on results (Varner 2006). "The department makes certain that all new jobs meet certain wage requirements and are in industries that provide Iowa with a comparative advantage in the marketplace" (Jobs for the Future 2006, 6). A cost–benefit analysis of the program by the Iowa Department of Revenue and Iowa Workforce Development is now being conducted, but the findings are not available at the time of this publication.

From 1983 to 2006, the New Jobs Training program provided job training assistance to over 140,000 Iowans in new jobs (IDED 2006). The number of projects per year has ranged from 29 to 149, and the number trained from 2,031 to 11,547 per year. Annual certificates totaled a high of $58,379.000 in fiscal year 2005. These 140,000 Iowans trained in jobs for new employers to the state, or with employers who were expanding in the state and were in need of workers with a new or upgraded skill set.

Current Ramifications

As a result of NJTP, Iowa's community colleges developed into regional economic and workforce development intermediaries, stepping up region-ally as the lead organization in serving both the skill needs of employ-ers and the career needs of workers. As intermediaries, throughout their communities, community colleges "align the economic and workforce development needs within their districts in order to develop demand-led regional growth strategies" (Prince 2006, 13). Two key features of NJTP described above have been major contributors to this development: the sustained nature of the funding and the allowance of an administrative fee to the community college. A direct outcome of this funding is the 140,000 Iowans trained in new jobs with employers located in the state.

In an attempt to mirror Iowa's success in developing general obliga-tions bonds as a funding mechanism for regional economic and workforce through its community colleges, the legislatures of Missouri and Kansas followed with comparably modeled legislation. As Heath Prince (2006) concluded in his analysis of these three states, there are a number of rea-sons why the practice of using bonds to finance job training is relatively rare in the workforce development field. They include

> the complexity of the legislative process; the high level of capacity needed to administer bond-financed programs; the need for a means to guarantee the bonds; their tendency to be demand-driven rather than population-focused; the requirements of a state income tax as a repayment mechanism; and equity concerns over the diversion of state taxes. (12)

These are not insurmountable factors as the recession of the 1980s bears witness; economic crisis provided the catalyst for the establishment of an innovative funding mechanism for community colleges in Iowa, followed by Missouri and Kansas.

The authority to issue bonds to provide customized training as a means to attract new and expanding industries to the state, has provided Iowa's community colleges with a sustained funding source for regional economic development leadership and coordination. State systems of community colleges seeking a sustainable funding source to support workforce training and regional economic development may find Iowa's pioneering work in general obligation bonds a model to replicate.

References

Anderson, E. 2008. Personal communication interview with the Former Chief, Bureau of Community Colleges and Workforce Preparation, Department of Education on 16 April 2008 in Iowa by Janice Friedel.

Friedel, Janice. 2009. "Engines of economic development: The origins and evolution of Iowa's community colleges." Paper presented at the Organization of Educational Historians Annual Conference, Chicago, IL, September 18, 2009.

Department of Education. 2007. *The Annual Condition of Iowa Community Colleges Report.* Des Moines, IA: Department of Education.

Department of Education. 2006. *Shaping the Future: Iowa's Community College Statewide Strategic Plan 2006 Annual Progress Report.* Des Moines, IA: Department of Education.

Department of Education. 2010. *Community College Tuition and Fees Report.* Des Moines, IA: Department of Education.

Iowa Code 260E (2009). Accessed from http://coolice.legis.state.ia.us/Cool-ICE /default.asp?category=billinfo&service=iowaCode&ga=83#260E

Iowa Department of Economic Development. 2006. *Annual Report 2006.* Des Moines: IA: Department of Economic Development

Jobs for the Future. 2005. *Building Skills, 2005. Increasing Economic Vitality: A Handbook of Innovative State Policies.* Boston, MA: Jobs for the Future.

Prince, Heath, ed. 2006. *General Obligation Bonds as a Financial Mechanism for Regional Economic and Workforce Development Authorities: Lessons from Three States.* Washington, DC: National Center for Education and the Economy.

Prince, Heath. ed., 2007. *Strategies for Financing Workforce Intermediaries: Working Papers.* Boston: Jobs for the Future/National Fund for Workforce Solutions.

Varner Jeremy. 2006. "Forty Years of Growth and Achievement: A History of Iowa's Community Colleges." In *Forty Years of Growth and Achievement: A History of Iowa's Community Colleges,* ed. J. Friedel. Des Moines, IA: Department of Education.

Case Study 5

Planning and Implementing a Voter-Approved Capital Bond Issue for the Alamo Community College District

John W. Strybos

Background

The Alamo Community College District (ACCD), now called the "Alamo Colleges," is the second largest community college system in Texas and the eighth largest in the United States. ACCD's enrollment increased 36 percent from 38,850 credit students (headcount) in the fall 1998 to 52,781 in the spring 2005. During this time of unexpected dramatic growth, no new buildings had been completed, even though there was a need for them. Financial demands on the operating budget limited the availability of funds to use to rent or lease additional classroom space and the real-estate market did not have sufficient available capacity to meet the demand for classroom space. There were other options that could be used to finance the lease, purchase, or construct new classroom buildings. However, the board of trustees selected to use financing methods that had worked in the past. The preferred method to finance the new building construction was through the sale of general obligation (GO) bonds that would require a referendum approval by voters of the taxing district for a property tax increase for a period of 30 years.

Governance of community colleges varies across the country. Some community colleges have appointed boards and in Texas the board of trustees is elected. Alamo Colleges have nine trustees whose six-year terms are staggered, with no term limits. At the time of the bond referendum, several of the trustees were in their first term and were relatively new to the board.

In October 2004, the board of trustees called for a bond referendum to be held in February 2005, which was proposed by administration and reviewed by a citizen committee. The voters rejected this bond referendum due to concerns over combining the nursing and allied health programs at San Antonio College and St. Philip's College at a new medical center campus, concerns over a property tax increase, and by low voter turnout. The eligible voters were residents of Bexar County and each region of the county had specific concerns about the impact of the bond on the college that services a particular area. Although the Alamo Colleges serves a large region, this bond referendum then became about local issues.

Steps for Reform

From this defeat, Alamo Colleges learned that the capital improvement program (CIP) projects had to be thoroughly explained and defined to the community. The biggest challenge was to define CIP priorities such as which projects should be constructed on which campuses and what budget allocations should be used. Defining the CIP would be a complex process that would involve five steps driven in part by the needs at each college. The steps were as follows:

Step one involved project budget definition. Alamo Colleges used Texas higher education coordinating board construction cost data as the base line for the estimated costs of the buildings. In the summer of 2005, these were reasonable cost estimating values. The values used were $100 per square foot for renovation projects, $210 per square foot for new academic building construction, and $300 per square foot for nursing allied health career buildings. These are total project cost dollars that include hard construction costs and soft costs such as architect and engineer fees, and furniture, and fixtures and equipment.

Step two related to project definition. The project definition was driven by academic needs, workforce needs, and growth projections. New plans were developed that were unique to each college, but most importantly were defined by the college users including students and showed building shape, size, mass, and academic functions. A board appointed a knowledgeable and highly influential citizens group who was directly involved in the master plan development and helped guide the final product. For example, for Northwest Vista College, the master plan specifically identified the number of classrooms needed for different academic programs as well as defined academic program space for programs that essentially did not currently exist in the fine and performing arts areas. All of the colleges had additional surface parking and physical plant and utility infrastructure improvements that would be necessary to support the new buildings. The project definitions were matched to building sizes and the project budgets and then presented by the college presidents to the chancellor. The needs of Alamo Colleges were not distinct, but the process of developing understandable project definitions was a critical part of making this step a success.

Step three occurred simultaneously with the project definition step and prepared additional data to support the CIP. This step consisted of updating Alamo Colleges design and construction standards that were then used by the architects and engineers A district-wide facility condition assessment was completed that identified which facilities needed to be renovated and their priority, and provided budgets for these projects. Detailed workforce studies were prepared for several key programs including diesel mechanics, veterinary technology, and nursing allied health careers. A space inventory and space utilization study compared ACCD space to our Texas peers and recommended a goal of 92 square foot per full time student equivalent. An overall service area demographics study showed student growth and capture rates. A socioeconomic benefit study showed the very dramatic economic impact of Alamo Colleges and San Antonio.

Step four was the public review of the projects. Chancellor Daniel Derrico reviewed and presented the CIP and their budgets to the board of trustees. The board of trustees then appointed an independent 27-member community-wide committee to review all of the projects. Two independent facilitators, one of whom was a well-known and highly respected retired judge, were used to assist in this committee process. The committee met during June and July 2005 and reviewed all of the projects. On August 3, 2005, the ACCD Citizens' CIP Committee unanimously recommended to the board of trustees that they should call for a general obligation bond referendum. The use and involvement of a citizens' committee was an innovation that was critical to the passage of this bond referendum. Many entities that have bond referendums use political action committees or some type of citizen oversight committee. The unique part of this citizens' oversight committee was the use of facilitators to keep the process moving forward and to ensure that all opinions of the committee membership were considered.

Step five was the general obligation bond referendum. The board of trustees called for the bond referendum to be held in November 2005. In order to ensure the passage of the bonds, a separate bond committee was formed. In Texas, public funds cannot be used to support these types of referendums. This bond committee was separate from ACCD and was composed of interested and concerned private citizens. This group coordinated and funded marketing, advertising, and fundraising efforts. The trustees, chancellor, vice chancellors, and college presidents took the lead in making presentations to a variety of community groups. As part of the "contract with the voters," the board agreed to appoint a citizens' bond oversight committee and that bond funds would not move between colleges without approval of this committee. This was a critically important pledge to make to the various community groups with special interests in each of the ACCD colleges. In addition, the board adopted a property tax freeze for senior and disabled citizens. Promotional activities included billboards, radio and television spots, and soliciting endorsements from influential citizens, politicians, and community organizations.

The referendum asked the voters to approve the sale of $450 million general obligation bonds to be paid back over a 30-year period and a tax increase of 30 cents per $1,000 of assessed valuation. We promoted the fact that this tax rate increase would amount to only $30 per year on a house valued at $100,000, which was the median house evaluation in Bexar County in 2005; and that the bond proceeds would only be used to improve the four existing Alamo Colleges, and to build a new fifth college. Media coverage of the November 2005 referendum was more favorable than the February 2005 referendum coverage and the CIP had widespread support among the community. It was important to maintain community support to set and maintain the amounts of capital construction bond funds to be spent on each of the district colleges with $ 17,500,000 reserved for district-wide information technology improvements. This bond referendum was approved by an overwhelming majority of voters. The voter approval was approximately 60 percent, with a much higher voter turnout than for the first bond referendum that had been defeated nine months before.

The Alamo Colleges property tax rate consists of two parts. One part is for operations and maintenance and is set at $0.91105 per $1,000 valuation. The other part of the tax rate is for interest and sinking tax rate. The interest and sinking tax rate funds are used to redeem long-term debt such as maintenance tax notes and general obligation bonds. The interest and sinking funds are not used to redeem revenue bonds. Prior to the referendum the interest and sinking rate was $0.1475 per $1,000 valuation. After the referendum, the board of trustees voted to increase the interest and sinking tax rate to $0.4475 per $1,000 valuation, while maintaining the operations and maintenance tax rate at the current level.

Strategic Decision Points

The bond referendum was approved by the voters, but Alamo Colleges essentially had no prior experience managing or implementing a project of this scope and size, nor the personnel resources in place to effectively control the project. Alamo Colleges examined other capital improvement programs to determine why some were a success and others were not and noted success involved key decisions that involved faculty, staff, and students, citizens' bond oversight committee, the chancellor, and the board of trustees.

In comparison, at the same time, Dallas County Community College District had a similar $450 million successful bond referendum on May 15, 2004 with several projects now scheduled to be completed in the fall 2009 and spring 2010. These projects have taken more than five years to complete while the Alamo Colleges projects were completed in less than four years. The delays in completing the Dallas projects would result in significant schedule and budget impacts when compared to the original proposed projects. Likewise, Houston Community College District (HCCD) had a recent capital improvement program that encountered budget problems due to major changes in the scope and information technology projects. These budget problems limited the success of HCCDs.

The first critical decision was to appoint a citizens' bond oversight committee. Alamo successfully applied key decisions from other construction projects to help minimize schedule and budget impacts. This included getting the design consultants and program managers under contract as soon as possible. In January 2006, the board approved a committee charter and appointed a 20-member committee, with some members selected by influential community groups. They meet monthly. Committee members are appointed for annual terms, but may be reappointed by the board of trustees each year. They prepared an annual report to the board. As the eyes and ears of this community, this committee relays the concerns of the community to the colleges and vice versa. The committee reviewed and approved recommendations for consultants, contractors, and changes in projects prior to their presentation to the board. The citizens' bond oversight committee meetings were televised on the local public access channel and recorded with presentations and meeting minutes available on the ACCD website.

The second critical decision was when to sell the bonds and for how much at each issue date. Under Texas law, contracts for design and construction services cannot be awarded without established funding. A commitment to sell bonds is insufficient to award a construction contract. Accordingly, the projects could not start until the bonds had been sold. While it would have been possible to sell all $450 million at one time, there was no specific need, nor any overriding financial reason to do so with respect to the financial markets. Scheduling these bond sales allowed the bond interest costs to be optimized, but also allowed all construction projects to be funded in a timely basis. The amounts varied based on the ability to spend the money and to construct the facilities in a timely and cost-efficient manner. Indeed, since progress was made rapidly, the second sale of bonds was moved forward by six months. The flexibility to exercise this option allowed the construction to continue rather than coming to a stop. In addition, the bond proceeds were invested until they were needed and cumulatively through November 30, 2009 earned an additional $31 million of interest income net of arbitrage liabilities. The additional interest income was critical in being able to construct CIP projects that were initially deferred due to funding constraints.

The third critical decision was how to staff the overall management of the CIP. Alamo Colleges did not have sufficient staff, or the funds to support a staff that could manage the design and construction of projects of this size. In addition, part of the "contract with the voters" was that all of the bond proceeds would be used on the CIP projects' direct construction costs and soft costs. No funds were to be used to support Alamo College's positions for the CIP. A business decision was made to outsource the program management and the architect and engineering services. Two separate program management firms were used with assignments for projects on specific campuses.

The program managers had day-to-day responsibility for the overall management of the design and construction of the projects and reported to the associate vice chancellor of facilities operations and construction management on the projects. Five different architect and engineering teams were selected, one for each college. Two different space programming firms prepared detailed programming documents for all the buildings. This project confirmed that it is crucial to have the right consultants working on the team to keep the projects on schedule and within the project budget. In addition to the above design and management firms, Alamo Colleges used an outside consultant on large-scale facilities projects, Chris Moran, to confirm that ACCD was on the right track and to highlight future potential problems that could adversely affect the final CIP product. Other consultants worked on Alamo Colleges business process analysis (BPA) to assist in improving overall operations. The design and management consultants that worked directly on the CIP projects were paid using bond funds. This was a planned cost of the projects.

The fourth critical decision was which construction delivery method to use. The board of trustees approved the use of five construction manager at risk (CMR) firms, one for each college. The CMR firms were selected in August 2006 and immediately began preconstruction services. The use of CMRs allowed guaranteed maximum price (GMP) contract awards when the construction documents, plans, and specifications were less than 100 percent complete. This allowed the CMR firms to begin the "buyout" of the construction project and helped to control construction costs. This process has resulted in more than $1.8 million of GMP reductions through January 31, 2010. These GMP reduction funds have been used to fund other CIP deferred projects. At the same time, the risk that the project costs may exceed the guaranteed maximum price (GMP) is the construction manager at risk's (CMR) and not the owner's risk.

The fifth critical decision was how to manage the budget for each college. Although the initial construction cost estimates were reasonable at the time of the formulation of the bond projects, by the time contractors were ready to begin preconstruction services, unprecedented construction inflation was adversely affecting all of the project budgets. The teams consisting of the college administration, program managers, architects and engineers, construction manager at risk, and Alamo Colleges worked to value engineer all of the projects. The colleges identified projects that could be deferred. Building sizes were reduced to stay within budgets. These hard decisions were made by the colleges with input from faculty, staff, and students as the 20-year old building were in dire need of upgrade. The rescoped projects that were 25 percent smaller than the original proposal were then presented to the citizens' bond oversight committee and the board of trustees. The redesign helped avoid the adverse impacts of San Antonio construction inflation.

Project Outcomes and Assessments

All projects of this size and scope have their share of opponents and this one is no exception. Although, ACCD had a good track record of using small, minority, women-owned business enterprise (SMWBE) firms, the ability to implement this on a program of this size was questioned and a key staff role to fill was a SMWBE diversity administrator. In retrospect, more time was spent on this topic than any of the other citizens' bond oversight committee meetings. The diversity administrator position was first recommended in December 2006 and was filled in March 2008. The delay in hiring was due to a combination of operating budget constraints and that this was a new position within ACCD. For the first two years of the CIP, the data gathering and reporting were not clear and concise. The hiring of a full-time SMWBE diversity administrator paid off in that the data reports were clearly understood and answered core questions that the committee had been asking. The data also clearly showed that Alamo Colleges had exceeded and continued through 2010 to exceed the SMWBE goals. In retrospect, this position should have been filled at an earlier date.

Communication with internal users is always a challenge on building projects. It is frustrating and at times impossible for end users to take two-dimensional plans and visualize three-dimensional spaces. While three-dimensional modeling has been available for some time, it is still the exception rather than the rule in developing building projects. This resulted in confusion with the users when they enter completed spaces and found that the room was not everything that they had imagined that it would be. In order to address internal communications issues, additional design review meetings were held and more frequent site visits with the users were implemented at which the construction manager would address user-identified concerns. This worked to help ease the users discomfort and to keep the projects on schedule with minimal impacts to the budget and the schedule. Another key element of the internal communications was the need to identify six months in advance when a building would be 100 percent complete with all furniture, fixtures, equipment, and information technology installed and operational so that classes could be scheduled for the building. The colleges had to have very clear and specific dates so that class schedules could be prepared, new faculty hired, and personnel moved to the new buildings.

Sustainable design is a critical element for projects of this size. A business decision was made to not have any of the buildings be leadership in energy and environmental design (LEED) certified. At the time of starting the design and construction projects, the added initial cost of LEED certification would have resulted in the reduction of additional square footage. While the lower operating costs of LEED certified buildings are well documented, the higher initial cost for the certification could not be supported by the budgets. This decision has worked for ACCD in that the utility costs to operate these buildings are lower than older buildings. Sustainable design is achievable without having LEED certified buildings. Alamo Colleges applied the LEED checklist to all of the projects and incorporated sustainable design features throughout. For example, Northwest Vista College included the construction of a water feature that serves the purposes of storm water retention basin, rainwater runoff collection, air handler unit water collection, and recycled water collection and storage for landscaping irrigation and chilled water supply. All buildings were located to take advantage of natural lighting and to optimize the energy demands of the buildings. Texas engineering experiment station energy systems laboratory assisted Alamo Colleges in implementing energy saving devices throughout the new projects including submeters for all buildings so that facilities that are wasting energy can be identified.

Value engineering was a critical element of the success of this CIP. When the construction managers at risk were contracted for preconstruction services they began a critical review of the plans and specifications. For almost all of the projects, the CMRs projected that they would come in over budget, unless modifications were made. The only way to keep the projects within the budget was to value engineer them. This process involved the faculty, staff, and students to resize projects and to identify projects to be deferred. This process kept the projects within the budget and on schedule.

Lessons Learned

The six lessons learned from this successful capital improvement program (CIP) project are listed below.

There needs to be a total support from the leadership of the institution. During the time of the CIP from the first referendum in February 2005 through January 2010, Alamo Colleges had three different chancellors and four different vice chancellors of administration. The board of trustees had a change of two trustees. The associate vice chancellor of facilities operations and construction management was the same individual throughout this process and was able to provide constant strong leadership with a vision of the final product that was a key to the success of the capital improvement program. The role of the associate vice chancellor of facilities operations and construction management was critical in the success of this project. The associate vice chancellor of facilities operations and construction management had direct day-to-day operational control and responsibility for the capital improvement program. The key functions of this role included responsibility for communications, budget and schedule. The communications role was critical as the single point of contact for the program managers, college presidents, chancellor, vice chancellor of administration, and citizen bond oversight committee. Filling this position with the right individual is critical to CIP success.

All key stakeholders need to be identified. Identifying the key stakeholders, working with and keeping them informed every step of the way through communication, transparency, openness, and integrity facilitated the success of the capital improvement program. Faculty, staff, and students were involved throughout the planning processes and made tours of the facilities as they neared completion.

There needs to be constant communication among all stakeholders. Constant communication with the citizens' bond oversight committee kept the public informed of all aspects of the program. The local newspaper, *The San Antonio Express News*, and the student newspapers, primarily the San Antonio College Ranger were provided copies of all documents given to the board of trustees and the citizens' bond oversight committee. It is critical that the membership on this committee be committed to the CIP as a whole and open to discussion of different and even opposing views.

There need to be preplanning. Preplanning was a key to the success of the bond. The preplanning has to be clearly defined, yet flexible enough to deal with changes in the construction economy and academic changes. During the life of some of these projects, four to five years, information technology needs and instructional methods will change significantly at least once. This has a direct impact on the design and construction of the facilities. Preplanning includes conducting work force studies, updating master plans, conducting demographic studies to estimate future student enrollments, and developing concept plans for the proposed buildings.

Another lesson learned is to develop consistent design and construction standards. This allows the architects and construction managers at-risk to have a very good idea of what the owners expectations were with respect to the final product.

There needs to be a schedule, quality, and cost controls. Schedule, quality, and cost controls are critical on projects of this nature. The use of outside consultant program management firms was fundamental to implementing schedule, quality, and cost controls. These consultants facilitated value engineering on all projects, kept them within budget, and delivered to the users the key facilities they needed. They were a critical link between the building architects and contractors and the college administration, responsible directly to the associate vice chancellor of facilities operations and construction management.

Conclusion

The elements required for a successful CIP project, as for any major project, include integrity, dedication, competence, support, cooperation, flexibility, transparency, constant communication, continuous evaluation, good planning, and excellent execution. The economy in 2010 is very different from 2005. There are increased demands on community colleges for new academic programs and increased enrollments due to changes in the labor market. The lessons learned in this case are even more relevant now, due to the budget constraints on higher education institutions, than they were in 2005. The single most important elements would be to ensure that the right personnel, consultants, and contractors are selected to plan and implement the capital improvement program. This CIP was unique for ACCD in that ACCD had no prior experience managing and implementing projects of this size and yet was able to successfully complete the CIP without major modifications to the administrative structure of the organization.

Case Study 6

Using Student Fees to Support Education Abroad

Michael Giammarella

In 1989, the Borough of Manhattan Community College (BMCC) developed an innovative initiative that provides student scholarships for short-term, faculty-led study abroad programs through funds generated by student activity fees. The initiative, the first of its kind in The City University of New York (CUNY), and for any US community college, was done in accordance with the university's by-laws. However, given the peripheral status of education abroad programs, very few community colleges have repeated this effort. The life-altering benefit of education abroad is well documented and is the cornerstone for many community college internationalization efforts (Raby 2008). The following pages document the process at BMCC to facilitate the implementation of a similar program at other colleges and universities.

The objective of the 1989 BMCC funding initiative was to alleviate the financial barrier that kept the college's diverse and economically disadvantaged student population from participating in education abroad programs, and thus enriching their educational and personal experiences. The BMCC student enrollment continues to reflect that profile. For the spring and fall semesters 2010, an average of 22,723 students enrolled at the college. Approximately 33.5 percent of the students were African American, 37.8 percent Latino, 14.2 percent Asian, and 0.2 percent Native American. Additionally, 59 percent of the students were women. Approximately, 66 percent of the students received either a Pell grant, and/or New York State tuition assistance or both financial aid awards. Education abroad programs cost more than typical community college tuition/fees, and thus, creative means to help fund these programs are required for continued student access and program success.

Historical Context

To understand the significance of this initiative and the impact that it can have as a model throughout the United States, a chronological understanding of the opportunities and challenges in passing the initiative are highlighted. The roots of a study abroad component at BMCC were planted in the early 1970s with an increased racial and ethnic awareness that many nontraditional students brought to the college and which helped support BMCC to be the first community college to offer short-term study programs to Nigeria, Israel, and Puerto Rico. The College Open Admissions Policy was used as the foundation for partially funding these programs by the BMCC Association, a college-wide committee made up of faculty, administrators, and students, whose role was to review and supervise the college student activity fee budget including the disbursement of student government fee allocations.

At that time, the process for approving funding for study abroad programs was informal and inconsistent. Budget requests were subject to the whims of student government leaders and college administrators who were careful to avoid being accused of favoritism and mismanagement of student funds. The obvious weaknesses of lack of transparency led a group of faculty members and students to propose a permanent funding formula to partially finance the three-summer study abroad programs and a new fourth program to Italy. Each program offered three credit courses in academic departments, a key requirement for a viable, faculty-led study abroad component.

It took numerous meetings to explore various funding formulas, including fund-raising events at the college, private corporate sponsors, foundations, and the use of student activity fee monies in accordance to CUNY's by-laws. In the end, the group opted for the student activity fee option as the best way to bring about a permanent formula to fund the college's study abroad programs. The other options required considerable, time-consuming work that most members of the group were reluctant to do, and, most importantly, provided no guarantee of obtaining adequate and permanent funding.

The proposed funding process relied on provisions in Article 15 (Student Activity Fee), Section 15.10 of the university's by-laws which provided for the use of a referendum "to earmark the Student Activity Fee for a specific purpose...without changing the total Student Activity Fee." The provision served the purpose in that it obviated any criticism from the Student Government Association and the college administration with having to deal with an increase in the student activity fee to fund the college's study abroad programs. Article 16, Section 16.2 also provided a specific expenditure category: extracurricular educational program to justify a rationale for the allocation and expense of student activity fees to fund study abroad programs.

In the fall of 1988, a referendum called for the permanent, annual allocation of $93,600 to fund 72 partial scholarships of $1,300 each. The funding formula reflected the average cost of program expenses per student (air fare, room and board, excursions, etc.) at the time the referendum was finalized. Each scholarship represented the BMCC Association 60 percent share of each student program expenses with 40 percent to be paid by the student. Students were also responsible for all course tuition/fees and pocket money.

Early in the 1989 spring semester, volunteers circulated petitions and made efforts to convince all stakeholders of the educational benefits of supporting the referendum. At the same time, three new faculty members including this chapter's author, were elected to the Ad Hoc Study Abroad Committee by the College's Faculty Council, which helped solidify support among faculty. At the first meeting, the committee members agreed that its most important role was to promote international education programs at the college, and that the study abroad scholarships were essential to any campus internationalization efforts. The by-laws Article 15.10 required 10 percent of the "appropriate student body" signatures, which that semester was 12,874 f/t and p/t students. In April 1989, the committee delivered approximately 1,300 valid student signatures, which was more than the 10 percent required by the by-laws. On May 9, 1989, during the annual student government election, the referendum was placed on the ballot and passed overwhelmingly in a vote of 168 to 26. The referendum earmarked 24 percent of the total student activity fees collected in the 1988 fall and 1989 spring semester, respectively, for the four summer study abroad programs, which amounted to $93,600 annually.

After the Student Government Association (SGA) election, some of the newly elected SGA leadership tried to undermine the hard-won victory of the study abroad referendum. Although these students initially supported the referendum, they then realized that there would be less monies for their own pet projects. The SGA president, an international student from Nigeria, whom I knew at the time while serving as the College's Coordinator of International Student Services, in one of his memoranda, noted that earmarking $93,600 for study abroad programs "would be wasteful at best." Because of these few students, it took until April 17, 1990 for the College's Election Review Committee to validate the study abroad referendum "the 168 to 26 student body vote in favor of the permanent, annual allocation of US$93,600 to the Study Abroad Committee by the BMCC Association, Inc. is legitimate and should no longer be questioned." The vote reflected the support given by students for the referendum.

For the next two years, due to other internal problems at the college, including student protests about possible tuition increases and budget cuts, President Augusta Kappner did not authorize action on the referendum. Although student opposition ended early in spring 1992, President Kappner did not openly support full implementation of the referendum. Moreover, President Kappner did authorize partial funding and in spring 1992, the BMCC Association only authorized US$10,000 to fund the Latin American Heritage (PRN 475) program, which combined cultural experiences in Puerto Rico and the Dominican Republic. In 1993, $20,000 was allocated to help fund the Black Experience in Africa (BLK 253) program to Senegal. In each case, the amount helped provide scholarships, but was short of the required full allocation. The limited funding led the members of the ad hoc Study Abroad Committee to rotate the four summer study abroad programs annually rather than offer them concurrently.

In fall 1993, dean of faculty, Stephen Curtis, became acting president of BMCC. In fall 1994, Dr. Marcia Keiz replaced Dr. Curtis as acting president of the college. During Drs. Curtis and Keiz's brief tenure as presidents, the BMCC Association allocated more funds that supported four summer programs, although these funds were still less than the $93,600 earmarked by the 1989 referendum. Full funding was still a few years away, as the problem had to do more with a turnover in the college's administration and bureaucratic wrangling mostly within the Study Abroad Committee over issues pertaining to study abroad course(s) requirements and related matters. In 1995, Antonio Perez was appointed the new BMCC president and administrative continuity and support for the Study Abroad Referendum with full funding was implemented. Moreover, because study abroad was perceived as an integral part of a student's educational experience at BMCC, I was asked by the college's dean of students to provide study abroad related services to students which also included raising awareness of our summer study abroad programs at BMCC (Giammarella 2005). This additional responsibility was to be carried out in conjunction with my responsibilities as coordinator of Foreign Student Services.

Current Efforts to Sustain
International Education

As of this writing, under the leadership of President Antonio Perez, the college's international education component has flourished. Since 1995, full funding has been in accordance with the 1989 referendum, and the number of short-term study abroad program offerings increased to seven. In recent years, President Perez provided additional funding for two, one-week global seminars in Salzburg, Austria, offered during spring break for students and in July for faculty. In addition, both Perez and vice-president for academic affairs, Sadie Bragg, were the first college administrators to undertake on-site visits of study abroad programs so as to get a firsthand view of how the programs function as well as meet with students and administrators from our host institutions.

Currently, the $93,600 annual allocation for education abroad represents only 6.8 percent of the total Student Activity Fees budget ($1,384.396) for the academic year 2010–2011, which are fees collected from the students at the time of registration each semester. While these fees currently meet the needs of three of the original four programs, it does not meet the expenses of the new summer programs. As a result of the insufficient funding, the BMCC Study Abroad Committee, which has become a full-fledged committee of the BMCC Academic Senate, is considering an additional referendum to increase the funding formula. In addition, other internal sources of funding like the college's Auxiliary Enterprise Board, which raises money from vending machines (snacks, soft drinks, etc.) and rental of college space are being considered to help support international education efforts.

The Study Abroad Committee still considers it vitally important that any monies be from a permanent funding source. Therefore, there has not been serious consideration for raising funds from sources like corporate sponsors, foundations, donations, and other related activities. In addition, the absence of a study abroad office with full-time staffing coupled with considerable time-related constraints on the part of faculty and students continues to make the pursuit of these options difficult. However, it is noteworthy that the financial constraints relating to additional monies for study abroad programs has been alleviated by funding from a private foundation, the Wallace Fund of the New York City Community Trust. This foundation has for several years provided funds to The City University of New York Office of International Programs to provide grants ranging from $1,000 to $1,500 to qualified students participating in a university-sponsored summer, winter, and semester-long study abroad programs.

The program known as Study/Travel Opportunities for CUNY Students (STOCS) has been an additional benefit to BMCC students participating in its study abroad programs. For example, in the Summer of 2010, 12 of the 33 BMCC students who participated in the China, Costa Rica, and Italy programs received awards under this program in addition to the BMCC Association Scholarship.

Since the inception of the BMCC study abroad scholarship program, over 400 students have qualified and received scholarships to study in the college's summer study programs: Dominican Republic/Puerto Rico, Senegal/Ghana, Italy, Spain, France, and Switzerland. A seventh summer study program to China was approved in May 2009 by the BMCC Academic Senate. The China program was offered for the first time in the summer 2010. Although full funding as per the 1989 referendum is in place, the amount is insufficient to support the offering of seven programs concurrently, thus requiring an annual rotation of programs.

Since most of the students who receive scholarships are members of underrepresented groups in higher education and economically disadvantaged, the scholarships make it possible for them to participate in a life-changing experience that is readily available to those with higher incomes. The BMCC 1989 Study Abroad Referendum supports open access because it provides opportunities without causing students to incur additional debt. Clearly, because our students face the challenges that many community college students cope with: attending college full-time, working full-time and raising a family, among others, the BMCC study abroad program initiative has allowed them to experience another culture in a four-week period at an affordable price.

Learning Outcomes/Assessment

The education abroad experiences have been very rewarding for students as documented by course evaluations, personal statements, and learning outcomes, the following of which have been identified and evaluated: (a) knowledge of the language and culture of the country that was visited, (b) improved cross-cultural skills, and (c) an understanding of what it means to be a global citizen. Academically, the education abroad programs have promoted the study of languages such as Spanish, French, Italian, and Wolof. Other subjects studied include literature, geography, history, the business of travel and tourism and the local culture. The in-class experience was supplemented with seminars, lectures, excursions, and visits to places of historical and cultural importance. Oversight of the study abroad programs is conducted periodically by college administrators including the college president and the senior vice president for academic affairs, the Study Abroad Committee, and annually by each program coordinator. Stakeholders agree that the investment of a portion of student activity fees to support education abroad continues to be an important educational goal.

The study abroad program benefits are experienced by all students regardless of their majors and personal backgrounds. Ismael Padua, who studied in the Dominican Republic in Summer 2005, noted that "I was able to realize that studying history goes beyond what we read in a book. Readings give you an overview of what a country is about; however, being there all this time gave me the opportunity to relate more to what Dominicans face on a daily basis. I was able to touch the sensibility and suffering Dominicans go through." Gabriela Sanchez-Bravo, who studied in France in summer 2008, wrote "there are tiny pieces of the puzzle of my life that have started to come together after this travel." Moreover, Gabriela stressed the importance of the financial support she received through the BMCC Association Scholarship, which covered 60 percent of her program expenses and allowed her to study abroad.

The exposure to other cultures has allowed BMCC students who participated in the college's programs to view the world as a "global village," and therefore, to think globally when discussing pressing issues, such as economic development, poverty, and disease. In the more than 25 years that I have been directly involved in the college's study abroad programs, unquestionably they have contributed academically and culturally to the enrichment of the education of our students by making their participation financially more affordable for the largely minority student population at BMCC.

The study abroad component at BMCC is part of a larger objective to internationalize the campus. It is the belief of stakeholders that giving our students an opportunity to participate in overseas study experiences prepares them to become informed and better global citizens. Additionally, program participants have contributed in sharing their experiences with other students and faculty on campus through their participation in study abroad fairs, classroom presentations, predeparture orientation sessions provided to students participating in future study abroad programs, and related activities. These activities have also been accompanied by student feedback on their overseas experiences through different evaluation methods. Study abroad faculty coordinators require students to meet in a group session to discuss how their experiences have contributed to their personal growth, whether their academic expectations were met, the extent of cultural learning in the host country, and related matters. Students who received STOCS awards also are asked to answer additional questions about their study abroad experiences in a survey soon after returning to BMCC. In addition, program coordinators submit a written report to the associate dean of academic affairs in which different aspects of each study abroad program are evaluated. Additional program evaluation methods are being considered by the college's Study Abroad Committee to improve student feedback.

The feedback and ideas generated by students participating in BMCC study abroad programs have found their way into the *BMCC Global Pedagogy Handbook* first published in 2007. The handbook lists pedagogical best practices adopted by BMCC faculty to bring global insights to its academic curricula. So far, the handbook, which is periodically updated includes course descriptions, assignments, lessons and projects in thirty-one courses that are part of career programs like Nursing and Business Administration/Management, and courses in the Liberal Arts. Thus, the active participation of students in the study abroad evaluation process will continue to enhance the BMCC mission as it relates to internationalizing the curriculum and the campus.

Conclusion

In conclusion, The Borough of Manhattan Community College is very proud of what it has accomplished for its students; we have broken down barriers to implement and sustain education abroad programs by providing students with study abroad scholarships. It is our belief that we have succeeded in opening doors and creating study abroad opportunities that the college will continue to honor and promote for our students. Despite current economic conditions, the BMCC Association Scholarship Program will remain intact and will continue to be one of the principal components of BMCC internationalization efforts.

Following are current goals that the BMCC Study Abroad Committee plans to maintain and pursue with regards to the college's study abroad funding formula: (a) continue to promote and engage all students at BMCC in viewing the study abroad experience as a very important component of their education in today's global economy, (b) maintain an on-going dialogue, a good working relationship and partnership with current and future college administrators, the BMCC Academic Senate as well as the leadership of the Student Government Association, (c) maintain and support its role in reviewing current and future study abroad program proposals, (d) encourage Study Abroad Program coordinators and student participants of past study abroad programs to raise awareness college-wide of the benefits of the study abroad experience, (e) consider a second referendum in accordance with current CUNY by-laws to increase the funding allocation for BMCC's expanding short-term study abroad program offerings, and (f) encourage the BMCC Study Abroad Committee to explore additional sources of funding BMCC's study abroad programs from other college-based sources such as the Auxiliary Enterprises, the college's Grants Office, and funds raised through fund raising events sponsored by the Office of the President.

Since 1992, the innovative study abroad funding formula and administrative financial support for additional international programs for students have contributed in making BMCC a unique institution. This process provides a model that can be replicated in other institutions. Much can be accomplished by the collaboration of various college constituencies. At the same time, sustained effort and commitment are required in order to assure full implementation of a BMCC-type study abroad funding model. As BMCC seeks to expand the current funding formula, the historical backdrop of this process will ground decisions and guide future efforts.

In retrospect, my experience with the process of funding BMCC study abroad programs has been challenging and satisfying. I have derived and continue to derive much satisfaction in working closely with other faculty members, administrators, and students in bringing to fruition an innovative funding formula that has benefited many students at BMCC. Yet, I have learned the importance of being vigilant, and educating others so that the hard-fought study abroad opportunities I have helped to create will continue to be made available to future generations of students at BMCC.

References

Giammarella, Michael. 2005. "Financing Community College Education Abroad: Best Practices." Paper presented at the NAFSA Annual Conference, Seattle, Washington, May 29 to June 3, 2005.

Raby, Rosalind Latiner. 2008. *IIE Study Abroad White Paper Series Issue Number 3: Expanding Education Abroad at U.S. Community Colleges.* New York: Institute for International Education.

Case Study 7

Revenue Generation through Training a Global Energy Workforce

Gordon Nixon

Context

Southern Alberta Institute of Technology, known as SAIT Polytechnic, is Canada's oldest technical college, established in Calgary in 1916. For over 90 years, SAIT has met the needs of students and the economy by offering a wide range of programming from apprenticeship, one-year certificate, two-year diploma, degree programs, and a variety of continuing education, distance education, corporate training, and international training programs. Today, SAIT serves 15,000 full-time students and 55,000 part-time students in over 100 programs. The college has enjoyed remarkable success with 97 percent of graduates being employed within nine months of graduation and employers being 90 percent satisfied with the quality of the graduates according to college research.

SAIT's annual operating budget is approximately CDN$275 million (revenue), of which approximately 55 percent comes from the provincial government as an annual operating grant. The next highest source of revenue is SAIT's for-profit training business (continuing education, corporate training, and international training), which makes up about 16 percent of the institution's revenue (CDN$42 million), followed by student tuition fees of 15 percent, which are regulated by the provincial government. Revenue from commercial services (parking, bookstore, residence, food operations) generates 8 percent of SAIT's revenue. The remaining revenue from sales, rentals, and services along with donations and invest-ment income comprise the remaining 5 percent of revenue. This case study will describe SAIT's for-profit training business (referred to internally as the "earned-revenue" business) and its recent success in making this part of the business more profitable.

As a public higher education institution, SAIT's shareholders are the citizens of the Province of Alberta. All profits generated from the earned-revenue business are reinvested in SAIT to supplement the government operating grants, maintain lower student tuition fees, address deferred maintenance requirements, upgrade lab and shop equipment, and main-tain greater stability in its revenues despite fluctuating government grants. SAIT has provided for-profit training for more than thirty years; it is deeply engrained in its culture and business model.

In the last five years, SAIT has transformed its revenue-generation capacity. It has done this in two ways by (1) delivering energy-related train-ing globally and (2) implementing the findings from *Good to Great* research (Collin 2001). Collins's three stages to greatness are: *discipline people* (level 5 leadership and first who, then what), *discipline thought* (confront the bru-tal facts and the hedgehog concept), and *discipline action* (culture of disci-pline and the flywheel). The five-year journey has resulted in greater focus on generating new revenue from both domestic and international energy-related training. The administration and staff now have a clearer direction in both the business process and decision-making. SAIT's transformation is continuing; other higher education institutions globally can now use the model and lessons learned to generate new revenues for themselves.

SAIT's programming business model is divided into two sections. One section is the full-time, publically subsidized traditional academic program-ming that is regulated by the provincial (state) government. Internally, this is referred to as the "grant" business because of the annual funding grant from the provincial government. The other section, internally referred to as the "earned-revenue" business, has a, market-based approach in which students and corporations pay the full cost of training and there is less regulation by the provincial government. The earned-revenue business is expected to cover not only direct costs, but also all overhead costs and generate a profit. For accounting purposes, the grant and earned-revenue businesses are internally separated because while the government approves and encourages public higher education institutions to operating for-profit businesses, it needs to ensure that public taxpayer dollars are not used to subsidize the for-profit side of the business.

SAIT's earned-revenue business has resulted in several tangible ben-efits beyond generating new revenue. The benefits include a closer link with industry and a higher profile and stronger image, both locally and internationally. In this context, SAIT can respond quickly to the needs of industry by launching new programming such as individual continuing-education courses in the fast-changing information technology sector to three-month preemployment trades training to a new diploma in energy asset management. This maneuverability has laid the foundation for cash and equipment donations from industry partners who recognize the benefits of working with an institution that can meet their need for skilled workers. In addition, because the earned-revenue program is market-focused, it has contributed to the strong entrepreneurial culture in SAIT and is a key factor in attracting employees.

Over the past few years, SAIT has strategized to increase earned revenue by employing a more disciplined and businesslike approach and ensuring that this part of its business contributes to the college's vision. Limited by reduced government funding and restrictions on tuition-fee increases, SAIT has adopted an "academic capitalism" approach. Academic capitalism, as defined by Slaughter and Leslie (1997), is the alignment of the activities of higher education with the needs of the marketplace. It involves engaging elements of the college with the market (for-profit activities) and market-like (competing for funding) tactics.

SAIT's academic structure is aligned to certain industry sectors. The eight academic schools are: business, construction, energy, health and public safety, hospitality and tourism, information and communications technologies, manufacturing and automation, and transportation. The head of each academic school is the dean, who is responsible for both grant programming and earned-revenue programming and for achieving annual target key performance indicators (KPIs) in student, employer, and employee satisfaction. SAIT's structure is a centralized-decentralized model with each dean responsible for grant, continuing education and career development programming and for delivering domestic and international corporate training. A centralized corporate training department is responsible for the sales of domestic and international training programs; business development managers are the single point of contact with corporate clients. To achieve success, the academic schools and corporate training department must work together to ensure that high-quality programming is delivered to corporate clients. To encourage collaboration between the grant and earned-revenue sides of the business and ensure that the tensions of these different operating models do not result in a destructive "us vs. them" mind-set, all the deans and corporate training directors report to the vice president academic.

Each dean and corporate training director is part of a pay-for-performance bonus system that rewards growth in student numbers and increased revenue generation while ensuring high-quality programming.

A maximum bonus of 25 percent of annual salary is paid at year-end to each dean and director. Managers in the schools are eligible for annual performance bonuses of up to 10 percent of their annual salary based on the same criteria. Factors that have created an entrepreneurial culture at SAIT include (a) the centralized-decentralized organization, (b) accountability for financial performance, (c) ensuring high quality in an area of responsibility, and (d) the opportunity to run a businesslike unit in an academic organization. This culture rewards innovation and risk-taking and has promoted a model of successful college leadership (Nixon 2003).

The Case for Change

Good to Great begins with "Good is the enemy of great... The vast majority of companies never become great, precisely because the vast majority become quite good—and that is their main problem" (Collins, 2001, 1). Since the late 1990s, SAIT has been transforming from "the local trades school on the hill" to its new vision of "Canada's premier polytechnic." This transformation was led by the new president and a management team who exhibited the level 5 leadership behaviors as defined in the first stage in *Good to Great:* Discipline people (Collins 2001, 17–40) and who have methodically built their teams using the principle of "first who, then what."

SAIT's executive believed that although the earned-revenue side of the business was successful, it could do better. Thus, in 2005, the vice president academic, deans, and corporate training directors met to review the performance of the institution's earned-revenue business. On the surface, it appeared to be performing satisfactorily by generating a reasonable profit. However, after employing Collins's second stage of *Good to Great*—disciplined thought and the principle of "confronting the brutal facts"—it was discovered that parts of the business were, in fact, operating at a substantial loss. Upon further review, it was discovered that while the *gross revenue* had increased by 20 percent in the previous five years, it had reached a plateau; the *net revenue* (after direct costs and overhead expenses) had increased by only 13 percent. After conducting a strengths, weakness, opportunity, and threats (SWOT) analysis, it was evident that the status quo in the earned-revenue business was no longer acceptable, that SAIT's earned-revenue products were not always aligned to changing customer needs, that competition was increasing, and that while the profile of its customers was changing, SAIT's earned-revenue program was stagnating. Following Kotter's (1996) *Leading Change* principles, the vice president academic stimulated the sense of urgency needed for change and action. A task team was struck to ensure that the current year's earned-revenue budget was exceeded. In addition, it was decided that a comprehensive external review of the structure, operating model, and operating procedures of the earned-revenue business was required. A request for proposals (RFP) was issued and an international consulting firm was selected to conduct the review and report back within six months.

The objective of the external review was to lay the foundation of a sustainable high-growth, earned-revenue program by 2010 by asking the following five questions:

1. What is SAIT's earned-revenue business and what are its characteristics?
2. What is the current and potential share of the market?
3. What are SAIT's opportunities for growth?
4. What are the current organizational capabilities, and what operating model and organizational capabilities does SAIT require to realize its growth objective?
5. What is the two-year business plan, including the executable implementation plan?

An earned-revenue steering committee was established with a small group of deans and corporate training directors to guide the external consulting firm's work, establish review questions, and approve a comprehensive plan. The plan included (a) interviews with SAIT employees, stakeholders, and partners; (b) an online survey with current and potential corporate training customers; and (c) interviews with the consulting firm's contacts with SAIT's competitors. Secondary research was to be conducted with a comprehensive trend analysis to establish market size and opportunities. A review of comparable operating models in both higher education and the private sector was established. In addition, SAIT's financial and customer satisfaction information and previous earned-revenue plans and documentation were under review. During the six-month review, four planning sessions were held with the deans and corporate directors to examine the external consultants' work, validate research findings, and test ideas and hypotheses. Regular status reports were provided to SAIT's senior executive and board of governors.

The findings from the online survey and interviews with SAIT's current and potential customers revealed seven major points:

1. Earned-revenue program needed to operate more like a business and less like an academic institution to respond to industry's needs

2. Need to improve its corporate training results by targeting large markets with well-priced products that were aligned to customers' needs

3. Need to improve its communications and responsiveness to customers

4. Need to improve its product pricing in order to differentiate itself from its customers

5. Was most successful with its off-the-shelf products; energy-sector organizations offered a growth area

6. Internal approval processes were tremendously slow, which added to the perception of the organization being bureaucratic and a business-unfriendly institution

7. Had a strong reputation for offering high-quality programs that met industry's needs.

A review of the financial performance of the earned-revenue program concluded that the domestic and corporate training business was performing below that of the individual-learner business (ILB). The ILB business included the revenue streams of continuing education, career development (earned revenue from full-time programs of less than one year), and distance education.

The external consulting firm then conducted an organizational assessment that examined governance, processes, culture, competence, and capacity as well as a high-level review of the supporting functions of finance, customer service, and information technology. The organizational assessment identified several themes limiting future earned-revenue program growth. It noted that the organization had certain strengths such as a clear commitment to fixing the earned-revenue business, a strong ability to ideate and start-up market opportunities, an entrepreneurial spirit, and efficient delivery and coordination of the continuing education and career development programs. They concluded that SAIT's earned-revenue business was not constrained by the market but by capacity and capability. The consultants reported that the current earned-revenue program go-to-market approach could be characterized as trying to be "all things to all people all the time, everywhere" with an operating model that was deeply embedded in the academic departments. The consultants recommended that SAIT needed to focus its earned-revenue program approach on market opportunities where it could clearly differentiate itself.

The consultants and the steering committee then identified the market opportunities SAIT's earned-revenue business needed to prioritize. The following nine earned-revenue program assessment criteria were used to evaluate its potential:

1. Is the business aligned with the organization's strategic plan?
2. Does the business add value to or improve the satisfaction of SAIT's customers?
3. Will the business improve SAIT's brand and reputation or differentiate it in the market?
4. Does the business have the organizational and key stakeholder commitment?
5. Is the business aligned with market, social, and customer trends?
6. Executives need to analyze whether there is a clear and demonstrable market and customer need.
7. Does the business leverage SAIT's grant capabilities?
8. Does SAIT have the capability to be successful in this business?
9. Will this business add value to SAIT within a reasonable timeframe?

Using the nine criteria above, the executive evaluated many options. The committee concluded the following:

1. SAIT needed to focus its current earned-revenue program only on individual learners and energy-sector organizations.
2. SAIT should establish an ILB functional group with the mandate to deliver a seamless yet differentiated experience to learners using off-the-shelf courses and programs meeting the needs of learners.
3. SAIT needed to establish an energy-sector business (ESB) functional group with the mandate to deliver a seamless yet differentiated experience to global energy-sector organizations using off-the-shelf courses and programs meeting the needs of the energy-sector organizations. This would reorient the domestic and international corporate training section by dealing with the energy sector rather than all industry sectors.
4. Finally, SAIT should leave the customized corporate-training business both internationally and domestically because of the many resources required to excel in this field.

By redirecting SAIT's earned-revenue program to individual learners and energy-sector organizations, the college would achieve several tangible results: (1) there would be no confusion as to which business SAIT was in, (2) from a resource perspective (people, investment, time), the program would become less complex and easier to manage, and (3) focusing resources made it more likely that SAIT would develop expertise in these two areas and therefore succeed in the market. Once these two tactics were operating efficiently, other markets would be considered to expand SAIT's earned-revenue program. It was concluded that one of the success factors of SAIT's earned-revenue program was the separation of the sales and delivery functions. It was determined that the development and delivery of the ILB and ESB programs would remain under the auspices of the academic departments, thus capitalizing on existing intellectual property and maintaining the centralized-decentralized model that had fostered SAIT's strong entrepreneurial spirit. To turn recommendations to practice, SAIT's executive management agreed that it needed to move forward with a managed "big bang" approach and prioritize the energy-sector business over the individual-learner business. The ESB then concentrated on areas with the greatest potential for growth, which (based on SAIT's location, expertise, and other factors) was the oil and gas subsector.

The Transformation

Adoption of the new earned-revenue business model was rapid and the original consulting firm was retained to aid in the implementation of the new model. An executive director was seconded from within the institution to lead a small, dedicated full-time team to work with the consulting firm so that internal knowledge and expertise on the transition would be retained. Together, options were developed so that SAIT could concentrate on the energy-sector business. A new structure created the position of associate vice president energy to head this initiative.

Following Collins's (2001, 13) principle of "first who, then what," the first step was to reorganize and staff the new earned-revenue business by getting "the right people on the bus, the wrong people off the bus, and the right people in the right seats." The transition team formulated each of the earned-revenue job descriptions.

The second step was to identify the earned-revenue "hedgehog" (90–119). For an organization to move from good to great, it requires a deep understanding of three intersecting circles: (a) What can your organization be the best in the world at? (b) What are you deeply passionate about? and (c) What drives your economic engine? The intersection of these three concepts becomes an organization's hedgehog. By focusing on the hedgehog, an organization can move from good to great.

In reviewing the energy-sector spectrum, it was determined that while SAIT had some expertise across the spectrum, it possessed the greatest expertise and experience in the oil and gas sector. This expertise was based largely on a product line known as the SAIT Open Learning Instructional System (SOLIS). SOLIS was developed in the early 1980s with funding from the federal government. The concept was to develop a series of stand-alone learning modules in partnership with industry that would train oil and gas workers in the field. SOLIS now includes 700 learning modules in 50 subjects covering technical areas, health and safety, and soft skills; it can be customized by the learners, corporation, or based on one of the six preset certificates. SAIT has developed a database of 600 task competencies to complement the theoretical SOLIS modules with practical learning. The competencies are generic operating procedures that were developed by working with industry to define essential field and maintenance functions for production facilities and equipment. Funded by the energy industry, some of the modules were put in an online format complete with multimedia components.

Based on market research, the transition team determined that the production sector represented the largest market opportunity and was an area in which SAIT had already enjoyed success in the Canadian market. In the production component, SAIT decided to focus on the operations and maintenance area. SOLIS had technical modules developed in each of the operation and maintenance areas: operator, electrical, mechanical,

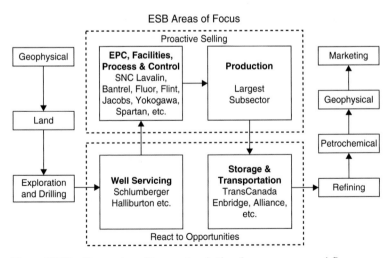

Figure CS7.1 Domestic and international oil and gas company workflow.

and instrumentation training. The team determined that this was SAIT's earned-revenue hedgehog (see Figure CS7.1). The third and final step in Collins's (2001) journey is "discipline action," creating a culture of discipline when "you combine a culture of discipline with an ethic of entrepreneurship, you get the magical alchemy of great performance" (13). By using this principle, SAIT developed a management system that was transparent. As SAIT's programming encompassed other industry sectors, the committee determined that SAIT would pursue profitable opportunities in other sectors on a reactive basis.

While the earned-revenue business was changing, SAIT embarked on a complementary institution-wide project management initiative to improve practices throughout the college. An advisory team was created to design a framework with common language, tools, templates, and processes. A twenty-hour project management course was developed, based on the type of projects found in both the grant and earned-revenue areas. The initiative was hugely successful, with over 300 employees completing the course. Two factors led SAIT toward a project execution culture: the critical mass of employees completing the course, and the insistence on all projects that required institutional resources following the project management approach.

To activate the ESB functional group, SAIT established an ESB council. This provided strategic and tactical guidance to domestic and international corporate training units. The ESB council meets weekly to assess the risks associated with new project proposals and to make go or no-go decisions based on the following five criteria:

1. The project's compatibility with SAIT's strategic plan and its ability to generate a high level of profit for SAIT.
2. The clarity of the project in terms of program content, learner need and abilities, customer goals, timing, and certification requirements.
3. SAIT's ability to provide the resources including curriculum, facilities, equipment and instruction.
4. The likelihood of generating follow-up business.
5. The risk to SAIT's personnel, financial well-being, reputation, and intellectual property as well as liability risks.

The ESB project lifecycle provides a disciplined management system for the ESB council. The lifecycle is a standard stage-gate process (common in the private sector) that has been customized to fit SAIT's ESB business. The ESB council makes go or no-go decisions at the "assess" stage, when projects are reviewed with the criteria of the preliminary

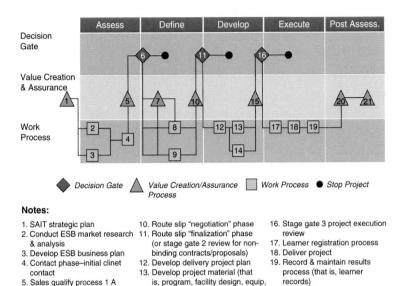

Figure CS7.2   ESB project lifecycle.

financial expectations and the organizational fit; at the "define" stage, projects are reviewed using the criteria of organizational fit, the project's clarity and suitability, the ability to resource, the detailed financial estimates, and the associated risks and mitigations. For each criterion, the council evaluates the project proposal against five defined levels (see figure CS7.2).

The Successes

SAIT's earned-revenue business transformation has generated new revenue for the college by providing greater focus and clarity. By saying "no" to unprofitable business and by doing "better business better," net revenue has substantially increased (gross revenue has fewer direct and overhead costs). Figure CS7.3 shows the ten-year earned-revenue business financial performance. During the first six years, despite an increase in net revenue, the performance was erratic with some years showing an actual decline in net revenue. However, since the earned-revenue transformation started in 2005, there has been a steady increase (144 percent) in net earned-revenue profits from CDN$3.6 million to CDN$8.8 million. This equates to Collins's flywheel principle in his final stage toward greatness—discipline action, where an initiative begins to take off after having time and resources invested in laying its foundation.

SAIT has been able to capitalize on the needs of emerging countries in the Middle East and of North Africa's multinational oil companies to provide a holistic approach to international workforce development. SAIT's approach includes the following:

1. Baseline assessments: SAIT conducts a complete suite of assessment tests for English language proficiency and foundational knowledge to assess the starting point of trainees.
2. Foundations training: SAIT gives in-country and in-Canada English language training and foundational training in mathematics, chemistry, physics, and computer fundamentals.
3. Travel: SAIT provides logistical assistance for students traveling to Canada.
4. Training settlement and orientation: SAIT employees meet students at the airport, provide accommodation at the SAIT residence, and introduce them to Canadian daily life and culture.
5. Technical training: SAIT provides operations and maintenance training in the technical areas of production, mechanical, electrical and instrumentation based on the SOLIS learning modules.

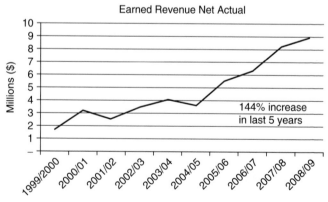

Figure CS7.3   Financial Results Multi-Year Trend Line.

6. Health, environment, and safety training: SAIT provides embedded and specific health, environment, and safety training to multinational-company standards.

7. Graduation: Formal graduation ceremonies conclude the process.

After its success in designing and delivering operations and maintenance training and in the earned-revenue transformation, SAIT searched for continual improvement and ways to expand this part of the business. One outcome is that SAIT has now formed a joint venture with another large international petroleum training provider to offer its SOLIS-based operations and maintenance training in an online format. Through the joint venture, SAIT aims to share with the world the operations and maintenance training that it has been delivering in Canada for many years. With the energy-sector business well on its way to success, SAIT is now analyzing the next industry sector to target for revenue generation, using the lessons learned from the energy-sector business.

Lessons Learned

During the five-year earned-revenue transformation, SAIT has learned several lessons that may be useful to higher education institutions considering a similar transformation.

Need to Confront the Brutal Facts and Not Accept the Status Quo

Jim Collins's (2001) *Good to Great* research concluded that "good is the enemy of great" (1); therefore, to achieve greatness, an organization must take bold steps and not be afraid to challenge the status quo. For SAIT, this meant having the courage to hire an external business consulting firm and allow it full access to financial and historical business records. SAIT had to remain open and nondefensive when the brutal facts were discovered and presented. During the transformation, the organization had to be tenacious in its pursuit of change, not just for the sake of change but to achieve greatness.

Engaging Needed People

Having the right people on the bus and in the right seats is critical; equally critical, but even more challenging, is getting the wrong people off the bus.

Major transformations such as SAIT's journey to a new earned-revenue model meant that some people resisted the changes and were not able to make the journey because of their adherence to the old ways of doing business. Helping these people exit the organization in a respectful manner was necessary for the transformation process.

Sustain Organization First Culture

The need to encourage an "organization first" culture rather than an academic "school first" culture, common in many public higher education institutions. The success of SAIT's earned-revenue transformation can be attributed in part to encouraging the discipline that everyone must follow common business practices. At SAIT, this included standard project management processes, the widespread use of a common decision support package at all levels of the organization, and a standard budget process that used transparency to drive compliance through open quarterly reviews. During these quarterly reviews, each component of the business is exposed and open to critiques from all deans and directors for efficiency and effectiveness. While this process was challenging for some at first, the high level of transparency and accountability to their peers soon forced everyone to understand the details of the business and what was and was not working.

Staying Focused

Real transformation to greatness requires that an organization determine its "hedgehog" and have the discipline to stay focused and not be distracted by other business opportunities that do not fit with the hedgehog. For SAIT, its hedgehog is operation and maintenance training in the energy sector; it has built a business model to sell its products globally. Although SAIT does not sell proactively into other business sectors it does examine other business opportunities outside the energy sector as they arise. The college evaluates these opportunities using a disciplined approach to ensure that they do not distract from the main business of operations and maintenance, and that they are profitable.

In conclusion, the president and CEO, Irene Lewis, described the development in SAIT Polytechnic's for-profit business as being transformational. She noted:

> Through the five-year journey we have become more strategic, more focused and more disciplined in our approach to this part of our business. We are now more responsive to the needs of our local industry while extending

our global presence. As a result of this transformation, we have been able to reduce our dependency on government funding and become more self-sustainable.

References

Collins, Jim C. 2001. *Good to Great.* New York: Harper Collins.

Kotter, John P. 1996. *Leading Change.* Boston, MA: Harvard Business School Press.

Nixon, Gordon. 2003. "Academic Capitalism Forces and Successful College Leadership." PhD dissertation, University of Calgary, Canada.

Slaughter, Sheila, and Larry Leslie. 1997. *Academic Capitalism: Politics, Policies, and the Entrepreneurial University.* Baltimore, MD: Johns Hopkins University Press.

Case Study 8

Response to a Financial Crisis: Case Study of CCAC 2003-2008

Stewart E. Sutin

The Community College of Allegheny County (CCAC) faced intermittent financial challenges on several occasions since its founding in the mid-1960s. Perhaps none were more serious than those in the fall of 2003. CCAC's operating expenses were approximately $107 million in fiscal year 2002–2003, while serving full time equivalency headcount of an estimated 18,000 students in its degree and certificate programs (CCAC 2003). Its noncredit community education program was also substantial, and was attended by thousands of students. Local residents were served by a network of four campuses and several smaller centers in Allegheny County, the hub of which is Pittsburgh, and an additional center in Washington County. The following case study highlights CCAC's financial challenges that became a source of special concern between 2003 and 2008, while summarizing a comprehensive three-year stabilization plan proposed by administration and approved by the board of trustees and the achievement of two successive administrations in successfully meeting financial challenges. The overall objectives of financial stabilization plan were to sustain the quality of education, maintain affordable tuition, and consistently balance the budget. CCAC's leaders, faculty, staff, and board of trustees were made aware of the need to adopt an improved financial model. The study includes data contained in CCAC's externally audited financial statements for the years 2002–2008, a special report delivered to the board of trustees in February 2004 titled *CCAC: Three Year Financial Plan 2004–07*, and minutes of the Board of Trustees Meeting, February 19, 2004. The financial statements and board of trustees minutes were generously provided by CCAC leadership to the author for purposes of this analysis.

Origin and Dimensions of a Financial Crisis

What constitutes a financial crisis? Perhaps a few background comments on accounting terminology and financial management merit attention. When annual operating expenses exceed annual operating revenues, an institution evidences an operating loss, or, in the case of fund accounting terminology applicable to educational institutions, a reduction of net assets. Operating losses may be dealt with in the short term through borrowing money or by drawing upon the financial reserves of a college. But the negative consequences of sequential operating losses become a serious matter unless addressed, and the accumulative consequences of several years of operating losses may eventually impair an institutions' capacity to function. In this context, CCAC was confronted by a financial crisis that peaked during 2003–2002 school year.

According to externally audited year-end financial statements for 2002–2003, CCAC evidenced reductions of net assets, or operating losses, of $2.37 million (CCAC 2003). CCAC's already weakened financial condition was exacerbated in the fall of 2003 when the state government, which had to deal with its own budget problems, reduced funding for community colleges by an estimated 10 percent relative to the prior years' operating budget. While community college operating revenues, therefore, suffered as a result of lower appropriations from the state government, certain operating expenses continued to rise. Contractual agreements with two labor unions assured their members of annual wage increases and benefits coverage. Overall salaries had increased by 11 percent, in part due to staffing increases, and fringe benefits increased by 28 percent (CCAC 2003). Health care insurance premiums increased well above historic norms. The stage was set for another year of operating losses.

The historical context for state funding of community college in Pennsylvania is worthy of attention. For the first time in its history, the Commonwealth of Pennsylvania did not meet its statutory funding obligation to community colleges in 2003–2004. State statute required one-third each funding from the state, the local sponsor(s), and tuition. Several local sponsors had long since failed to adhere to this statutory requirement, including CCAC's sponsor, the government of Allegheny County. This resulted in increasing student tuition above the one-third statutory limit. The financial consequence to CCAC of state action in the fall of 2003 was projected by the college chief financial officers as a potential reduction of $2.1 million in funding to CCAC relative to normal appropriations based upon its funding obligations (CCAC 2004b). This occurred after the colleges' board of trustees had approved the annual budget, inclusive of tuition rates for school year. To compound matters, the state had audited student attendance records of noncredit continuing education programs dating back four and five years. The historical audits resulted in "disallowances" of previously funded operations at many community colleges, including CCAC. The state government decided that disallowances would net out from state appropriations to community colleges over time. As a result, the overall financial consequences from lower state appropriations, when coupled with de facto reductions of funding due to audits, presented CCAC with concerns relative to balancing its budget.

CCAC faced an array of challenges to its operational environment and financial condition. As previously noted, in the fall of 2003, the college was notified that its health care insurance premiums would rise by 39 percent in 2004 for an increase of $1.8 million in the cost of coverage while contractually mandated salary increases were set to go up by an estimated $1.5 million (CCAC 2004b). Energy and facilities maintenance costs were rising. The chief financial officer's (CFO's) study of registered nursing and allied health programs, reportedly the third largest of all community colleges health care programs in the country in terms of numbers of graduates per year, revealed operating losses of $2.3 million for 2002–2003 (CCAC 2004b). Its largest campus, Allegheny Campus, required costly emergency repairs and refurbishment of aging buildings. The system-wide technology platform or bandwidth was "maxed out," and affected the colleges' ability to accommodate instructional and operational technology needs. The chief technology officer and the CFO reported to the CEO that the cost to remedy this situation could be as much as $5 million (CCAC 2004b). Funds were needed for important professional development of faculty and administrators. The high cost of sustaining a multicampus multicenter system further strained the limited financial resources.

The president invited the CFO to develop three-year financial projections in order to quantify the potential financial condition of the college in the absence of an effective plan of action. The result of that forecast indicated that an operating loss of up to $15 million in the third year was possible in the absence of implementing a financial stabilization plan. Based upon this data, the president notified the board of trustees in fall 2003 that the financial model of CCAC "was broken" (CCAC 2004c). A commitment was made to deliver a comprehensive plan within three months with the objectives of stabilizing the colleges' financial condition and improving its overall capacity to perform. In the months that followed, the president, the CFO, and other key administrators gave attention to the range of options worthy of consideration. Thus began a transformative experience at CCAC that ultimately brought about a more durable and improved financial model for the college.

Three-Year Financial Plan

The leadership team agreed upon guiding principles for development of a stabilization plan. Three components were deemed essential. Budgets would have to balance. Educational quality could not be impaired. Tuition would have to remain affordable. While it was apparent to the colleges' leaders and the board of trustees that an advocacy campaign to restore state funding was imperative, it was also evident that other sources of revenue would have to be found, and costs would have to be contained. The president advised the board of trustees: "This is just the beginning. We feel we have to be disciplined and judicious in the use of money that we do get and use that money as effectively as we can to support our educational and workforce missions" (CCAC 2004c, 6653).

Revenue Generation Plans and Initiatives

Several measures were proposed to generate incremental revenues. In addition to lobbying in Harrisburg, the plan recommended a $6 per credit hour increase in student tuition, beginning with the second summer session of 2004 as a one-time emergency measure. When enacted, it brought tuition to $77.50 per credit hour in 2004–2005, an 8 percent increase over the previous year (CCAC 2004a). Since tuition in 1994 had been $64 per credit hour, the increase represented an average annual increase of 1.35 percent over 10 years—and was well within the increase in the consumer price index over that time frame. The increase in tuition and student enrollment brought about a $2 million increase in tuition revenues (CCAC 2004a). In view of the high cost of nursing and allied health care, the plan called for a 20 percent premium in tuition for students enrolled in health care courses (CCAC 2004b). Grant generation targeted at the foundation community and federal government became a priority. Finally, CCAC operated the largest continuing education program among community colleges in Pennsylvania, and the college created a costing model that was applied to all noncredit courses. This permitted CCAC to make upward adjustments to those courses where tuition had remained static for years, and to assure a reasonable profit margin for the college. The plan signaled a shift to an aggressive bottom line approach to administration of community education. All courses were subject to periodic review of fees alongside evaluation of instructional quality. Subsequent annual operating plans called for generating an average increase of $1 million of revenues in excess of expenses in community education for years 2005–2007 (for three years; CCAC 2004b).

CCAC leadership and its board of trustees were aware of the need for more aggressive advocacy with leaders in state government in both the executive branch and legislature in an effort to assure that future budgetary allocations would comply with statutory obligations. Collaboration with other community college presidents and the Pennsylvania Association of Community Colleges ultimately did result in a restoration of most operating funds from the state. Regrettably, the formula for allocation of operating funds became more complex and funding for mandated and nonmandated capital projects remained problematic. The state insisted upon predictability of its funding allocations to its community colleges, but solved its problem by transferring unpredictability to those colleges. This action accentuated the need for community colleges to become increasingly self-reliant.

Cost Containment Plans and Initiatives

The financial plan resolved to save personnel costs by a minimum of $1million per annum through a 10 percent reduction in the nonacademic workforce over a three-year period of time (CCAC 2004b). Staff attrition and retirement incentive programs for administrators, faculty, and other staff were identified as ways to help achieve that objective. Restructuring to achieve improved operating efficiencies, and administrative effectiveness were equally important. One component of operational effectiveness called for an organizational shift to a "one college" system in which campus administrators would assume additional system-wide functional responsibilities. An analysis of student attendance per class section identified instances of low enrollment class sections. The CFO advised the president that CCAC could save approximately $1 million annually by increasing student enrollment per course section (CCAC 2004b). Instructional deans and department chairs were empowered to make decisions on enrollment per class section, with special consideration afforded to disciplines that might be adversely affected by higher enrollments (such as English Composition) and lower enrollment courses required for graduation by students about to receive their associates degree.

The cost containment plan touched many operating functions of the college. Travel, dues, and memberships were reduced in 2003–2004 by 30 percent per annum relative to the 2002–2003 budget (CCAC 2004b). The president's travel budget was reduced by 40 percent in order to set an example for others. The plan called for similar restraints in years two and three. The college elected to reduce its reliance on outsourced security services by hiring a public safety officer at each campus, at savings of $500,000 per annum, according to CFO estimates (CCAC 2004b). An evaluation conducted by the CFO concluded that limited in-sourcing would result in improved security on campus, at the same time lowering costs. The plan called for a review of cost containment options on an ongoing basis. These areas included health care insurance costs, energy, procurement of vendor services, refinancing bond obligations during historically lower interest rate cycles, and increasing use of CCAC facilities for continuing education as opposed to renting locations from others. CCAC reviewed its leased properties from a strategic and cost–benefit model perspective. In one case, the college opted to exit the fixed cost of operating its own center and to colocate with a school district on the basis of paying for classrooms used per semester. CCAC did not elect to increase reliance upon adjunct faculty as a means of lowering operating overhead. Investments were made to build out its technological platform and bandwidth. Funding for professional development of faculty and staff was increased. The board of trustees unanimously approved the three-year financial plan. Several members of CCAC's board expressed concerns about the increase in tuition and fees that were called for in year one, but understood that the college had no viable alternative in the short term if the budget were to balance.

Internal Stakeholders Respond to Challenges

College leaders disclosed information about the financial challenges faced by CCAC and the three-year financial plan. Once the board approved the comprehensive financial plan, town hall meetings were held at all campuses. The president shared with attendees the full report provided to the board. The financial condition and challenges faced by CCAC and remedies were presented at these meetings. Attendees were alarmed by the cutbacks in state funding, yet most understood the need to find solutions in order to stabilize the college.

The reactions by union leadership and the memberships of the collective bargaining units representing faculty and staff, namely the American Federation of Teachers (AFT) and Service Employee International Union

(SEIU), were mostly collaborative. Some agreed to support the lobbying effort in Harrisburg in an effort to restore state funding, while others expressed the view that CCAC was overstaffed at the administrative level. The AFT leadership welcomed the president's commitment to gradually increase the number of full-time faculty. Twelve full-time faculty members accepted the retirement incentive plan and 15 new full-time faculty members were hired. Its leadership worked constructively with administration to gain entry for CCAC into a health care insurance consortium of the Allegheny Intermediate Unit, a move that saved the college substantial money over time.

SEIU leadership worked closely with college leadership throughout the financial crisis. After a retirement incentive plan was offered to faculty and administrators, SEIU asked for a similar package for its membership. College and union leadership agreed upon an implementation plan that would allow the college to save money above and beyond the cost of the retirement package. In addition, brainstorming sessions were held at which union members introduced revenue generation and cost containment initiatives. For instance, CCAC had never charged students or alumni for transcripts to be sent to third parties. SEIU members studied practices of other community colleges and universities in our region, and recommended a fee of $5.00 per transcript. The dean of enrollment services calculated that this initiative would generate an estimated $300,000 per year based upon historic usage. Its members worked with administration to evaluate workflows in enrollment services and financial aid, resulting in improved service for students and lowering costs for the college.

Administrator response was mixed. Structural reorganization, staff reductions, and shifting of responsibilities required behavioral changes in an institution accustomed to a set way of doing business. Understandably, many were concerned about the prospect of job loss. Campus-centric planning and behaviors were expensive and complicated the task of agreeing upon system wide educational, student services, and physical plant priorities. A consultant was hired to help design a new administrative structure. David Peirce, former chancellor of the Virginia Community College System and former president of the American Association of Community Colleges, undertook a hands-on study of CCAC and tendered his recommendations. The presidents of Borough of Manhattan Community College, Metro Community College (Kansas City, MO), and San Francisco Community College District served as a sounding board in vetting the restructuring plan. This plan called for structural reorganization and adoption of a "one college" system. It was intended to reduce administrative overhead, improve operating efficiencies, define educational and student service standards, and support system-wide planning and priority setting. It called for fewer administrators overall, and a shift of certain senior leadership responsibilities. For example, the chief academic officer, the chief financial officer, the head of workforce development, and the head of student services were given system-wide accountability and authority for their respective areas of functional responsibility in addition to campus-based administrative responsibilities. A new performance evaluation system was put in place for administrators, one that included "management by objectives" along with evidence of behaviors consistent with articulated college values. Special recognition was given to teamwork skills. Some administrators and faculty experienced difficulty in adjusting to realities in which concerns for institutional priorities trumped campus-centric concerns, and resentment manifested itself in a variety of ways.

The board voted unanimously in favor of the plan as described. Implementation of this plan caused discomfort to some administrators and faculty. Matrix management or dual administrative duties and reporting lines put a premium on teamwork and focus on needs of our students needs throughout the system. Assumption of system-wide responsibilities rather than a primary focus on campus priorities was a complex undertaking. Its adoption represented a significant implementation challenge.

Did the Financial Stabilization Plan Work?

The aggregate quantitative results of the financial stabilization plan show that over a seven-year time line, that in 2002–2003 there was a negative $2.4 million net asset that grew to positive $6.6 million net asset in 2007–2008 (Independent Auditors' Reports of CCAC 2004). In order to evaluate the success of implementing the financial plan approved by the board of trustees, one may consider certain data points as taken from the externally audited financial statements of CCAC between 2002–2003 and 2007–2008. For example, the cost of instruction reached a high point of $45.4 million in 2002–2003 (CCAC 2003), and remained steady at $45 million five years later despite annual increases in contractually mandated base pay for faculty. Ongoing management of class section attendance contributed to this favorable result. Institutional support accounted for $19.4 million of the 2007–2008 expense base (CCAC 2008) compared to a high point of $21.8 million in 2004–2005 (CCAC 2005), evidencing the results of restructuring and reduction of administrative staff. While tuition increased somewhat in 2007–2008 (CCAC 2008), the average annual increase in tuition for the most recent three years was 1.9 percent—a figure below increases in the consumer price index during the same period. Refinancing long-term debt during lower interest rate periods permitted the college to spend $2 million to service interest payments on $68.3 million of debt in 2007–2008 (CCAC 2008) as opposed to $2.1 million to service $39.9 million of debt in 2002–2003 (CCAC 2003). Moreover, improvements were made to the technological platform of the college, professional development programs for faculty and administration was funded, emergency repairs were completed on the Allegheny Campus, and a center for workforce development opened in the West Hills, the fastest growing area of Allegheny County. In addition, incremental monies were added to academic support and student services for the purposes of improving rates of student persistence and graduation. The success of adopting a more viable revenue growth/cost containment model continued from one presidency to the next. This underscores an ability to institutionalize a more effective financial model, while maintaining fidelity to community college mission and educational standards.

Conclusion

Empirical data validate the beneficial results at CCAC from implementing a comprehensive multiyear financial plan. The college found ways to contain cost, increase operating revenues from nontraditional sources, balance the budget, and sustain affordable tuition. Was implementation of a financial stabilization plan an option? Not really. Were certain components of expense containment such as staff reductions painful? Surely. Might college leaders have adopted a more deliberate and collaborative response to problem resolution? Perhaps. But the magnitude of revenue losses and expense increases in the fall 2003 prompted decisions to act swiftly. The weakening financial condition of CCAC was of paramount concern and created a sense of urgency to act among leaders and the board of trustees alike. Did CCAC develop an improved financial model that sustained the quality of education while maintaining affordable tuition? The body of evidence suggests an affirmative.

Several lessons may be gleaned from CCAC's response to challenging financial circumstances. Full, honest, timely, and effective communications with stakeholders are imperative whenever material adverse financial news emerges. Transparency is essential in its own right, and because it provides a substantive foundation for communicating a case for change. Advocacy with public officials remains a priority for community college leaders, yet is likely to prove insufficient by itself. Instead, a decisive and comprehensive financial intervention plan must be implemented. Union leaders are capable of collaborative approaches to problem-solving, provided the direct financial interests of their constituents are not in jeopardy. Problem-solving among a broad constituency is likely to unearth revenue generation and cost containment ideas and support the sustainability of change through consensus building. Periodic reviews of administrative staffing, organizational structure, and operating procedures are constructive in identifying revenue generation and cost containment options. Changes of behavior can be invigorating, and essential, but take time and may precipitate countervailing rearguard actions by some who resist change. Finally, complex financial challenges require comprehensive multiyear responses if the benefits are to bring financial viability, improvement to the quality of education, affordability of tuition, and access for students.

References

Community College of Allegheny Country (CCAC). 2003. *CCAC: Financial Statements for the Years Ended 2002–2008 and Independent Auditors Reports.* Pittsburgh: CCAC.

CCAC. 2004a. *CCAC: Financial Statements for the Years Ended 2002–2008 and Independent Auditors Reports.* Pittsburgh: CCAC.

CCAC. 2004b. "CCAC Special Report: CCAC Three Year Financial Plan 2004–07." A report shared with the Board of Trustees of CCAC at its Monthly Meeting, February 19, 2004. Pittsburgh, PA: CCAC.

CCAC. 2004c. "CCAC: Board Meeting Minutes. CCAC Board Meeting." Held on February 19, 2004. Pittsburgh, PA: CCAC.

CCAC. 2005. *CCAC: Financial Statements for the Years Ended 2002–2008 and Independent Auditors Reports.* Pittsburgh, PA: CCAC.

CCAC. 2008. *CCAC: Financial Statements for the Years Ended 2002–2008 and Independent Auditors Reports.* Pittsburgh, PA: CCAC.

Case Study 9

The Expensive Dream: Financing Higher Vocational Colleges in China

Yingquan Song and Gerard Postiglione

Since 1999, China began to move from elite to mass higher education. During the rapid expansion in the last decade, two-to-three-year higher vocational colleges (HVCs) have played an indispensable role in achieving mass higher education objective by providing higher education opportunities for roughly half of all college students in the country. In short, the rapid growth of the higher vocational colleges is one of the most impressive landscapes in China's higher education development. However, such a rapid expansion requires a collective financial responsibility among central, provincial, and local governments, especially as it determines how expensive it will be to individual student. Our case study assesses the financial support strategies that China's governments at various levels employ to enhance the development of higher vocational colleges. Particularly, it describes two financial initiatives that the central government recently put forth: (1) the model vocational college construction project and (2) the national financial aid program. Our case study argues that it is too complicated to evaluate the effectiveness of these policy initiatives in terms of efficiency and equality due to the lack of data and the limitations of empirical studies in literature. Consequently, employing financial data from some 100 "model HVCs" at an institutional level and aggregate data at provincial and national levels permits us to explore the role of tuition and fees in the revenue structure of HVCs and its inequality implications for both institutions with weak financial foundations and students from economically disadvantaged families.

The Changing State of China's HVCs

During the rapid expansion in the last decade, HVCs have shared roughly half of all college enrollments in the country. The rapid growth of the HVCs is one of the most impressive phenomena in China's higher education development. However, rapid expansion requires a collective financial responsibility among provincial, municipal, and central government as they determine costs for the individual student. The intent of this case study is to assess the financial support strategies that China's government at various levels employs to enhance the development of higher vocational education institutions. Particularly, it describes two financial initiatives that the central government recently put forth: (1) the model vocational college construction project and (2) the national financial aid program. It is premature to evaluate the effectiveness of these policy initiatives in terms of efficiency and equality due to the lack of data and a scarcity of empirical studies. By employing financial data from some 100 "model HVCs" at the institutional level and aggregate data at provincial and national levels, this chapter explores the role of tuition and fees in the revenue structure of HVCs and their unequal implications for institutions with weak financial foundations and students from economically disadvantaged families.

Rapid Growth of Higher Vocational Education Institutions in China

The last decade has seen a remarkable transformation in higher education. Since 1999, China began to devote more attention to mass higher education. The gross enrollment rate of college students for 18- to 22-year-old increased from 9.3 percent in 1998 to 23.3 percent in 2008. The enrollment in higher education institutions (HEIs) increased from 3.3 million in 1998 to 20.2 million in 2008 (MOE 2009). This achievement was accomplished by the internal reform of higher education system and increasingly unmet demand for higher education opportunity in the county as the nation's economy grows.

The number of HVC institutions more than doubled from 431 in 1998 to 1,184 in 2008, with enrollments of HVC students increased 12.5 times from 0.73 million in 1998 to 9.17 billion. In contrast to HVC, the regular four-year universities enrolments increased fourfold, from 2.6 million in 1998 to 11 million in 2008. HVCs account for 51 percent of higher education institutions, enrolls 45 percent of all college students, and graduate students 56 percent of all tertiary education students (MOE 2009).

Some scholars have viewed HVCs as community colleges (Cheung 1996; Kong and Gimmestad 1999). In fact, China's HVCs resemble US community colleges in some respects. For example, they provide higher education opportunities to those who otherwise would not be able to access it; offer multiple programs with flexible curricula suitable for students with different levels of academic preparation and career interest. Moreover, admission criteria is relatively relaxed in vocational colleges, making them better able to serve local or regional economic and social development needs by training skilled workforce needed in the labor market.

Financial Challenges of HVCs

While HVCs have successfully extended opportunities to many of those who otherwise would not be able to attend higher education, HVCs have long been challenged financially. Many HVC institutions were transformed from adult higher education institutions, upgraded from vocational high schools, or specialized worker universities (Kong and Gimmestad 1999; Niu et al. 2006). Traditionally, local governments (municipal and/or provincial) took the primary financial responsibilities for those institutions.[1] The central government has no role in financing these higher education institutions (Zhao 2006). In fact, most HVCs are historically rooted in financial austerity. It is no wonder that some researchers argue that the governments allocation to higher vocational colleges (Niu 2006) is insufficient. The dramatic regional variations in HVC finance cause some to argue that this amounts to unfair treatment, especially in terms of the expenditure per student difference between HVC and regular four-year universities (Hu and Ma 2006). Education expenditure in HVCs is only one-sixth to one-fifth of that in four-year universities during 2005–2007. Education expenditure in HVCs accounts for only 4–5 percent of the nation's total education expenditure, while spending on regular four-year universities accounts for some 25 to 30 percent.

Consequently, relying on high tuition and fees as the main revenue source differentiates HVC in China from community colleges in the United States. Therefore, the HVC challenge is to provide affordable higher education for those students from economically disadvantaged families. After the transformation of higher education system in the late 1990s, most HVC had to increasingly finance themselves with tuition and fees. We estimated that on average around 50 percent of HVCs' total revenue came from tuition and fees in 2006.[2] This national average covered the variations of HVCs revenue across different provinces. With data at provincial level, we compared the percentage of tuition and fees vs. that

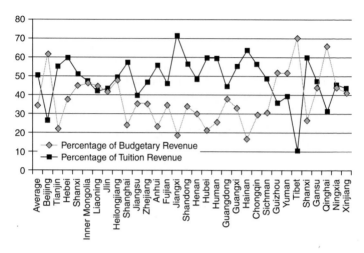

Figure CS9.1   Variations of percentage of tuition and fees vs. governmental funding in total HVC revenue, 2006.

Source: Authors' tabulation based on financial data at provincial level (MOE 2007).

of governmental funding in total revenue in figure CS9.1. It shows that tuition and fees account more than 50 percent of revenue in more than half (16) of China's provinces. In five provinces (Hebei, Jiangxi, Hubei, Hunan, and Shanxi), tuition and fees account for more than 60 percent of revenue.

Two Financial Policy Initiatives Launched by Central Government

In order to enhance the development of HVCs and to make them more affordable for students from economically disadvantaged families, the central government launched two important policy initiatives since 2006: (1) model HVC construction project, and (2) the new financial aid system.

Model HVC Construction Project

One of the most important policy initiatives that central government put forth to enhance the development of HVCs is called the "model HVC construction project." In 2006, the Ministry of Education and Ministry of Finance jointly announced the project, signaling the message that the central government would begin to financially support HVCs. The project would identify 100 higher vocational colleges that have a relatively strong foundation, and provide then with financial support to develop internship bases, facilities, and teacher training. In 2006, 28 colleges were selected. Another 42 colleges were selected in 2007, and 30 more in 2008. The total funding from the central government amounted to RMB 2 billion (approximately $350 million). This occurred as part of the 11th five-year plan period and required that matching funds be provided by provincial governments (Zhao 2006). Until now, no official statistics are available on the extent to which matching funds have been provided by provincial governments. In the case of Zhenshen Vocational College, the total investment has reached RMB 226 million, of which RMB 45 million came from the central government, RMB 166 million came from provincial and municipal governments, and RMB 15.2 million was received from industry and other sources (Shenzhen VC Report 2009).

The National Financial Aid System

In 2007, the State Council of China released new financial aid policies. The objectives of the policies are to help students from economically challenged families have access to higher education, and to complete their college careers. This package of financial aid includes need-based grants, merit-based fellowships, work study programs, and a college student loan scheme (Li 2007; Wei and Wang 2009; Yang 2009). The significance of this aid program is that it makes HVC students eligible for all forms of financial assistance for the first time. In comparison with the old financial aid system, coverage was dramatically increased by 20 percent on average.[3]

Empirical Evidence on Tuition and Financial Aid Policies

What is the impact of the Model HVC Construction Project on the financing of HVCs? How would the financial aid system affect students' access and affordability in higher education? Admittedly, it would be empirically challenging to directly assess the effectiveness of these policy initiatives due to the lack of data, the difficulty in dealing with selection bias, and complexity of these policy packages in design. However, the empirical evidence we have suggests that (1) the Model HVC Construction Project tends to support those HVCs with stronger financial foundations and

(2) the current financial aid system does not lower the "net cost" (tuition minus aid) of HVC education in comparison to the most selective four-year universities.

In this section, we empirically demonstrate the role of tuition and fees in the revenue of HVCs at institutional level to see if there is significant difference in the revenue structure among model HVCs, nonmodel HVCs, and four-year universities. Also, we explore whether or not HVC students are being charged lower tuition than students of four-year higher education institutions.

Data

Two data sets are employed in the current study. The first is the financial data of 2004 at institutional level for three types of higher education institutions, including 70 model HVCs,[4] 103 non-model HVCs randomly selected from all the nonmodel HVCs in 2004, and 108 prestigious four-year universities that are "211 project institutions."[5] The second data set indicates the range of tuition and fees in 2009 for the above three types of institutions. The 2004 financial data at institutional level include variables of total revenue and percentage of five categories of income (government funding, of tuition and fees, of income of services, of donations, and other sources) in total revenue, respectively. One of the unique strengths of these data sets is that they represent the financial situation before the central government implemented the model HVC Model Construction Projects. The 2009 tuition dataset are compiled from all those institutions' admission documents.

Preliminary Findings

Tuition and fees are the most important sources of revenue for both model HVCs and nonmodel HVCs. However, model HVCs have a stronger financial foundation and thus come to receive a higher percentage of revenue from government and other sources. In 2004, as shown in Figure CS9.2, tuition and fees accounted for about 50.02 percent of model HVC revenue, whereas it accounted for 54.73 percent for nonmodel HVCs.

Secondly, in contrast, government funding is the most dominating component of income for four-year universities. There is a statistically significant difference in revenue structure between HVCs and four-year universities. For these most selective four-year universities, only 22.75 percent of total revenue came from tuition and fees.

Finally, there were no significant differences in tuition and fees are found to have been charged to students of HVCs and those of four-year universities. That is, in 2009, HVC students had to pay tuition and fee as high as those students attending four-year universities. As indicated in Figure CS9.3, the median lowest tuition and fees of "Model HVCs" is 4,600 RMB, which is 100 RMB higher than that of most prestigious four-year universities (211 project institutions). When it comes to the median highest tuition and fees, four-year universities seem to be higher than HVCs. It should be noted that those upper band of tuition and fees are normally for majors related to arts or international programs.

Discussions and Implications

Admittedly, this empirical study suffers from several weaknesses. One of the limitations is that we only have tuition and fee data at institutional level instead of individual level. This keeps us from an accurate conclusion on the relationship between students' socioeconomic status (SES) and actual tuition charged to them. Another limitation is that we only compare simple statistics like average percentage and median of variables of interest among different types of HEIs. This may lead to only crude findings. Even with these limitations, the preliminary findings above have the following policy implications.

First of all, it is an ironic finding that pursuing a higher education in HVC is such an expensive dream. HVC students, who tend to come from more economically challenged families, are being charged a higher "net price" for attending HVCs than would be the case if they attended the most selective four-year universities. This is because existing data seems to indicate that students from affluent families are more likely to attend more highly selective HEIs and, they are more likely to receive financial aid, and receive financial aid in larger amounts than those who attend HVCs (Ding 2006; Song 2008; Yang 2009; Loyalka et al. 2009a).

Second, it is inequitable to have such a pricing strategy in higher education, one in which tuition and fees of HVCs are as high as that in the most prestigious four-year universities. From an economist's perspective, "high tuition" policy may harvest efficiency, but it leads to inequity if not supplemented by "higher levels of compensatory financial aid" (Nelson and Breneman 1981). A high-tuition, low-aid strategy "punishes" the poor. Ironically, the current tuition and fees of HEIs have been frozen for several years for political reasons (Cui 2007). Examples are shown in figures CS9.2 and CS9.3.

Third, the "Model HVC Construction Project" might be inefficient financially in supporting model HVCs with better revenue sources, since these institutions have been better able to generate sufficient revenue through diversified sources than nonmodel HVCs. According to the law

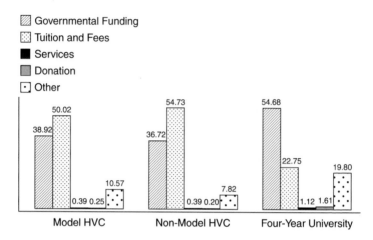

Figure CS9.2   Variations of revenue structures among three types of HEIs.
Source: Authors' tabulation based on financial data at institutional level (MOE 2004).

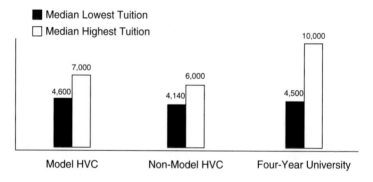

Figure CS9.3   Comparison of tuition range among three types of HEIs.
Source: Authors' tabulation based on 2009 data on tuition and fee from various institutions.

of declining return in economics theory, the gain from the investment in those colleges might be smaller than that from an alternative where funding is given to HVCs with a weaker financial foundation.

Lastly, further empirical research on the impact of tuition and financial aid to HVC education is critically needed in China to help policy makers fix the current financial aid system. While there has been ample research on effects of tuition and financial aid on college attendance (Kane

1995, 2003; Heller 1999; Dynarski 2002; 2003; Linsenmeier et al. 2006; Long 2008) on aid distributions (Grubb and Tuma 1991; Boschung et al. 1998;), on persistence in community colleges (Dowd and Coury 2006; Mendoza et al. 2009), on those who missed financial aid opportunities (King 2004) in the United States, there is scant research available in China on the causal link between financial aid and college enrollment. The exceptions are Loyalka et al. (2009b) and Liu and colleagues (2009) who employed experimental methods of randomized controlled trials to examine the financial aid. Even though there have been studies of aid distribution (Loyalka et al. 2009c; Yang 2009) and on financial constraints that cause students to give up the opportunity to attend college (Wei et al. 2010), few of these studies focus directly on HVCs. Therefore, we need to know more about how potential HVC students respond to different levels of tuition and aid, and how financial aid influences poor students' access, and their choice of colleges.

New Development and Potential Transformations for 2010–2020

As we neared completion of this case study, the government released one of the most important educational documents of the reform era: *Outline of the National Medium- and Long-Term Program for Education Reform and Development (Outline)*. This document calls for the rapid improvement of HVTE. Among its provisions are the following:

1. A modern vocational education system shall be established by 2020 to meet the requirements for transition in methods of development and adjustment in economic structure, to embody the idea of life-long education, and to include coordinated contents at both secondary and advanced levels.
2. Government at all levels shall earnestly substantiate its duty in quality by establishing and improving a quality assurance system for vocational education. Assessment must involve employing enterprises in educational quality assessment. Vocational skill competitions shall be widely held.
3. Establish and improve integrated system of curricula for vocational education. Encourage already employed graduates to continue their studies; improve a system where graduates from vocational schools are allowed to directly seek higher education in an effort to broaden the channels for continuing education.

4. Entrance testing for undergraduate study in general colleges and universities shall be conducted by the state authority while those for higher vocational education shall be conducted by provinces (autonomous regions and municipalities).
5. Explore the possibility for schools of higher vocational education to independently conduct entrance tests, or enrollment by registration based on results from proficiency tests.
6. Improve the financial assistance policy system for students from economically disadvantaged families in schools of secondary vocational education, general undergraduate education, and higher vocational education.
7. Offer supports to the building of vocational schools of higher education.

The final two provisions about financial assistance have the most relevance to our argument in this case study, namely that it is currently far too complicated to evaluate the effectiveness of the policy initiatives for efficiency and equality due to the lack of data and the limitations of empirical studies in literature. Nevertheless, the *Outline* does place a major stress on assessment and evaluation of results, for example: (a) to improve assessment on teaching in universities and colleges, (b) to establish scientific assessment and incentive mechanisms, and (c) to encourage professional agencies and intermediary organizations to perform assessments on disciplinary structures and curricula in colleges and universities. If benchmarks and time lines were added to the *Outline*, it would be extremely useful for charting the rate of progress over the 10-year period 2010–2020.

Summary and Conclusions

During the dramatic transformation and rapid expansion of higher education in the last decade, two-to-three-year HVCs have played an indispensable role in providing higher education opportunities for roughly half of all college students who otherwise would not be able to access higher education in China. However, this achievement was made possible by high tuition and fees that generated more than half of total revenue for HVCs. The level of tuition and fees charged to HVC students is as high, if not higher than that charged to students attending the most prestigious four-year universities. This tuition policy, if without sufficient public subsidies and financial aid, will comprise the realization of the goal of equality of educational opportunity assigned to HVCs.

While the central government has launched the "Model HVC Construction Project" and financial aid policy initiatives to help make the dream of higher education more achievable for most students, it is empirically challenging to assess the effectiveness of those policies in terms of equity and efficiency. Available empirical evidence seems to suggest that the current pricing (tuition) policies for HVCs and the financial aid system are somewhat flawed. One of the consequences of these policies and their implementation is that it is more likely for financial aid with higher amount to be received by those from more affluent household who attend four-year colleges where tuition and fees are lower than that at HVCs.

In short, preliminary data suggests that the current financial support system is somewhat flawed. The recently promulgated *Outline of the National Medium- and Long-Term Program for Education Reform and Development* Outline has the potential for improving this situation. However, further research is needed to address the specific financial implications of the new policies regarding the development of the HVC system in China.

Notes

1. Due to lack of the national financial statistics that separate local (municipal) and provincial spending in HVCs, we don't know the percentages of financial contribution to total HVC revenue from provincial and local governments, respectively.
2. This figure is higher than an estimate by a task force on investment strategy of HVC from China Youth Political Science University where they found that tuition and fees are something below 30 percent of total revenue over time from 1997 to 2002. However, it is obvious that they underestimated the contribution of tuition and fee on total revenue because they just simply employed the percentage of HVC students in total university and college enrollment times various revenue sources of four-year universities when no official statistics on HVC revenue were available before 2005.
3. For a brief review of the financial system in China, please refer to Li (2007).
4. There are only 70 of 100 model HVC institutions with financial data in 2004 since some HVCs were merged with other institutions, and some of them were missed in the 2004 dataset.
5. There are 112 "Project 211 institutions," which are very selective in China. There are only 108 in our dataset since we missed three military universities, and one specialized university for which financial data are not available.

References

Boschung, Milla D., Deanna L. Sharpe, and Mohamed Abdel-Ghany. 1998. "Racial, Ethnic, and Gender Differences in Postsecondary Financial Aid Awards." *Economics of Education Review* 17 (2): 219–222.

Cui, Bangyan. 2007. *Jiaoyubu: Gaoxiao Xuefei Biaozhun Pingjun 4500 Yuan (Ministry of Education: College Tuition Standard Averaged at 4500 RMB).* Beijing: Ministry of Education. Available online at: http://www.moe.edu.cn.

Cheung, Eleanor. 1996. "Higher Vocational Education in China in Response to the Changing Needs of the Labor Market Beyond 2000." *Industry and Higher Education* 10(4): 261–263.

Ding, Xiaohao. 2006. "Scale Expansion and Equalization in College Access." *Peking University Education Review* 2: 25–33.

Dowd, Alicia C., and Tarek Coury. 2006. "The Effect of Loans on the Persistence and Attainment of Community College Students." *Research in Higher Education* 47: 33–62.

Dynarski, Susan M. 2002. "The Behavioral and Distributional Implications of Aid for College." *American Economic Review* 92 (2): 279–285.

Dynarski, Susan M. 2003. "Does Aid Matter? Measuring the Effects of Student Aid on College Attendance and Completion." *American Economic Review* 93 (1): 279–288.

Grubb, W. Norton, and John Tuma. 1991. "Who Gets Student Aid? Variations in Access to Aid." *Review of Higher Education* 14 (3): 359–382.

Heller, Donald E. 1999. "The Effects of Tuition and State Financial Aid on Public College Enrollment." *The Review of Higher Education* 23 (1): 65–89.

Hu, Xiujing, and Shuchao Ma. 2006. "On Policy Analysis on Higher Vocational Education." *Vocational and Technical Education Forum.* 23: 8–11.

Kane, Thomas J. 1995. *Rising Public College Tuition and College Entry: How Well Do Public Subsidies Promote Access to College?* National Bureau of Economic Research (NBER) Working Paper No. 5164. Cambridge, MA: NBER.

Kane, Thomas J. 2003. *A Quasi-Experimental Estimate of the Impact of Financial Aid on College-Going.* NBER Working Paper No. 9703. Cambridge, MA: NBER.

King, Jacquelin E. 2002. *Crucial Choices: How Students' Financial Decisions Affect Their Academic Success.* Washington, DC: American Council on Education.

Kong, Xiangping, and Michael Gimmestad. 1999. "US Community Colleges and China's Counterpart Institutions." *Community College Review* 27 (3): 77–91.

Li, Wenli. 2007. "Family Background, Financial Constraints and Higher Education Attendance in China." *Economics of Education Review* 26 (4): 725–735.

Linsenmeier, David M., Harvey S. Rosen, and Cecilia E. Rouse. 2006. "Financial Aid Packages and College Enrollment Decisions: An Econometric Case Study." *Review of Economics and Statistics* 88 (1): 126–145.

Liu, Chengfang, Linxiu Zhang, Renfu Luo, Scott Rozelle, Jennifer Adams, Brian Sharbono, Yaojiang Shi, Ai Yue, Hongbin Li, Xiaobing Wang, and Thomas Glauben. 2009. *Early Commitment on Financial Aid and College Decision*

Making of Poor Students: Evidence from Randomized Evaluation in Rural China. Rural Education Action Project (REAP) Working Paper No. 207. Palo Alto, CA: Stanford University.

Long, Bridegt T., and Erin K. Riley. 2008. "Financial Aid: A Broken Bridge to College Access?" *Harvard Educational Review* 77 (1): 39–63.

Loyalka, Prashant, Yingquan Song, and Jianguo Wei. 2009a. *Institutional Mechanisms and Sorting Across China's Higher Education System.* China Institute for Educational Finance (CIEFR) Working Paper Series. Beijing: Peking University.

Loyalka, Prashant, Yingquan Song, and Jianguo Wei. 2009b. *Information, College Choice and Financial Aid: Evidence from a Randomized Control Trial in China.* CIEFR Working Paper Series. Beijing: Peking University.

Loyalka, Prashant, Yingquan Song, and Jianguo Wei. 2009c. *Is Aid Reaching Poor Students? The Distribution of Student Financial Aid Across China's Higher Education System.* CIEFR Working Paper Series. Beijing: Peking University.

Mendoza, Pilar, Jesse Mendez, and Zaria Malcolm. 2009. "Financial Aid and Persistence in Community Colleges: Assessing the Effectiveness of Federal and State Financial Aid Programs in Oklahoma." *Community College Review* 37 (2): 112–135.

Ministry of Education, 2004. Year book for Educational Fiscal Data in China.

Ministry of Education, 2009. Year Book for Educational Statistics in China.

Nelson, Susan C., and David W. Breneman. 1981. "An Equity Perspective on Community College Finance." *Public Choice* 36 (3): 515–534.

Niu. Zheng. 2006. "On Resources Allocation among Higher Vocational Colleges." *Vocational and Technical Education Forum* 19: 23–27.

Shenzhen Vocational College. 2009. Summary Report of Model HVC Construction Project in Shenzhen Vococational College. Accessible May 8 2011 http://shifan.szpt.edu.cn/

Song. Yingquan. 2008. Tuition and Affordability of Students Attending to 2-Year Colleges and 4-Year Universities in China. CIEFR Working Paper Series. Beijing: Peking University.

Wei, Jiangguo, and Rong Wang. 2009. "Student Loan Reform in China: Problems and Challenges." *Higher Education in Europe* 34 (2): 269–280.

Wei, Jianguo, Prashant Loyalka, and Yingquan Song. 2010. "Determinants on High School Students Who Gave Up Higher Education Opportunities." *Journal of Educational Development* 21 (1): 15–21.

Yang, Po. 2009. "Who Gets More Financial Aid in China? A Multilevel Analysis" *Economics of Education Research (Bei Da)* 23 (7): 1–31.

Zhao, Lu. 2006. *Remarks on the Opening Ceremony of Model Higher Vocational College Construction Project.* Beijing: Ministry of Education.

Case Study 10

The Unintended Consequences of Funding Policies on Student Achievement at Colleges of Further Education in Wales and England

Martin Jephcote

Introduction

The processes of policy making and implementation are not linear or unproblematic but, on the contrary, are based on complex social interactions, often giving rise to unforeseen outcomes. Thus, matters such as colleges' organization and curriculum are open to negotiation and renegotiation over time. Within these processes, control over funding is regarded as a key lever for ensuring policy change, but the consequences, especially in social terms, are rarely thought through in advance. This chapter draws attention to this fact, depicting how changes to the governance of the Further Education (FE college) sector in England and Wales are underpinned by a "marketized" approach, in which colleges have to compete with each other to attract students. Their funding largely depends upon enrolment.

Background

In England and Wales there are three separate educational sectors. Education up to the age of 18 is free to all but after 18, fees are payable depending on personal circumstances. Schools provide for compulsory, mainly general and some vocational education up to the age of 16, and many offer advanced academic and vocational courses for 16–18-year-olds. Higher, or university education, is available from the age of 18 onwards and individual institutions set their own prior qualification entry requirements. The Further Education sector takes students from the age of 16 and increasingly, some at the age of 14 who are dual enrolled at school and work training programmes. Depending on location, some students have the choice of studying from 16 to 18 at either a school or an FE college.

In terms of student profile and subjects provided, FE colleges are similar to American Community Colleges (ACCs). Most students are adults who study part-time. But, unlike ACCs, the majority of students would not be aiming for entry into universities or completion of foundation (associate) degrees, and their success or otherwise would not be judged in these terms. Those students at an FE college wanting to get into a university are more likely at the age of 16 to be engaged on a program providing requisite qualifications, or later in life be on an FE "access" program. Although FE colleges do offer two-year foundation degrees, their mission is more centered around the acquisition of vocationally relevant qualifications by their students.

Government funding, which accounts on average for about 80 percent of a college's income, is derived from providing approved courses. For those aged under 18, it would be common not to pay any fee, and some might be eligible for grants and loans. Extra help is available for learners with special circumstances, such as students who have a disability, or who have caring responsibilities. For adult learners, grants, loans, and reduced fees are available depending on individual circumstances such as age, and income, if they or a family member receive state benefit payments, or if they are seeking work (see notes). The remainder of a college's income comes from a variety of sources including fees paid by employers and/or individuals mainly for vocational courses that contribute to labor-market upskilling.

Overall, central (federal) government is in a relatively powerful position to make macrolevel adjustments, but without the insight and reach to make adjustments at the local level. As a recent report highlighted (Schuller and Watson 2009, 224), in the UK, from all sources per capita expenditure on formal and informal learning is around £8,000 (about $10,500) for those aged 18–24, £283 (about $400) for those aged 25–50, £86 (about $115) for those aged 50–75, and £60 (about $80) for those over 75. As Schuller and Watson (2009, 100) commented: "The current distribution of resources for learning is heavily weighted towards initial education. It is inevitable that the system should be 'front-loaded'...However, the weighting is too strong."

The Research

This case study draws on existing published work (see notes) based on fieldwork research undertaken in the period of the two academic years 2005–2007 and subsequent ongoing analysis and dissemination of findings. It took place in three colleges, dispersed geographically over seven sites, chosen to reflect the cultural, social, and economic diversity evident across Wales. As a constituent country of the UK, together with England, Scotland, and Northern Ireland, the college system is similar, and especially so in Wales and England. Within the limitations of any qualitative work, the extent that findings can be generalized is limited, but the findings are particularly pertinent to England, which has experienced similar policy regimes.

The research followed a core group of about 45 students and 27 of their teachers for a two-year period. It employed a variety of approaches including one-to-one in-depth semistructured interviews, structured journal writing, and on-site ethnographic observation carried out over 65 days. Focus groups interviews were undertaken with additional groups of students. The details of the research are widely reported, and see, for example, Jephcote et al. (2008) for a comprehensive account.

Finding

How Funding Impacts on Students

The results of funding FEs were a recurring theme throughout the findings. Even for those students aged under 18 and who paid no fees, there was often mention of difficulty in meeting their living and travel costs, or implicit reference of the opportunity cost of going to college rather than going to work. Funding adversely impacted students' possibilities to enroll and remain in courses, and the ways in which they engaged in learning. For full-time students, real and perceived lack of funding combined with the need to undertake paid employment, lessened time spent on study. Similarly for part-time students funding was an issue, sometimes exacerbated by family commitments, and balancing competing pressures for time and money. For some it led to protracted periods out of college, so that being at college was a fragmented experience, often described as a "revolving door." Thus students joined courses, some left early, some returned at a later date. Indeed, it is the very nature of FE colleges and courses that they "scaffold" learners' opportunities to engage in learning in flexible ways at different stages of their lives. Indeed, one of the largest groups that further education supports is that of women aged 24–40 who, for a variety of reasons, do not reach their potential at school, disengage from learning, but reenter at a later time.

A focus group interview with one group of female adult returners was particularly revealing. Group members were enrolled in an Access to Nursing and Health Professions course and hoping to progress to local universities. The area in which they live is characterized by the disappearance of heavy industry and coal mining, has a high rate of economic inactivity, and is engaged in major economic regeneration efforts. With gross domestic product (GDP) across Wales at only 80 percent of that in England, this is a particularly deprived area, with high rates of debilitating long-term illness and a drive to raise the qualification and skill levels of the population. Furthering one's education and qualifications is increasingly associated with wider benefits. For example, adults who participate in learning are 14 percent more likely to give up smoking, potentially saving the health service in Wales over £30 million a year, or if the proportion of the working age population with no qualifications was reduced by one percentage point, the saving in reduced crime in Wales would be £37 million each year (Schuller and Watson 2009). The point here is that extra funding for education could result is less expenditure on health and ameliorating social disadvantage.

As we reported (Jephcote et al. 2009a) the importance of these contextual factors was evident when these women reflected on their earlier lives. They vividly described the constraints and disruptions in schooling arising from family circumstances: Sue Keane (age 31) had "been brought up in an environment where girls are not really looked upon to go far in education." Di Nissons (age 38), out of education for 22 years, was twice divorced and had five children: "my parents were divorced...I grew up in domestic violence, I experienced domestic violence...and it's made me stronger and it's made me want to go out and prove to the world—that I can do it." Carrie Morris (age 27), who described herself as "always in trouble as a child," had been a teenage mother who was not allowed to resume her studies: "I've just been determined right the way through that I'm going to finish this course no matter what."

These women gave testimony to how wider-life influences conspired to thwart or interrupt their studies and a main part of their effort and struggle was about money. Everyone in the group reported financial hardship. None of the women who were divorced received maintenance payments from their former partners. Several learners received £500 grants, including coverage of travel costs. Nevertheless, a number still needed to work part-time, evenings and weekends, and they described the stresses and pressures on them resulting from this. Molly had two part-time jobs, and

Elly Amos (age 33), a single mother, worked two night shifts each week, while Carrie Morris was married and received no grant because of her husband's income. Sue Keane (age 31) and Molly were full-time students on the Access course. Sue was ill and unable to work and was conscious of the effects on her children. For Shelley, the stress was that her employment consumed vital study time, making her frustrated: "I work as a part-time customer assistant...and I also work (in the health sector)...But I don't get a grant because I still live at home with my parents and they take in their wages into account even though I'm 20...I've got my own things to worry about and it's just not fair and I mean I do work. I work all weekends, it's seven days a week constantly for me, it's not a day off. I don't get the option to have a day off!"

These learners were juggling college attendance, the demands of study and course work, paid employment and family responsibilities, displaying immense determination and tenacity. Like Sue, above, they were not unaware of the costs, including the effects on others, including experiencing some alienation within the family, and having less time to devote to care and "service" within the family. Molly said that she was "a bad mother at the moment because I don't get to spend time with my daughter. I haven't seen my mother for a fortnight 'cos I'm there every night on the laptop, you know."

Unconditional support from family members was not universally available, some experienced little help, while some did report support from both their neighbors and relatives living nearby, with mothers, sisters, or even 19-year-old daughters to collect their children from school and baby-sit while they studied or did paid night or weekend shifts. In their turn, college teachers and systems responded by straining to provide the support that would retain the students on the course and to foster constructive and nurturing responses and group relationships. Almost all students admitted to feelings of self-doubt about their abilities as well as personal difficulties relating to wider outside lives and situations.

Learners of all ages reported to us that the need to support themselves financially impacted on their engagement in learning and their capacity to remain at college. In our interviews, we came across one partner, of a couple both aged 18, living off state benefits, supporting two children while at the same time being full-time students. He illustrated how they prudently managed their finances and shopped for budget lines at a local supermarket. They succeeded in balancing their private lives with their lives as students but, like many others, found the tensions problematic. We came across numerous cases of young people on so called "full-time" courses at the same time engaging in "part-time" employment, up to 44 hours a week. Many openly declared to us that they attended their college courses on an irregular basis, and/or that they did little study outside of college. In one of our regular journal correspondences we asked students to account for a typical day. We were shocked at how little time a minority, but substantial number, admitted to spending on college related work. Financial reasons were common, but in some cases students engaged in part-time paid work not out of necessity but to fund their consumerist lifestyle choices.

How Funding Impacts on Managers and Teachers

Central government aims and their seeking to use the education system, especially the further education college sector to promote social cohesion and economic growth are laudable. A ministerial foreword to a recent key policy document stated:

> Skills and employment are the foundation of a successful life, and they are essential for a more prosperous and more equal Wales... Further education institutions must be key drivers of skills... If we succeed, we will unlock people's talents, regenerate some of our most deprived communities, help families and children to escape from poverty, encourage businesses to grow and the Welsh economy to prosper... While our focus here is on economically-valuable skills, we recognise that learning has a broader role. It enriches our culture, helps preserve our heritage, and transmits our values to the next generation. Young people need a broad foundation of general and vocational learning to become well-rounded citizens. (Welsh Assembly Government 2008, 2)

There continues to be a misfit between the needs and interests of individuals, employers, and of the wider society. Some would position students as "clients" in a student-led model, in which colleges provide courses and qualifications to meet their demands. In other cases, colleges operate in a provider-led model, where they put on courses that they perceive to be important to the labor market and to fulfill institutional interests, such as meeting running costs. The point is that neither properly functions to meet the needs of the labor market. A recent UK government report (Leitch 2006) has called for the system to be "demand-led," namely, one in which employers interests are met. This approach has been criticized as "a one-sided analysis" (Schuller and Watson 2009, 231).

So, as in many other systems, the UK college sector has become rigid and resistant to change. To a degree, they operate to meet their own self-fulfilling interests, driven externally by the demands of efficiency, value for money, and performativity. Our research evidence (Jephcote et al. 2009b) has pointed to how external funding regimes and the wider mechanisms of regulation and accountability have impacted on the roles of managers and teachers and the relationships between them.

College leadership is forced to operate in a competitive, marketized environment, acting as independent incorporations whose main income derives from students, heavily dependent on government, and directly subject to government funding policy. Essentially, their income is based on the number of students they recruit, the numbers retained and the results (qualifications) attained. Managers have, in the main, to adopt the practices of "new managerialism" (Gleeson et al. 2005). They have to take tough decisions to "balance the books" but some observe that many are more concerned with financial management than student learning, creating something of a divide between the two (Shain and Gleeson 1999; Jephcote et al. 2008).

In all our work with teachers and especially in our interviews, they told us of how the mantra of "recruitment-retention-results" pervaded every aspect of their working lives. They were required to maintain detailed records of attendance and some even implied that such data were manipulated. If students were not retained, teachers faced the threat of their course being withdrawn if it fell below a "viable" number. To ensure the best results possible, some teachers reported how they received and commented on "endless" drafts of students' coursework assignments. Many teachers felt under threat, their working and home lives under stress, and added to this, for colleges to maintain or increase income, they expanded numbers taking on what some teachers described as "more difficult to teach" and "more challenging" students.

How Funding Contributes to "Negotiated Regimes" of Learning

Given the ways that funding impacts students, teachers, and college management, it became evident that funding adversely impacts teaching and learning transacted in classrooms. It would of course be untrue to suggest that funding was the only factor determining how teachers and students interacted, but it did seem to generate the wider conditions in which this transaction took place.

In response to financial pressures, sometimes faced with larger class sizes, and often a reduced amount of time to teach their subjects, teachers looked for different ways to engage their learners. Some, who had previously adopted more participatory styles of teaching and learning decided to move to more "traditional" transmission modes arguing that they had to cover more ground in less time and that larger classes meant that they had to abandon more learner-centered approaches. Conversely, others used the very same conditions to argue for the adoption of more learner-centered approaches, where they took on the role of facilitator, requiring students to engage in self-directed learning, commonly supported by e-learning technologies in "open-learning" centers. Thus, these changing conditions forced many teachers to reconsider their instructional practices. In most cases, their solutions were based on what they thought to be in the best interests of their students, and not a response to management directives. Indeed, our work with teachers revealed what we have referred to as an "ethic of care" (Jephcote et al. 2008, 2009b; Jephcote and Salsbury 2009), which privileged students' interests, their professional identities leading them to compensate for students' prior educational disadvantage and give primary responsibility to their social well-being. But this was not without cost and they invested heavily in "emotional labour" (Hochschild 1983) as a way of coping with the pressures from managers and external regulators, and from challenging learners (Salisbury et al. 2006).

Teachers and students bring to the college classroom their own sets of circumstances that impact on their engagement with each other. For students, difficulties in their outside college lives had to be managed, but often, as described above, not without cost to the ability to engage in learning. For teachers, they have to manage competing demands and be attuned to the lives and needs of their individual learners.

College classrooms are, therefore, to be thought of as social contexts for learning, contingent on the conditions that shape what teachers do, and the dispositions that students bring. In these terms, learning is a "negotiated regime" (Jephcote and Salsbury 2008). Learning can only be understood when viewed in the cultural, economic, and social settings in which it is generated and when it encompasses the interactions of both teachers and learners (Jephcote and Salsbury 2008).

Conclusion

Funding and associated policy regimes have impacted on teachers' work and students' lives and, more generally, on how teaching and learning is transacted. As in the case presented, the processes and their consequences are quick to act and have long-term implications. They determine the social relations between educational "managers" and "workers," teachers and students, and give rise to unstable conditions for all. As a result, solutions to these new problems are complex and overcoming them might, somewhat paradoxically, be dependent on new policy initiatives, thus contributing to further change and risking more destabilization.

In a rapidly changing world, with changing conditions of work and new technologies, it seems odd that "front-loading" education and training and the funding that goes with it is taken-for-granted. More attention has to be given to the different phases of people's lives, and more importance and more funding attached to supporting those in and out of work.

Acknowledgments

The research was cofunded by the ESRC and Welsh Assembly Government as part of the Teaching and Learning Research programme (see http://www.tlrp.org). Co-researchers were Dr Jane Salisbury and Professor Gareth Rees, Cardiff University School of Social Sciences, and Mr John Roberts, University of Wales, Newport.

Notes

For further information about the research project and publications are available online at: http://www.FurtherEducationResearch.org

For full details of funding for FE students in Wales are available online at: http://wales.gov.uk.

References

Gleeson, Denis, Jenifer Davies, and Eunice Wheeler. 2005. "On the Making and Taking of Professionalism in the Further Education Workplace." *British Journal of Sociology of Education* 26 (44): 445–460.

Hochschild, Arlie. 1983. *The Managed Heart: Commercialisation of Human Feeling.* Berkley, CA: University of California Press.

Jephcote, Martin, Jane Salisbury, Gareth Rees, and John Roberts. 2008. *Inside Further Education: The Social Context of Learning.* Teaching and Learning Research Briefing No. 52. London: Teaching and Learning Programme. Available online at: http://www.tlrp.org.

Jephcote, Martin, Jane Salisbury, and Gareth Rees. 2009a. "The Learning Journey: Students' Experiences of Further Education in Wales." *Contemporary Wales* 23: 141–157.

Jephcote, Martin, Jane Salisbury, and Gareth Rees. 2009b. "Learning and Working in Wales: An Overview and Initial Findings." *Welsh Journal of Education* 14 (2): 18–28.

Jephcote, Martin, Jane Salisbury, and Gareth Rees. 2009c. "Further Education Teachers' Accounts of Their Professional Identities." *Teaching and Teacher Education* 25 (7): 966–972.

Jephcote, Martin, Jane Salisbury, and Gareth Rees. 2008. "The Wider Social Context of Learning: Beyond the Classroom Door." *The International Journal of Learning* 15(6): 281–288.

Jephcote, Martin and Jane Salisbury. 2008. "Being a Teacher in Further Education in Changing Times." *Research in Post-Compulsory Education* 13(2): 163–172.

Leitch Review of Skills. 2006. *Prosperity for All in the Global Economy: World Class Skills.* London: The Stationery Office.

Salisbury, Jane, Martin Jephcote, Gareth Rees, and John Roberts. 2006. *Emotional Labour and Ethics of Care: Work Intensification in FE Colleges.* Learning and Working in FE in Wales Working Paper No.5. Cardiff, UK: Cardiff University. Available online at: http://www.FurtherEducationResearch.org.

Schuller, Tom, and David Watson. 2009. *Learning Through Life, Inquiry into the Future of Lifelong Learning.* London: National Institute of Adult Continuing Education (NIACE).

Shain, Farzana, and Denis Gleeson. 1999. "Under New Management: Changing Conceptions of Teacher Professionalism and Policy in the Further Education Sector." *Journal of Education Policy* 14 (4): 445–462.

Welsh Assembly Government. 2008. *Skills that Work for Wales: A Skills and Employment Strategy and Action Plan.* Cardiff. Wales, UK: Welsh Assembly Government, Department for Children, Education and Lifelong Learning and Skills.

Chapter 11

Going Forward

Edward J. Valeau, Stewart E. Sutin, Daniel Derrico,
and Rosalind Latiner Raby

Community colleges now function in an era of extraordinary global sociopolitical, economic, and communications connectivity. Intellectual capital, workforce effectiveness and productivity are valued. Hence, community colleges and their global counterparts have become a key vehicle of economic development and for educating their residents across cultures. The rapidity with which new challenges emerge and the wide scope of those trends increase the need for responsive and transparent institutional behaviors. *Increasing Effectiveness of the Community College Financial Model: A Global Perspective for the Global Economy* is written at a time when community colleges and their global counterparts are experiencing unprecedented reductions to their budgets while the expectations are increasing for affordable tuition, highly functioning workforce development programs, and improved outcomes measured by student success within and beyond the classrooms.

A fundamental tenet in the book is that community colleges must make hard choices in pursuit of an improved financial model. They must evidence the ability to translate planning into positive, measurable, and sustainable outcomes. Towards this end, the chapters describe ways to improve the community college financial model, while the case studies illustrate that the seemingly impossible is indeed viable. The authors draw upon a body of knowledge and experiences to show that systematic change to the community college financial model is both realistic and attainable. We position this book as a guide for community college leaders, boards of trustees, senior administrators, and faculty and staff in search of creative and sustainable solutions to address current and future financial needs.

Charting Our Way

Several compelling themes emerge from the chapters and case studies that help chart a new path for change. There is an ample body of knowledge about institutional reform. Some of these ideas have already been adopted by community colleges around the world. Other opportunities either remain untapped or underexploited. Enduring change results not only from idea generation, but from consistent and comprehensive application of these ideas to forge a more vibrant financial model. Combining creative thinking with effective follow-up will enable collective experiences and expertise of community colleges and their global counterparts to be harnessed.

Role of the New Generation of Leaders

The first theme is the need for transformational leaders to be just as committed to improve financial models as they are to learning outcomes for their students. Leaders are the catalyst for developing, sustaining, and implementing the institutional mission, vision, and values and hence are stewards for the college's financial well-being. The leadership agenda must rise above handling day-to-day issues. Strategic and evidence-based decision making, and effective advocacy coexist with consistent application of sound budgeting, planning, fund-raising, and process management. Leaders must maintain a passion for lifelong learning as role models for continuous improvement of their financial, international, and budget literacy skills. Such leaders must be clear, pragmatic, and creative in sustaining accountability and holding others to a like standard of performance.

The task of finding and supporting such leaders belongs to the board of trustees, while the task of cultivating them for the future is dependent upon current community college leaders. Such development is critical to leadership succession. This is a promotional sandbox for those who evidence positive results on progressively more senior and complex assignments.

Sustainable change is requisite for the new paradigm and requires strategic leadership, identification of medium- and long-term priorities, data-based decision-making, alignment of strategic and annual operating plans with financial, physical, and human resources, to generate incremental revenues from nontraditional sources, and actions intended to contain costs. No less important are processes to monitor progress, and a performance-based evaluation system built largely upon a composite of personal behaviors aligned with college values and delivery of yearly measurable objectives. Finally, financial decisions must be consistent with beneficial impact on students, respect for employees involved, and open, timely, informative, and honest two-way communications. Collectively, these measures will improve institutional effectiveness and create a paradigm for planned sustainable change.

It is critical for leaders to embrace equity and respect for others, while striving for good ideas and a membership reflective of our increasingly global community of learners. Sustainable change and creation of an institutional culture of self-reliance is achievable to the extent that community college leaders are inspirational and strongly committed to fostering environments characterized by idea generation, team play, agility, decisiveness, creativity, delegation of authority, accountability, transparency, and an unrelenting desire to delivery on agreed upon goals and outcomes.

Educational and Institutional Revitalization

The second theme explores how the new financial reform model can foster educational and institutional revitalization through comprehensive actions that sustain organizational change. All the authors in this book underscore the importance of defining and communicating priorities, planning, and follow-through. A results-driven environment requires fidelity to make difficult decisions, the courage and the tenacity to implement them, commitment to priorities, recognition and support for those who perform well, and accountability for those who fail to do so. The standards and expectations for community college performance have risen, and so too must institutional responsiveness. However, all answers do not always lie only in the United States, as exemplary practices are occurring at community colleges and their global counterparts around the world, as evidenced in this book.

Supportive boards of trustees play a key role in sustainable financial reform. Thoughtful, board-adopted statements of institutional mission, vision, value, and goals will define "what we are here to accomplish." Multiyear strategic plans and priorities should be a matter of public record, along with annual operating goals. Boards are well positioned to support organizational changes and sound human resource and financial management practices to assure administrative accountability, improve institutional effectiveness, and support leadership amid push back from change-resistant staff.

Many of the authors in the book comment upon how globalization has changed the world economy, job market, and social skills and how community colleges must realign, or in some cases, reinvent their technical, occupational, vocational, and academic programs to remain relevant. On a microlevel, adaptive changes integrate multiyear planning and new approaches to budget management that decrease reliance on public funding through increasing revenues from ancillary operations, while containing costs. These changes facilitate affordable tuition, enhanced student retention, workforce development, capital bond projects, facilities management, internationalizing the curriculum, and entrepreneurship.

This book underscores the need for management by objective performance evaluation systems and sophisticated budgeting practices. While not a panacea for building, monitoring and assessing the success of the budget plan on intended outcomes, performance-based budgeting offers a viable mechanism to affect change and ensure results. Its usage by the Western Association of Schools and Colleges (WASC) in their accreditation standards increases its prominence, and emphasis upon decisions based on comprehensive data, rather than superficial and anecdotal information. Since administrators have varying roles and responsibilities in carrying out work of the college, financial planning should be transparent, comprehensive and strategic. A data- and priorities-based mindset offers a sound basis upon which annual operating goals and budgets are defined, while planned outcomes and performance are evaluated.

Revenue Generation and Cost Containment

The third theme relates to improvement of financial self-reliance through revenue generation from ancillary enterprises and cost containment. It begins with asking the right questions to stimulate productive discourse, analysis, and solution creation. Is there a business plan in place to grow revenue-generating ancillary enterprises? Is it inventive and aggressive? Is the leadership of ancillary enterprises entrepreneurial-, market-, and performance-driven? On the cost containment side of the house, are administrative and "back shop" staffing levels appropriate relative to the size and overall staffing of the institution? Are operations and services efficient and effective, or time-consuming and labor-intensive? Can services be delivered at lower costs? Do certain approval processes require too many administrators? Can processes be both soundly controlled yet expedited by empowering middle management to make certain decisions? Are certain administrative and staffing positions redundant and compressible in multicampus and multicollege districts? Can peer group information-sharing and problem-solving task forces identify cost-saving and service improvement opportunities without regard for turf building? Do administrators, faculty, and support staff participate in process improvement, revenue generation, and cost containment forums?

The impact of reduced funding from public sources and an unpredictable future is a source of great concern across community colleges and their global counterparts. As an example, Scott Lay (2010), the executive director of Community College League of California (CCLC) explained in a communiqué to the field that in 2009, California community colleges took $382.8 million in cuts. He used a picture taken of empty seats in an auditorium to muse that "this will be what graduation looks like if California continues to divest from public higher education." As Sutin (chapter 10) recommends, we need to find the place where creativity and practicality converge. This book provides many examples of such convergence and illustrates that change is constantly occurring. The consequence is that community colleges have the potential to assume increasing control over their own destinies or run the risk of continued subjugation to state financial models that could potentially bankrupt some of the nation's community colleges.

Plan for the Unexpected

The fourth theme relates to the ability of organizations and their leadership to anticipate the unexpected and to develop tools needed to perform in conditions increasingly characterized by material and sudden swings in global economics, shocks to the sociopolitical and economic environment, and lack of respect for discourse and reason between persons of differing views and origin. Our colleges exist in a rapidly moving world, whose effectiveness is visible through shifts in manufacturing services to knowledge-based economies, cultural and linguistic transitions in service populations, and the pace of technology where knowledge and innovation arise amid massive amounts of information, ideas, and possibilities. Globalization, as discussed by the authors, affects the economic, social, and political stability of communities that rely upon a trained workforce and an educated citizenry for their economic well-being. Community colleges are profoundly influenced by such exogenous influences and the rapidity and often unanticipated emergence of new challenges.

The norm must be for leaders to set the tone and the foundation for collaborative ownership and accountability, thus sharing responsibility for annual operating goals. Persons incapable of effective collaboration and teamwork will be source of needless conflict and a drain on the energies of those around them. Going further, role definition and responsibilities, as outlined by the authors throughout this book, show how change agents can function and how their effectiveness can be evaluated. In this context, not only must we become better than our competitors, but each day, we must improve upon ourselves.

Best Practices

The fifth and final theme is that community colleges and their global counterparts should consistently examine and deploy best practices. Some of our authors advocate that community colleges must adopt businesslike approaches to development of revenues from nontraditional sources, and comment upon ways to do so. Others have described ways to contain costs. An entrepreneurial culture must supplant thinking that it is somehow illegal or immoral for public institutions to engage in "for-profit" businesses. Some warn that while this approach is warranted, it should be with an appreciation for the historically unique mission of the community college. Selected examples offered below should stimulate the reader's interest, thinking, and actions on ways to reduce the financial dependency of community colleges and their global counterparts on public funding.

1. Document and disseminate information related to the financial gains associated with student retention.
2. Aggressively develop international education as a revenue producing enterprise, on a larger scale, yet understand, like all small, labor intensive programs, profit may not be the ultimate goal.
3. Revise fee schedules for all non-credit courses to deliver minimum profit margins yet allow tuition and scholarships to be awarded on a financial need basis.
4. Design and operate in-person tutorial, distance education, and supplemental instructional services in direct competition with For-Profits who serve K-16 students.
5. Identify areas that lend themselves to innovative cost containment solutions. Opportunities could include energy conservation programs, contracts for services, open bidding, equipment purchase, and health care.
6. Invest in institutional leaders dedicated to being change agents.
7. Educate the board and the college constituency on strategic ways to control and enhance the institution's financial destiny.

A failing delivery system undermines the ability of the community college to fulfill its mission and meet its responsibilities. High-performance institutions find solutions to problems. In so doing, they become role models for their students by practicing what they teach. Successful community colleges inspire confidence among those who rely upon them to meet their educational and training needs to meet their dreams and financial goals. Responding to these demands require that colleges avoid as many mistakes as they can. In this book, a selected list of best practices emerges from the chapters and case studies. Many of them transcend national borders.

Connect Finance, Mission, and College Priorities

Maintaining the community equity mission that links college finances to their ability to serve their unique communities remains a basic challenge. Advancing equity must include real economic incentives that acknowledge the realities of the current market economy and their real-life affect on students, faculty, and curriculum. The authors in this book question the traditional argument, which defined equity as equal access to equal dollars. This premise does not take into consideration the diverse nature of community colleges, and their multiple, varied, and changing missions and constituencies. As editors, we suggest that sound financial management, pursuit of community college mission, and sustainable educational and student service, excellence are inseparable and compatible objectives.

Communication, Transparency, and Coordination

A common charge against most budget office's is a lack of transparency and a degree of insularity from those responsible for delivery of academic and student services. Mitigating this belief is both important and achievable by making all information common knowledge through existing modes of communication including social media. A financially literate constituency, along with collaborative budget preparation processes, is more likely to result in support for leadership undertaking systemic change. Effective leadership connects the dots between functions, and across the college. It supports laser-like action through relationship building and acceptance of a shared vision. It unites action in a collaborative manner to achieve specific outcomes.

Accountability and Shared Responsibility

Micromanagement or top-down decision-making typically fails in today's world of collaboration in which community leaders, administrators, faculty, and staff want to "own" idea generation and act as partners in change. This can be fostered by including stakeholders in communication and planning forums. Concurrently, accountability should be aligned with human resource policies and financial planning practices throughout the institution. Authority to make decisions must be commensurate with accountability and responsibility. Clear articulation of performance objectives, while essential, will be of little consequence if there is no system to recognize and reward those who exceed expectations or hold accountable those unable or unwilling to do so. Revenues and expenditures must be closely monitored after budgets are approved in order to make off-cycle adjustments as unplanned events occur and that can result in variances to the approved budget.

Multiyear and Multistream Planning and Institutional Performance

Planning must be connected to clear, time-sensitive, measurable, and realistic goals at the institutional and individual levels. Strategic planning must be aligned with resource allocation, set baseline priorities, describe the future directions of the institution, and provide the basis upon which to evaluate progress toward mission achievement.

Preparation and Forecasting

Skills preparation and a well-conceived set of assumptions about future cycles and future year program needs are essential for success outcomes. Forecasting "what if" scenarios will improve upon institutional and staff readiness to meet challenges as they arise. Those who assume that the future will only be an extrapolation of current events tend to buy into unwarranted positive or negative trend line analysis. Leaders need to be aware of enrollment prospects, public and private funding support, student tuition and fee levels, inflation rates, facilities construction, remodeling and maintenance, staffing requirements, energy costs, equipment purchases, health care, and other matters that impact revenues and expenses.

Stimulate and Motivate Leadership

We advocate creating a highly credible, diverse, and thoughtful constituency of team players, or steering committee, to facilitate the process of change. The CEO should appoint this group for the purpose of planning the change process, tendering recommendations, and overseeing the early stages of plan implementation. This group should include respected and credible change agents from administration, staff, faculty, and student leaders. This steering committee must embrace an improved financial model as integral to systemic change and a well-executed strategic plan. A systematic data-based approach to selecting choices upon which to act is preferable to intuition or reliance upon anecdotal information. Persons capable of sustaining a broad institutional and student-centric perspective, reflective thinking, global literacy, and effective teamwork can be invaluable to institutional reform efforts in general, and developing an improved financial model in particular. This book comments upon some known theories about institutional reform and applies them to a community college financial model. It sheds a spotlight on processes and solutions that should receive more attention as community colleges lead rather than react to change. It demonstrates ways to build upon prevailing strengths of adaptability and resilience, and judiciously apply them to a financial model that works for community colleges and their global counterparts in sustaining affordable tuition, and ensuring high-performance educational, workforce development, and student and community services enterprises.

We emphasize the importance of leaders who make a difference in the education of others. Such leaders experiment, are willing learners, and adapt to changing environments. They protect and guide the college and delegate authority to implement change so that accountability and decision-making ability are aligned. Such leaders may be charismatic. They may be humble. But they define success by results achieved.

Our book is ultimately for educators, those who teach, and those who lead, but all of whom are entrusted with the pedagogy and learning process that engages the students mind and creativity. Finally, it is for the community, who invests its dollars and trust in leaders to find the right things to do and do the right thing. Most importantly, this book recognizes the outstanding work already being done by community college leaders around the world, while suggesting that hard times remain and that continual change is required.

Conclusion

This book offers insights into leadership roles and responsibilities, shows how change agents can function, and how their effectiveness can be evaluated. We demonstrate how new processes require an understanding of the past and the imagination and vision to build for the future. The success stories clearly illustrate leaders who have embraced the skill set of 1980s management training that emulated private sector business models, demonstrated the 1990s emphasis on transformational leadership, and who have incorporated the 2000s emphasis on team work, accountability, and transparency for support of student access and success. This book underscores how and why financial literacy, business competencies, fidelity to community college mission and educational standards, and a global outlook need to constitute the institutional foundation going forward. Using this as a jumping off point, recommendations and case studies are offered with the overarching goals of keeping community colleges financially and educationally sound in order to better serve students looking to achieve their dreams in an increasingly global twenty-first century economy.

Reference

Lay, Scott. 2010. *Community College League of California Budget*, e-mail correspondence update sent from the Community College League of California, Sacramento, May 27, 2010.

Contributors

Stewart E. Sutin, PhD, is a clinical professor of Administrative and Policy Studies and associate director of the Institute for Higher Education Management in the School of Education at the University of Pittsburgh, where he also serves on the faculty of the Katz Graduate School of Business Administration. He is a former president and CEO of the Community College of Allegheny County, former senior vice president of Mellon Bank, and former president of Bank of Boston International.

Daniel Derrico, EdD, is the former interim chancellor and vice chancellor for Administration and Finance for the Alamo Community College District. He currently is an adjunct professor in the PhD Program in Higher Education Leadership at Barry University. He has 40 years of administrative experience in community colleges in New Jersey, Florida, and Texas, including several senior administrative positions at Miami Dade College, including district associate provost for operations.

Edward J. Valeau, PhD, is the superintendent/president emeritus of Hartnell College. He has served in higher education administration for 35 years. His professional leadership experiences include: president of California Colleges for International Education, chair of the American Association of Community Colleges Commission on International Education, and member of the board of directors for American Council on Education International Commission. He has also been a Fulbright community college specialist to India and Nepal.

Rosalind Latiner Raby, PhD, is a senior lecturer at California State University, Northridge in the Educational Leadership and Policy Studies Department of the College of Education and is an Affiliate Faculty for the Educational Leadership and Policy Studies EdD. Community College Program. She also serves as the director of California Colleges for International Education, a non-profit consortium whose membership includes 84 California community colleges. She is widely published on the topic of international education and community colleges.

Pamela D. Anglin, PhD, CPA, is the president of Paris Junior College, Texas and serves on the American Association of Community Colleges board of directors.

George R. Boggs, PhD, is president and CEO emeritus of the American Association of Community Colleges. He is also the superintendent/president and CEO emeritus of Palomar College.

Jenna Cullinane is a doctoral student of Public Policy at the University of Texas at Austin and Research Scientist at the Charles A. Dana Center.

Janice Nahra Friedel, PhD, is a professor in the Educational Leadership and Policy Studies Department at the Michael D. Eisner College of Education, California State University Northridge in the Community College EdD Program. For 11 years, she was the administrator of the Division of Community Colleges and Workforce Preparation at the Iowa Department of Education.

Robert A. Frost, PhD, is vice president of Student Learning at the College of Siskiyous. He has 20-plus years' in community colleges academic and student services administration in four states and serves on the Editorial Advisory Boards of the *Journal of Education Finance* and the *Community College Journal of Research and Practice*.

Michael Giammarella is a professor in Counseling and is the Coordinator of Study Abroad at Borough of Manhattan Community College.

Martin Jephcote, PhD, is a senior lecturer and researcher at Cardiff University School of Social Science, Wales, UK and is the director of Undergraduate Studies.

Steven M. Kinsella, DBA, CPA, is the superintendent/president of Gavilan College. He earned both his doctorate and master's degree in the field of finance.

Chris Moran, PE, was director for Facilities and Construction for the Miami-Dade County Public Schools and the vice provost for Facilities Management at Miami Dade College.

Christopher B. Mugimu, PhD, is a senior lecturer and head at the Department of Curriculum, Teaching, and Media at Makerere University in Uganda.

Christopher M. Mullin, PhD, is the program director for Policy Analysis at the American Association of Community College.

Gordon Nixon, PhD, is the vice president Academic at SAIT Polytechnic in Calgary and is in charge of both the Domestic and International Corporate Training Departments.

Steve Ovel is executive director of Governmental Relations for Kirkwood Community College.

John C. Petersen, PhD, is former president of four accrediting commissions: Western Association of Schools and Colleges, Northwest Commission on Colleges, Hong Kong Council for Academic Accreditation, and was Executive Director of the Accrediting Commission for Community and Junior Colleges, for California, Hawaii, and the Pacific Islands.

Gerard Postiglione, PhD, is professor and head, Division of Policy, Social Science, and Administration, and director of the Wah Ching Centre of Research on Education in China, Faculty of Education, The University of Hong Kong.

Edward "Ted" Raspiller, EdD, is an associate professor and director of the Doctoral Program in Community College Leadership and is Chair of the Educational Foundations and Leadership Department at Old Dominion University.

John E. Roueche, PhD, has completed 40 years as director of the Community College Leadership Program at the University of Texas at Austin. He is the author of 35 books on community colleges and is regarded as a leading authority on U.S. community colleges.

Yingquan Song, PhD, is an associate professor of educational finance at the China Institute of Educational Finance Research, Peking University and is a policy consultant for China's Ministry of Finance and Ministry of Education.

John W. Strybos, PE, is the associate vice chancellor for Facilities Operations and Construction Management for the Alamo Community College District and has 27 years of experience in the field.

John J. "Ski" Sygielski, EdD, is president of Mt. Hood Community College. He is currently the chair-elect of the American Association of Community Colleges.

Brenda S. Trettel is the dean of Academic Affairs, Community College of Allegheny County South Campus and is a doctoral student in the Higher Education Management Program at the University of Pittsburgh.

John L. Yeager, EdD, is an associate professor in the University of Pittsburg School of Education in the Department of Administrative and Policy Studies, and director of the Institute for Higher Education Management.

Index